TRAINING TEACHERS
Problems and Issues

TRAINING TEACHERS
Problems and Issues

R.P. Singh

GYAN PUBLISHING HOUSE
New Delhi - 110002

Training Teachers Problems and Issues

Rs. 650

ISBN : 81-212-0900-5

Published in 2006 in India by
Gyan Publishing House,
5, Ansari Road, Daryaganj,
New Delhi-110002
Phones: 23282060, 23261060,
Fax. 23285914
email : gyanbook@vsnl.com

Laser Type Setting by: Mega Graphics, Delhi
Printed at: Salasar Imaging System, Delhi

Contents

Preface

Writing books on Education can be a very rewarding experience provided what one writes is both relevant and interesting. Not only those who work in the area of teacher education but others too, I have found, are interested in education of the teachers. The present book is focussed on the state of teacher education today and the challenges it faces vis-à-vis virtual classrooms and E-learning. Over a period of time India has come of age technologically. The problem is not so much about technology but use of the same. When even the metropolitan towns do not get uninterrupted supply of electricity what could one say about the smaller towns or states like UP and Bihar where the entire State is forever short of its supply. The rural India is a classic case of utter neglect where any realty check would reveal that in most cases people live more by hope than performance or delivery on the ground. Consequently, both schools and society cannot take the advantages of what is already available for all. I have therefore talked in one of my write-ups of revolutionizing village life and school, especially because we have 24- hour educational channels supported by Edusat. It is not difficult to light the village streets with solar power and provide schools with simputers and television sets. Since money and power have as yet to be entrusted to the village panchayats the digital divide is a greater reality than what one would like to believe.

Teacher education in India has a long and exciting history. Éven before it was formally organized numerous experiments were made in the field. At least in this field India kept pace with the world trends. Europe for the first time felt the need to provide education to the common men during the Renaissance period –something Indians had always felt and provided. The earliest Indian teachers, whose presence is recorded in the Vedas, organized and offered teaching in their homes. It took considerable time for Europe to follow suit. The need to provide teacher training in England arose because of Industrial Revolution. All the big names of Europe and England we are familiar with are products of these times. It is the Renaissance, which gave us Rousseau, Pestalozzi, and Mill and numerous others. It is this time when India started lagging educationally behind Europe and consequently we became a British colony. The colonial rule has its own rules of the game. For instance, no colonizer would like the ruled to become leaders in any human endeavour vis-à-vis their masters. It is a matter of surprise that this law did not apply in the case of teacher education where Indians lend ideas like the monitorial system or the Madras system. It is we who gave the ideas of effective classroom instruction to the British, which they improved upon according to their requirement.

Considering the type of new demands of both the subject areas and instructional strategies one must think of preparing teachers for tomorrow. We know nothing about tomorrow beyond having some vague ideas; therefore, it is all the more necessary that we equip ourselves with a few extra tricks of the trade. In the meanwhile, the rate at which knowledge becomes obsolete is simply astounding. No matter what we teach teachers their knowledge shall have become obsolete in no time whatever. In such a situation what do we do? Perhaps we shall have to tell them techniques and ways to keep themselves up-dated. In other words, it is not the quantum of knowledge that is essential but its quality. How do we do that? Teachers in the days to come have not only to be innovative but must also learn lateral thinking methods to succeed in tricky situations.

In the hope that the present book will meet at least part of the teacher education's curricular requirements it is being offered.

R.P.Singh

SECTION A
TEACHERS AND TEACHING

1

Teacher Education — Old Problems, New Solutions

This section constituting five papers seeks to analyse the historical development of teacher education programmes in India and presents a comparative perspective of the same taking examples from the USA and UK, which have several striking parallels both in practice and ideology. While commenting upon the current 'mess' teacher education finds itself in the world over, a few suggestions have also been hinted at to improve it; should someone bother to think first and act thereafter and not the other way round which has been the usual practice.

The major problem that persons working in this area are currently facing (and one is not sure about its future scenario) is the ICT and the way it has placed demands on an unsuspecting class of professionals. We must quickly take number of decisions in the age of virtual classrooms and the virtual universities. The question in brief is: are we ready?

Teacher education in India faces crises on several fronts. Because of poor salary scales (are they?) teaching *per se* does not attract the very bright [men and women] at any level, much less at the primary or secondary levels. To some extent we in India share this universal phenomenon. Despite research findings that "(Paulsen and Feldman 1995: 21) no such care is noticeable in the organisation of educational institutions. While we all know that culture can be thought of" as a source of stability in organisations in many ways (Paulsen and Feldman 1995: 20), we in India find that in terms of 'learning' cultures students and teachers reflect a good deal of divergence. We have not been quite sure as to whose responsibility "it is to ensure teacher students' mathematical knowledge" (McIntyre and Byred 1996: *xvi*). Should a teachers' college limit itself to the professional part of teacher education or cover the subject matter too? This debate is part of an endless universal discussion and does not promise any immediate conclusion.

Equally importantly, we are not quite sure until this day whether teacher preparation belongs to 'skill' area or it constitutes only information-mongering. Of course, we are quite sure that teacher preparation has something to do with "pedagogical skills but what precisely these skills are and how could one identify and transmit them as well, we could not ever be more unsure. These skills are called 'competencies' and they have been itemised to include more than 1700 mini-abilities. With regard to information, which we consider extremely important and unavoidable, we have assumed that information, not unlike its finished product, can be selected, graded and packaged before it is transported. It is something akin to teaching Shakespeare at different levels with a variety of accompanying explanations and glossaries.

Curiously enough, until very recently we had an idea that a teacher, once trained is good enough for his entire service tenure. And when a desirable modification has been made in one's attitudes, it is the information part, which necessitates updating, and not the 'skill' area. What is even more interesting to observe is that in the teachers' colleges a number of 'new' papers have been added and put under 'optional' category. One wonders whether this has happened merely in response to some social necessity or something more. Instead of seeing that changes occur in teaching methodology/techniques, it is the quantity of information, which has undergone additional burden. It would appear that there is some confusion about the terms 'quantity' and 'quality' since they are commonly used, almost as synonyms.

And the worst part of it all is to have made a teacher education degree or diploma, something like a 'driving license'—irrespective of the competence one acquired or the ethics of the case having been carefully accounted for. No matter how much research may contradict the assumed idealised image of the teacher, we continue to accord it publicly a status, which no one could knowingly endorse, not even the teachers themselves. In a recent World Bank financed study it was discovered by NCERT that more than 29 per cent of the teachers were academically unsound, something, which had been endorsed in earlier surveys too

(Parulekar 1945: *xxvii*). We do not seem to acknowledge the reality that all teachers are not equally competent or willingly join the profession. There is no evidence either in ancient or medieval times to support the view that Indian society had ever been a 'learned' society. Learning in India had always had a social bias or caste bias, and we are not likely to get out of it in the near future either. We must learn to distinguish between a reality and its idealised version.

Interestingly enough, while everyone seems to admire innovations and experiments, one seldom comes across any attempts whatsoever on the part of teachers' colleges to offered nay encouragement in that direction. One is not sure whether there is any possibility to offer an incentive or a cue in this regard. In fact we are not quite sure whether an individual can be trained to be original or innovative. The closest one could come to it is both appreciated and rewarded: A few institutions could develop this kind of environment and sustain it through creative activities. This area seems to be totally unexplored.

We now come to the most important aspect of our problem. Do we really know: who is a 'good' teacher or what is 'good' teaching? If we know them both, which particular course of study leads one to become a 'good'/effective teacher? How do we decide that a given course of study would lead a prospective teacher to become an effective' instrument to transmit information for which society pays him? How does society know or distinguish which level of teacher performs with what efficiency and how does it grade teachers for the job they undertake?

It is a commonly held view that primary teachers perform the most exacting of teaching tasks. At this age are children moulded to acquire certain values and attitudes. Also, it is extremely difficult to attend to students of this level. Numerous researches are cited to support these views. But one does not find any effort on the part of society to pay these teachers accordingly. Instead, we even do not see the need to have the very best among enterprising and intelligent men and women to man positions at this level. While we expect them to perform at their optimal levels, we fail to have a motivation to think of compensating them adequately.

Indeed, we have failed to give reasons or defined our criteria to categories and label information. How do we define 'higher' or 'lower' knowledge/information?

If classification of 'concepts' according to the nature of their abstruseness is regarded as 'higher' knowledge, there is no reason to regard imparting of a complex skill like 'reading' or 'writing' 'lower' knowledge. After all, no one would dare say that weak or inadequate foundation was good enough to bear the structural load of a 'high'-rise building. If this analogy makes any sense, the 'lower' levels of teachers require as much, if not more, attention and care as the ones who teach at the so-called 'higher' levels. In fact, in terms of responsibility the latter class of teachers undertake to provide only polish to the structure, which has already been created on a certain type of foundation.

Once again we come back to the basic question: who is performing an onerous job and how do we prepare and motivate her/him? What evidence, whether of empirical or intuitive nature, do we have with us to endorse the opinions we hold? Also, how do we define 'higher' or 'lower' levels of education and what do we know of the complications a teaching job entails?

Interestingly enough, of late a class of intellectuals are being given considerable weightage for discovery that comprehension is superior to memory. Today's teaching allegedly lays a great store by 'memorisation' of content rather than understanding. Perhaps the logical corollary to this debate would be a Satre-like 'Either' or 'Or' situation. Teachers are being accused of relying too much on 'memory' and both the courses of study and their evaluation are said to be enhancing this dependence. Unfortunately, these wise men have overlooked the simple fact that 'memory' is the very foundation on which 'comprehension' could be developed. It is not an 'either'/or situation. Instead, the former is pre-requisite for the latter to develop. If this kind of confusion can cloud the reasoning power of a certain class of people, how could a poor teacher be expected to resolve it and much less differentiate it in his classroom? If one thought that this debate has no direct relevance for preparation of teachers, one doubts about the meaningfulness of any other controversy either. While it is being trumpeted as a great finding, no one has come out thus far with any accompanying course of study for teachers under preparation or even with an in-service programme. Also, someone must explain or demonstrate its preparation even with an in-service programme. Also, some one must explain or define steps to make everyone in the classroom 'understand' things/information, etc., and not memorise any item in their course of study. One wonders whether they are awaiting the arrival of yet another class of geniuses to help them get out of their self-inflicted misery.

In most of the advanced countries of the world there is a growing hiatus between the teachers and researchers. Researchers are generally believed to be better/superior to 'mere' teachers. Thus a kind of debate is going on about the primacy in teachers' functions. Recently three types of subcultures have been identified in the USA. (Paulsen and Feldman 1995: 25) They are: *enhancing, counter-cultural,* and *orthogonal.* While the *first* type attempts to state about "member's commitment to the basic beliefs of the dominant culture which "remains classroom teaching", the counterculture "presents a direct challenge to the core values of (the) dominant culture". In *"an orthogonal* culture, the members would simultaneously accept the core values of the dominant culture and a separate unconflicting set of values particular to themselves" (Paulsen and Feldman 1995: 25). This discussion does not include teachers who neither teach nor undertake research or even feel committed to their avocation. Teacher absenteeism and their basic indifference toward their job are serious problems in India, besides the dominance of a subculture very peculiar to her, which could be called *the phenomenon of teacher politicians.* No institution is free from this malaise in our country.

A few more problems, hitherto overlooked because of their peculiar nature, should at least invite our attention. One of these concerns is the question of development of reasoning among the teaching community. Being intellectuals does not necessarily imply that everyone is really capable of reasoning in areas, which are charged with emotionality. Teachers have generally been considered a class skilled in reasoning power, in making out a case logical enough to qualify on these grounds. In rarity does this faculty if it is one, or, the ability if it can be so called, seems to be obvious. Though not empirically validated, logic is not only an academic area; it is also an applied science which one can use for training purposes. In the USA, Edward de Bono's work *Lateral Thinking* has been in news. Though all the claims made by De Bono could not be substantiated despite extensive research, the fact that it showed some positive results is all too obvious and well publicised. A few experiments in this area in Mumbai/Delhi, etc., hold out a possibility unknown thus far.

The other questions are: how much should social concerns and problems bother a teacher? Is he free to express himself and where? Their academic leaders do not admit of the possibility for such a venture. Outside of their academic world do they have a right as teachers to voice their opinions? The Indian Constitution does provide this freedom. I wonder whether this right has been wisely utilised thus far. Teachers' unions are also not very democratic in their organisations and could hardly qualify to be very academic in their concerns. The questions related to the existing multiplicity of religion and cultural diversity is faced in our classrooms. Who is training our teachers to really cope up with this phenomenon? Do we teach that there are states in India with matriarchal systems? Does the meaning of 'secularism' ever encompass Christians, Jains, Buddhists, Sikhs *etc.* other than 'Muslims'? Related to this is the question of values. Which values are we teaching? The Truth takes on various shapes in India, eg. Ahimsa, cows, nationalism etc. mean very different things to different religious groups. Therefore, who defines them and how? What does a teacher do in this regard is not a simple problem which any one-time education/ training can really face up to.

I believe making Indian teachers 'creative' or even conscious of not steamrollering every child to suit a kind of homogenous society India is not, is decidedly a difficult matter. I do not know how does one resolve this complex problem. But then our teacher training programmes have neither been realistic nor imaginative, nor even accommodating. They have historically been irrelevant. Ever since a B.T., or its equivalent L.T./B.Ed., etc., was instituted, 'change' has been an unfamiliar commodity to these institutions. They have been more 'conformists' than 'future'-oriented or 'change'-prone. I have with me an advertisement of a book brought out in 1896 whose 'content-list' is as modern as any textbook we teach today. Does it mean that Education/Teacher Training is such an Eternal Reality like the Absolute that while several new disciplines may take birth in this century and the existing ones may undergo a sea change, both in concepts and illustrations, Education alone must retain its original lustre? If yes, why? Also, it is a relevant issue that while no outsider could enter M.Sc. or M.Com. streams, etc., unless trained in them specifically, Education alone is one area wherein anyone and everyone is not only welcome but can also hope to become its leader as well?

In very simple terms, Education is an 'open' area with no barriers or fences against any in-coming upstart. Whereas it is happy with any non-synchronised curriculum, it does not visualise itself as the leader in its own house.

Shorn of idealism and myths built around the social status and learning of the ancient and medieval teachers, teachers share their 'goodness' with a doctor who is able to diagnose a disease correctly and can administer the most suitable medicine to the patient. His eyes can detect the symptoms of a disease much better than any other common practitioner. Besides, his humane outlook puts him in a class all by himself. So does a good lawyer who knows the law and can interpret it to build a proper case in favour of his client. He studies and devotes all his attention to the work he chooses to undertake. A 'good' teacher, not unlike the said doctor or lawyer, knows his subject, is capable of thinking and can communicate in the manner most suited to the children under his charge. The 'bad' ness comprises inadequate command on the communication skills, perfunctory information and lack of devotion to one's job. *This should be true for any worker in any field.* Teacher is merely an employee hired by society to undertake a specific work.

Unfortunately, our teachers' colleges neither teach him any communication skills nor allow him guided practice for any length of time so that one comes to realise that teaching is *serious* business and one cannot afford to take it lightly or even permit the prospective teacher to become aware that newer methods of teaching should be adopted and researched and experimented and not go in for undertaking meaningless theoretical researches.

Also, should we not acknowledge that the history of modern teacher training in India is less than 200 years old and that the form in which we know it and are familiar with is only seventy odd years old? In a nation which boasts of learning traditions running into past thousands of years, have we ever tried to discover the methods of teaching our ancestors followed or assess whether anyone of these methods of preparing teachers in relevant for our times? Traditions have their own merit. They are neither to be scoffed at nor admired unwittingly. While change has its own place and value, change, as we all know, does not always mean progress.

Thus far the theoretical aspects of pedagogy have dominated teacher education scenario. In terms of weightage we cannot discover any significant value being attached to the skills of teaching. Why should this situation have arisen at all, has also not been analysed. Indeed, I have not come across a single research work of any substance on this aspect of the irrelevance of teacher education curricula. *Parrot-like repetition of its irrelevance helps no one.* Interestingly enough, the answer to this poser was always available. Only we have shown no inclination to acknowledge it. The overburdening of curriculum with unnecessary facts is the direct consequence of making education part of university system and giving designations to Education personnel similar to what others have in academic disciplines, ignoring completely the fact that on its own Education is no discipline and therefore does not need any profundity. Scholarship in Education invariably means information about some other discipline. The baneful influence of university initiated in India in 1919 by Sadler Commission has overshadowed Education's core importance of being skill-based.

In the West this debate is already on. In India a meaningless Ph.D. in Education commands mere respect than one's ability to communicate or teach. On the contrary the West can come out with a work like *Taking Teaching Seriously* and point out that 'good' teaching and 'good' research are not necessarily equal, nor should they command equal value. Good teaching is therefore defined in terms of one's functions in classroom. There is need to re-examine the location of 'Education' in universities where it is neither a fish nor a fowl. Education never had much of an 'academic' content. However, universities and teaching techniques do not go well with each other. For the latter objectives, one has to have IITs or ITIs, etc. I am only saying that the withdrawal of the 'academic' content from the existing relationships will only help Education to grow on its own.

What, however, a teacher may develop are the social concerns as part of his curriculum. Based on logic and systems analysis, a teacher could be equipped to think for himself, independently of the so-called academic disciplines, and thereby be able to acquire insights into children's behaviour, their interests, their outlook and socialisation processes, and also be able to cut, prune and present the flowers of his thought processes.

A teacher is fundamentally a thinking being. But when he does not face either a challenge in thinking or work, his faculties are dulled. Separated from the present day baneful influence of university academia and allowed to flower in his/her own area of work, a teacher could compete and compare with anyone with whom he hesitates at present to mix. A teacher is not to be overawed by the presence of 'superior beings' into some kind of coerced behaviour or conduct; instead he must be encouraged to recognise his own moorings.

Let us take an example. If a teacher of Mathematics has to learn about his subject area, university is the only place where he needs to go. But if he desires to become a teacher for acquiring skills in teaching, a teachers' college would be his correct destination. The marriage of the two is absolutely unnecessary and the argument that a teacher ought to know his subject as well as the skills of teaching is tenable only if we recognise that for a teaching job both are necessary and that the two different agencies could look after two different jobs. If a teacher does not know Mathematics, the university should be held accountable for its failure in its assigned function even as a teachers' college could be made answerable for his lack of skills in communication. I fail to understand why a Professor of History or Physics should be declared the norm to adjudge (in terms of equivalent academic merits) a Professor of Education except for purposes of salaries. While academic disciplines grow more on the strength of speculation, theorising or on experiments under laboratory conditions, the world of teaching requires very little theorising since its value lies mainly in the art and craft of holding students' attention, ability to explain a concept and the mastery in the art of communication. If the universities have done their job well, the rest could be taken care of elsewhere.

Toward a Fresh Look at Curriculum

Without entering into a fruitless debate about the unimaginative and non-competitive efforts at curricular reforms, we may acknowledge straightaway that there are numerous reasons why a fresh attempt in this direction has become 'imperative'. These challenges have occurred independent of any government decision or a public outcry or even because a professional group has woken up from some kind of beauty sleep. Instead, they have woken up because of technological revolution which has totally transformed our life-style, including the sources of information gathering, and also because the nature of competition too has changed. Compared to this scenario, time was when sources of information were limited. For instance, they were: (*i*) religious discourses, (*ii*) political campaigns, (*iii*) print media, and lastly (*iv*) the classroom teacher. Part of the respect a teacher received was because of his caste, the theological character of his teaching, but largely because of his possession in the form of some 'select' skill or information. Today modern technology overshadows any other form of information gathering simply because it has easy and inexpensive availability, it matches public curiosity and levels of comprehension besides being audience-paced and convenience-oriented. In other words, it is consumer-friendly, overcoming caste, age and other types of bars.

In brief, the all-pervasive nature of technology has changed classroom interaction in a manner unknown thus far. Even in India we use radio and television extensively at all levels and in all parts of the country. A highly structured society has become further structured and for once this division is on the lines of one who has access to 'quality' information and the other who is not so lucky. *These 'luck'-less ones are not necessarily illiterate, rural or tribal.* They may as well come from government and municipal schools and even colleges where they acquire outmoded skills and ideas which will not stand them in good stead at the time when they need them. In short, we have our society divided, both vertically and horizontally, directly in proportion to its various segments possessing early the quality information and skills which entitles them to cushy jobs or no jobs. Without unnecessarily drawing the attention of the reader to the eventual outcome of this reality, that is, increasing violence all around and demand for larger and larger protection of ignorance and poverty, we may as well limit our discussion to classroom teaching and the possibilities of preparing teachers who may take up the challenges posed before them. The nature of challenge also needs to be defined. The virtual classroom and the virtual universities are not going to permit the present system to remain as static as it has been thus far.

The second challenge to Indian education *per se* has come from advanced countries that are currently advertising their educational wares in the market. For example UK team which arrived in India shortly after an Australian team had left, proposed to offer the Indians 'skill-based' courses in place of the 'profession based' ones. They reminded Indians "that the government regards education as a giant industrial process whose products have to be managed, promoted, sold and brought out into line with adjacent industrial process, manufacturing, marketing as mass commodities" (*The Times of India,* November 20, 1996). While majority of Indian educationists still believe education to be a static, moral / social obligation and to be undertaken politically, a few are not overawed by the consequences of technology being unleashed everyday or the superiority of the 'Western' product. A large chunk of Indian talent is comparable with the best in the world. But, unfortunately, our semi-medieval society would eventually revert to barbarism if we did not quickly overhaul classroom interaction and changed the attitudes of our teachers. The sharp class and social cleavages in India would one day halt our march toward future if we did not give up our present day cliches, apathy and ignorance about the meaning of education and start valuing education as an instrument to fight poverty and ignorance with. In a relatively stable and non-technological world people could be happy even in poverty and could take their misfortune as part of fate. No longer now. The WTO and the IPR (world trade organisation and intellectual property rights) have already forced the government to sit up and learn to take steps. For instance, the NIEPA has now a unit on the WTO and a team is going to work out a plan to face up to the challenge of the intellectual property rights. But unfortunately not much is likely to happen. The schemes take too long to percolate down. Here also there is a class distinction.

Teacher education curriculum, therefore, cannot be unimaginative, static and class-oriented. It has to be imaginative, dynamic, class-less but competitive and technology-based, aimed at meeting the requirements of an uncertain world. Until something new came there is no chance that the information technology will not leave us alone.

We might as well remember that the social cost of inefficiency in teaching is enormous. There is enough evidence already which points out that Indian labour, which is unskilled and illiterate, as well as India's educated class is less than efficient. The result is that while daily wages and salaries, as the case may be are low in India, but in terms of their productivity are exorbitantly high. As it is, numerous professionals who are migrating outside India have to acquire a 'new' culture and work ethic to be able to adjust. Since, basically, Indians do not lack abilities to meet any challenge, they are able to compete and in some cases they also outshine others But have we ever examined the contribution Indian schools make to sustain, nurture and identify these abilities? The reason is very simple: our teachers are neither trained properly nor do they ever realise that their inefficiency, lack of imagination and conformism *etc,* are costing heavily already. I believe this realisation alone (if we had a social conscience) could take us a long way on the path of meeting the challenges of an uncertain future, if not fully at least half way down the road.

Also, let us not overlook the fact that while the contemporary association of teacher training with the universities is less than a century old, the criticism of the programmes for teacher education has been fairly vocal for several decades now, condemning it as both irrelevant and dysfunctional. Almost all attempts at using a variety of cosmetics have been miserably ineffective and ill advised. There is a possibility to identify a few reasons for it. For instance, it may be because what we offer in the form of an updated curriculum has really no empirical basis for being meaningful, necessary and motivating. Also, because of its association with university, and in its quest for becoming 'academic', it has ceased to be skill-based. Too much of theorising and lack of the 'real feel' of the classrooms has contributed to its gradual lowering down in actual status, without making it in anyway look even close to any of the existing disciplines etc.

The entire schools, curriculum being examination-oriented and the society having increasingly become conscious of the value of excellence in the examination results, we have, it would appear, ceased to possess the *elan* to suitably modify the purpose of teacher education. While we condemn the examination in teacher education programmes as being pernicious because of their undue emphasis on rote-memory and their one-time judgement, in practice we have done precious little to change it or accept the same if we cannot do anything else. Let us remember that classroom instruction cannot be easy and homogenous in a tightly unstructured society. Children with varying SES backgrounds, a wide range of mental and linguistic abilities and motivational levels cannot take equal benefits from the same class. No single teacher can face a class of students with this kind of variety. And when we know that all teachers have neither similar aptitudes, abilities, competencies nor the drive, the results are bound to be predictably uneven. Even this fact is not very clearly acknowledged.

The teacher education programmes depend on the existence, expansion and enrichment of the school organisation, curricular changes and systemic upgradation, *etc.* This dependence is one-sided and not even mutual. If it were so, that is, if both were interdependent, teacher education programmes would not have been all that static or unimaginative. We all know that numerous changes have occurred in the curricula, teaching aids, etc., in the school system but they have taken ages to be reflected in the teacher education programmes. How come teacher training is so backward looking and traditional and the system for which it exists is not so? In simple terms, teacher education need not be the leader. Surprisingly, it has accepted that role of being a second- class fiddler.

Perhaps one of the reasons why teacher education is no more than an 'official' or 'statutory' requirement has defined its role and character. Indeed, why was it initially decided to take on a passive role can be discovered by reading the history of any educational system. Teaching *per se* started quite independently of any deliberate attempt to organise even a system of education. From an unorganised, primitive system to living in a highly complex modern society with defined rules to govern specific social obligations it is really carries the story of the evolution and march of human organisations. It is in this process that teaching arose as a social function with whose help societies have been able to transmit, preserve and enhance the quality of information they gathered from experience—be it empirical, interactive or need-based. One need hardly be surprised that the elderly people commanded veneration because of the length of their experience. Later on propitiation of the gods acquired a ritualistic status and thereby added yet another dimension to teaching—even if this got restricted to group/family or a clan. Teaching as an independent profession arose much later when the body of information and skills to be transmitted grew both in volume and number. Here the quality of teaching depended on the quality and quantity of information. In ancient Indian Ashramas too one can easily discover the predominance of the 'selective', need-based teaching. While the fame of the teacher attracted students, the class of students was determined by the quality of information a teacher had. In no case the craft of teaching was considered distinctly different from the actual acquisition or transmission of either skill or information. We can thus discover the reason why teaching as a separate art or craft did not develop until we reached the 18th century.

All I am trying to say is that whereas educational system has a long history of having evolved numerous disciplines, education had to wait until the late 19th century to be recognised as a vocation for the few who developed some interest in teaching the basics to small children. Even here the interest had twin bases: (1) children have independent personalities and are not mini-adults, and (2) a recognition of the fact that some learn better than others if they are attended to properly. Therefore, a J.S. Mill would be taught by his father to learn Greek and Latin long before he attained the age of 10, a Rousseau had to open a school for experimenting with his newly developed philosophy of naturalism or a Tolstoy had to teach his own serf-children to show that love and freedom were excellent teachers. These men knew no pedagogy but they helped develop one.

Pedagogy has, therefore, grown into a distinct body of information, skill and knowledge because numerous scholars who wanted to transmit their own acquisition have left records of their efforts. We have thus inherited a tradition of teaching and become a body of pedagogues. Now a stage has come when the stock needs be taken and the future course of action clearly defined.

The future of curriculum development depends on its being socially and intellectually relevant, and this is not possible unless we undertake empirical research on a massive scale. It would be preferable if such research is carried out longitudinally. As it is, theoretical research in education is almost universal. Not much can be said about its quality. Data based statistical research also constitutes a major chunk of scholarly efforts. What we lack are both a critical analysis and a desire to empirically validate the theories we propose to hold. Elsewhere in this book I have seriously questioned the relevance of research for policy making. We are neither taught nor do we on our own have come to realise the importance of the chapter wherein a candidate must be made to define the relevance of a piece of research.

Landmarks in Development of Teachers' Colleges in India

In India we have so far failed to produce a proper history of teacher education. Still, whatever material, exists is enough to suggest that in almost all British colonies its total history does not span more than two centuries. For instance, in the USA too normal school grew with the common school. The first public (government) normal school was started at Lexington, Massachusetts in 1839. A study of its curricula, made in 1890 indicated that "no great change in the curriculum" of normal schools had been visible until then. The curriculum consisted of History of Education, Science of Education, Mental Science and Methods in the Elementary branches. In 1898 the USA had 127 normal schools in the public sector and almost a similar number in the private sector.

At the secondary level the first Department of Education was set up at Michigan University in 1879 where the first chair of Pedagogy was established. This followed the setting up of several other departments of education elsewhere with professors of education/pedagogy where a fixed curriculum was offered. Herein Philosophy of Education, Psychology, and Pedagogy were offered as far back as 1894; School Administration was added later on with an emphasis upon data gathering and statistics.

It should interest us to know that with the development of science of education, school classrooms were put on the back burner. Education was divorced from classroom as the focus of inquiry, both by John Dewey and Charles Judd, who laid great store by Psychology shifted from improved classroom teaching to examining its psychological bases. The result was that research started getting valued for its own sake. Specialisation in certain areas like Psychology of Learning, Statistics, etc., grew apace. In the process of developing science of education, Psychology received greater attention than the concerns for the quality of school teachers.

In the hierarchy of teacher education, university departments came to occupy a much higher pedestal than the normal schools, and the monopoly of universities, to the utter disregard of practical problems of school teachers, gradually became all too patent. University values came to dominate the area and "normal schools evolved from a single purpose institution devoted to training teachers into low status institution of teachers" college in the educational hierarchy.

By the 1920s, a full-fledged Foundation of Education movement started gathering momentum. The school foundation approach was widely adopted in many universities and colleges, though separate disciplinary courses such as history philosophy and sociology of education, etc., have not disappeared.

In 1980, in the USA, researchers came "to decry the low quality of students in teacher education programmes and the questionable academic credentials of the professors of education preparing them".

Conclusions of a study in the volume *Teacher Education as a Field of Inquiry* by Professor Wayne J. Urban of Georgia State University have relevance for us:

(*i*) Teacher education has always depended on market forces, which govern it supply and demand.

(*ii*) Normal school students come from more ordinary social class backgrounds than university students.

(*iii*) There is a view that gender and class have seriously affected teacher education programmes. (in the USA, school teachers are invariably women).

(*iv*) Reform in teacher education is dependent on the reforms in the occupation of teaching.

In brief, teacher education that is studied, conceptualised, analysed and "reformed without careful and critical attention to the social context in which teacher education exists, as well as the practitioners and the practice of teaching, will quite likely be an empty exercise."

Coming to an analysis of the Indian scenario of teacher education, we would be well advised to note each and every point raised thus far. Like the USA, India too has had the experience of British colonisation and their attitudes because until this day our institutions have not learnt to overgrow the past.

The landmarks now being detailed have marked similarities with the history of teacher education programme in the USA. We are in fact in urgent need of a proper history being produced in this area.

Before we undertake a historical survey of teacher education in India, we should remember that M. Liberman had found teaching a quasi-profession (Kuvernab 1956). In terms of rank order, Hoyle discovered it to be much lower than a doctor, an engineer or a lawyer, and specially primary teacher was found to rank 19 on a 25-point occupational scale (Bernbaum, Noble and Whiteside); and I found that as a discipline it has no standing at all (Singh 1969). With such a background it becomes even more interesting to record why were normal schools opened in India. The third report of Adam thus records the objectives: "the old race of school masters will thus gradually pass away and be succeeded by a race trained from the beginning under the operation of new system.... The general effect of this training upon the face of society, if steadily pursued, will be to increase intelligence, enterprise, and morality; to make the people better acquainted with their own interests and with the legitimate means of protecting and promoting them; and I confidently believe and hope, to attach them by gratitude and affection to the European rulers of the country as their real friends and benefactors" (Singh 1969: 181) He further recorded: "We are among the people but not of them...The consequence is that we have no hold on their sympathies, no seat in their affections" (Singh 1969: 237). His perception of the Indians, shared by the majority, was: "The truth appears to be that they are so completely bowed down by ages of foreign rule that they have lost not only the capacity and the desire, but the very idea, of self-government in matters regarding which the authority of the state is directly or indirectly interposed" (Singh 1969: 133).

If these observations are taken to represent a typical example of British attitudes, the introduction of teacher training in India had a political purpose of winning over the sympathies of the vanquished. When we recall that Bell and Lancester had learnt from India itself the first lessons in initial and inexpensive classroom pedagogy and vetted it in the economics of mass production, the 'models' suggested by Adam acquire a new meaning. Let us have a look at the three 'models' suggested by Adam for teacher training.

These models were suggested to an "inattentive government" which had taken no note of the work of the most enlightened parts of the 19th century Europe where "the practical science of education had been developed." Adam was thus citing Mr. B.H. Hodgson's opinions (Singh 1969: 152).

The first model suggested by Adam was of learning 4 school books in vernacular prepared by the authorities which were to form the basis of examination conducted by a mobile examiner of prospective teachers in 4 stages—i.e. one a year would be given monetary rewards. These vernacular series of books would consist of a given type of content by the government and would qualify a teacher for a class corresponding to the level of the book he is able to master.

The third model envisaged a normal school which, when defined, was to be located in "the vernacular department of the English School" (Singh 1969: 164). The admission was to be made open to all in-service teachers who came to it during their 'free' time and studied with stipends paid in full. "The normal school therefore should be open to native teachers throughout the year" (Singh 1969: 165). *The concept anticipated the District Institutes of Education for Teachers.*

If somehow we have an idea that teacher training in

England has been in a better state than in India or they have had better institutions than ours may be asked to revise our opinion. While tracing the history of teacher education in England, D'Souza and Chatterjee (1956: 4) said that it all started by being "simple, short and economical" in the 19th century. Under Kaye-Shuttleworth, the period of training got extended from 3 months to 2 years in the first ever teachers' college at Battersea. From the pupil-teacher system under which half-trained and half-educated teachers were being produced, in 1904 the curriculum was modified and improved to prepare them better. *As late as 1944*, the MacNair Committee had discovered that teacher education *"lacked professional status; had poor quality preparation"*, there were divisions, fissures and castes within the profession and there was no coordination in the various stages of teachers' preparation (D'Souza and Chatterjee 1956: 10). For the first time Sir T.P. Nunn (1932) had remarked that "as the reorganisation of the school system develops a corresponding new orientation in the Training College system develops a corresponding new orientation in the Training College system will necessarily follow" (D'Souza & Chatterjee 1956: 11). And not unlike India the social origin of the teachers in England remain "working and lower middle classes" (D'Souza & Chatterjee 1956: 40). A study by Miss Margaret Phillips confirmed this fact.

In brief, we in India are in excellent company as far as teacher preparation goes. Only we are less forthright in our analysis and are not very sure in which direction we wish to take it. And the way self-financing institutions are being opened and run should make us sit up and admit that things haven't changed for the better after all.

A comparison of our curricula with that of England reveals that there the emphasis remained on classroom practice and the theoretical studies are limited to being supportive and reinforcing the practice component (D'Sourza & Chatterjee 1956: 60-63).

Christian missions in India set up the first teacher training institutions. They were interested initially in elementary education but later on they came to feel drawn toward secondary education as well. Therefore, whether such institutions were started in Portuguese occupied territory of Goa, French ruled parts of Pondicherry or the East India Company government's portions of the rest of India; the missionaries were the first to start teacher education institutions. The obvious reason was "to bring light to the dark territories of India where people had sunk into social degradation and ignoble moral standards". Education was the tool to be employed for their all round upliftment. Teachers thus had to have religious goal-oriented training with the aim of converting the locals to superior forms of moral practices.

In India, Serampore (Bengal) was chosen by Danish missionaries to set up the first teacher training institution. Theology-laced proselytising-oriented Christian missionaries wanted India's poor, orphaned, lower-castes tribals, etc., to receive the fruits of their labour first. They therefore concentrated on elementary education area. The first institution to train secondary teachers was opened at Madras in 1856. The second was set up at Lahore in 1880. Even by 1902 there were no more than six training colleges and a few secondary training schools.

The fact that teacher's colleges and schools were mostly for men showed social discrimination and gender bias. However, missionaries were the first to enter this other area for the women too.

As a policy, teacher training started receiving encouragement from the officials of East India Company. In March 1825, the Court of Directors, while confirming the monthly grant of Rs. 500 to the Calcutta School Society, appreciated the measures adopted for the education of persons as teachers of native schools. "The Calcutta Schools Society appears to combine with its arrangement for giving elementary instruction arrangements of still greater importance for educating teachers of indigenous schools. This last object we consider worthy of great encouragement, since it is upon the character of indigenous schools that the education of the great mass of the population must ultimately depend. By training up, therefore, a class of teachers, you provide for the eventual extension of improved education to a portion of the natives of India, for exceeding that which any elementary instruction that could be immediately bestowed would have any chance of reaching" (Quoted in Fisher's Memoirs; see Basu 1952: 88).

The Native Society of Bombay followed suit and in 1826 it deputed 24 trained teachers in different primary schools (Srivastava 1955: 425).

The 1854, Wood's Despatch wanted these efforts to grow apace, and therefore desired: "to see the establishment, with as little delay as possible, of training schools and classes for masters in each Presidency in India." It recommended that the pupil-teacher system of England should be adapted to suit Indian conditions. The English system mainly consisted "in the selection and instruction of pupil teachers (awarding a small payment to the masters of the schools in which they are employed for instruction outside schools hours); their ultimate removal, if they prove worthy, to normal schools; and in securing to them sufficient salary when they are afterwards employed as school masters." The system in India could be open to both the government and grant-in-aid institutions. "The Directors wanted that the profession of the school masters may, for future, afford inducements to the natives of India as such as are held out in other branches of public service."

On 7 April, 1859 Lord Stanley, Secretary of State for India, dissuaded the administration from procuring teachers in England for India and desired the same to be made available locally. Until then, 4 normal schools functioned in Bengal, I in UP (at Banaras), and sanction for 3 more was accorded for UP area. Besides, in Madras and Bombay training was being offered to students for Anglo-Vernacular school positions also. How times change! Now it is the turn of the Indian teachers to go and man schools and colleges both in Great Britain and the USA.

Interestingly, salary grants were being given to teachers, whether trained or untrained. Those *not* trained and not wishing to be trained either were free to take tests to qualify for grades. The tests consisted of (*i*) General Education, and (*ii*) Principles of Education and School Management (suitable for the grade where a teacher was teaching). The latter consisted of methods of teaching English and vernacular such as reading, writing, *etc.*, Geography and History, (*iii*) writing notes of a lesson, (*iv*) organisation of a high school, and (*v*) Moral discipline related to conduct of pupils of a high school.

In the Punjab, written examinations had the same weightage as the practice of teaching (Singh 1990: 30).

The Indian Education Commission, 1882, also known as the Hunter Commission, made a few significant recommendations in this area. In fact, this Commission gave teacher education an impetus and direction for growth. By 1892 India had 116 training institutions for men and 15 for women. Training and certification were until then two separated functions. The certification followed 2 years of successful teaching in a school and that too after training.

In 1892 the Board of Examiners for Teachers' Certificates was created at Madras. Training certificates were awarded after 12 months of training at a normal school, provided a candidate passed both Theory and Practice examinations. Physical and Gymnastic training were started in 1892. At I.T. College, Lucknow in 1985, English Teachers' Certificate was introduced. Training for Drawing Masters was first given in Bengal in 1892.

The third Quinquennial Review, Vol. I (p. 238) recorded the unpopularity of training courses. "It has been the habit, not only of students, but also of the Inspecting officers who select them, to regard normal schools as Reformatories, to which objectionable teachers from village schools were sent by way of punishment, not perhaps for their shortcomings as teachers, but because of some reasonable or unreasonable hostility on the part of their Deputy Inspector toward them."

The turn of the century saw 6 training colleges in India—Saidapct, Rajamudry, Kurseong, Allahabad, Lahore and Jabalpur; 50 secondary schools and 54 primary teachers' schools (Mukerji 1968: 12).

The 1904 Government of India Resolution on Educational Policy desired that "teachers be trained in the art of teaching," and fixed the duration of training as *one* year for graduates and *two* for non-graduates.

By the 1913 Resolution on Education, teacher education had started showing all its currently known weaknesses. It made suggestions regarding (*i*) improvement of the economic condition of teachers, (*ii*) constant alertness about the improvement of the academic quality of teachers and a need for their regular in-service upgradation so that they may not become ignorant, (*iii*) attending to issues like the best size for a practising school, the nature and method of practical work, the relative importance of methodology and of psychological study, the best testament of educational history, the extent to which classroom subjects may be taught during training, to differentiate the course for graduates from that of undergraduates, and the extent of which students' work may be included in the award of the diploma etc. etc.

In 1917 the Calcutta University Commission recorded the poor quality of teacher training programmes in existence, wherein they did not learn to be either 'good' teachers or good administrators. Therefore, they recommended the opening of a department of education in a university where they proposed that a systematic study of science and art of education would be taken up. A Professor assisted by Readers and Lecturers should man these departments. These departments should get in touch with other departments like departments of Philosophy, History, Economics, Experimental Psychology, etc. Also, these departments of Education should have demonstration schools where practical trials of *new* methods of teaching, new combinations of school subjects and new plans of school organisations be experimented upon. The department should have an excellent library, bring out publications, undertake research and help professional growth of teachers in service. It may also serve as a link between Boards of Education and Intermediate Colleges and Committees of High Schools.

The Commission observed: *"the three essential components of teacher education* were *knowledge of the subject matter, practical training and theoretical training but under existing conditions the first is often unfulfilled, second rarely possible and third too little regarded by the university in framing the regulations*. Mysore was first to have a faculty of Education in 1925."

The Hartog Committee, which came in 1929, painted a dismal picture of teachers and their training. It said: *"The period of training is too short, the curriculum too narrow and the teaching staff inadequately qualified."* The Committee recorded the inefficiency of schools, the elderly teachers exerting a depressing effect on the younger and well-trained teachers. They also reiterated about the shortness of courses and showed dissatisfaction with old methods of teaching.

But of 18 universities, 13 had departments of Education until 1932 and Bombay was the first to launch an M.Ed. programme in 1936.

In the first decade of the twentieth century specialised training of teachers had started in areas like Technical Education (Madras), certificates for teaching Art, Agriculture and Industrial Arts (Bombay), Architecture and Building, Cabinet Making and Metal Work (Punjab), etc.

Although separate institutions trained teachers, the courses remained same for both men and women. Kindergartens had come to India and hence training for them had started on European lines.

The Abbot-Wood Report of 1937 is perhaps as important as Gandhiji's Basic Education Scheme, which attempted to transform the attitudes of teachers by proposing a new curriculum in schools and methods of teaching, which inevitably had an effect on teacher education.

The Abbot-Wood Report wanted the training of intending teachers in the technical arts of their crafts with the purpose of fortifying them against future disappointments. A normal school, according to them, should concern itself with the social "why" of education as well as with the technical "how" of teaching. They emphasised the arrangement for technical teachers on a regular refresher course basis but within a broad framework.

By 1940 the Basic Education scheme had caught on and specific institutions were opened to award degrees/ diplomas for teachers in this area.

The Central Advisory Board of Education (CABE) which had been revived in 1935, went into the question of 'Training, Recruitment and Conditions of Service of Teachers' in early 1940s. The Board made the usual recommendations such a training all teachers, fixing minimum qualifications for Nursery and Infant Schools. The Sergeant Committee of CABE wanted normal schools to award diplomas after 2 years of training, and that one who had special aptitude must have a third year for being qualified for Senior Basic Schools.

The University Education Commission (1948), The Secondary Education Commission (1953), and the Indian Education Commission (1966)—all looked into the question of teacher education. In the recent past the National Council of Teacher Education has been set up by an Act of Parliament, and is supposed to regulate the programme. But the achievements of the NCTE could easily make a sensitive and knowledgeable individual turn red in the face and look for cover.

Perhaps the most innovative as well as disturbing part of teacher education has been Distance Education, also mistakenly called Correspondence Education. I do not propose to anticipate the future except that I would like to reiterate the points, which India's history of education in this area has raised but which have remained unattended thus far. While no claims for originality are being made because they can hardly ever be sustained logically, even so they demand attention.

Points to Ponder

(1) The first requirement seems to be to make teacher training skill-based and less theoretical.

(2) The examination for certification purposes should lay emphasis on the quality of teaching and not on 'information-gathering'.

(3) The variety of teacher's required, such as for general subjects, science, and technical and vocational areas, should each have their individual, specific skills defined for success.

(4) The unmotivated and unskilled should be made to find teaching a difficult job to hold on to. Unproductively in teaching has to be avoided on all costs.

(5) We should accept the fact that teaching is 'quasi-professional,' skill-oriented and low-rewarding occupation. Therefore, its development on non-university lines may be encouraged. Organisations like AIATE should be involved in the training, selection and criteria-determining functions.

References

Basu, A.N. (Ed) 1952): Indian Education in Parliamentary Papers, Part I (1832), Asia.

Bernbaum, G., Noble, G. and Whiteside, J.: Intra-Occupational Prestige Differentiation in Teaching, Pedagogy Europe, 5: 1-59.

D'Souza, Austin A. and Chatterjee, J.N. (1956): Training for Teaching in India and England, Orient Longmans.

Hoyle, E.: The Professionalisation of Teachers: A Paradox, British Journal of Educational Studies. 30(2): 161-71.

Liberman, M. (1956): Education as a Profession, New Jeresey: Prentice Hall.

McIntyre, D. John And Byrd, David M. (eds.) 1996): Preparing Tomorrow's Teachers: The Field Experience (Teacher Education Year Book IV), Association of Teacher Education, USA,

Mukerji, S.N. (ed.) 1968): Education of Teachers in India, New Delhi: S. Chand & Co.

Parulekar, R.V. (ed) 1945): Survey of Indigenous Education in the Province of Bombay (1820-30), Bombay: Indian Institute of Education.

Paulsen, Michael B, and Feldman, Kenneth A. (1995): Taking Teaching Seriously: Meeting the Challenge of Instructional *Improvement, Washington: The George Washington University.*

Singh, L.C. (Ed) 1990); Teacher Education in India, New Delhi: NCERT.

Singh, R.P. (1969): The Indian Teacher, New Delhi: National Publishing House,

Srivastava, B.D. (1995): The Development of Modern Indian Education, Orient Longmans.

2
Teacher Education Challenges and the Emerging Trends

"Establishment of knowledge bases for a proactive critical information auto autopsy using 'Artificial Intelligent' for 'Knowledge Wars' through 'software soldiers' as predicted by Alvin Toffler is certainly on the cards."

The current physical and intellectual state of India's teacher education programme holds out no promise of a discernible improvement in the near future. I have been very unhappy about its programmes and functioning. There are quite a few reasons for my unhappiness. In fact, way back in 1998 I had raised a few points about the direction it ought to be going in one of the issues of the AIU Newsletter. The first Chairman of the NCTE and his faithfuls were far removed from the reality. They refused to be sensitive toward the world trends and learnt nothing from India's own cultural and literary history. Being a lone voice then and now, I am quite sure this paper is most likely to meet deafening silence – the fate it deserves.

The first point that I wish to raise is: Who in this country has tried to define the 'good' traits in a teacher? And who, I should like to ask, has devised any strategy to inculcate any of the desirable traits through their teacher education programme? Also, is there a system by which it is possible to assess and grade any of those traits consensually established? There is considerable discussion about the type of values teachers ought to have, but in reality the national dailies and private discussions suggest that few, if any, get displayed in the classrooms. India's dailies carry tales everyday of what teachers actually do and in no case those write-ups are very flattering to the image of the community. About the reading habits of the teacher educators too studies have revealed bleak pictures. Personally I have no answers but I do not come across many that even raise relevant questions.

In my knowledge the first and perhaps the last such definition had occurred to the Vedic seers. This is what they wrote:

"A teacher should have the ability to build up the students under his charge. He must never be proud of his knowledge. He should be as glorious as fire and possess qualities of leadership. He must be specialist of his branch of knowledge. Just as a cow collects milk in her udders after grazing grass, a teacher should collect knowledge through reflection and self-study. He should make teaching an enjoyable experience even as food items are made tasty and palatable before they are served. He should be popular among his students and be their benefactor. Sitting in the midst of his students he must look distinguished because of his knowledge". RIGVEDA 1/69/2

Since then there hasn't been any dearth of scholars trying to define a 'good' teacher but no one has bothered to tell us how to prepare one. All that we find are mere attempts to suggest 'models'. And in this area plagiarists abound. The acme of the great Buch-ian tribe offers itself as role model within the country. This is how an incident that took place in one of our university 'teacher preparation classrooms'. Once a university student stood up to complement the teacher for his recent publication, "Look Sir, the Americans are great plagiarists. They have copied verbatim from your book." Perhaps we Indians are the most original among the plagiarists. While the Europeans theorize, Americans innovate but none comes up with a model that can successfully replicate its Indian namesake.

I cite now a few problems concerning the theme that a UNESCO publication raises.

Presented in six chapters the UNESCO publication* addresses squarely the problem of professional development of teachers across the globe. In the opening chapter the author defines the area and gives background information. It acknowledges the double role of teachers in educational reforms – being the subjects and objects of change. "This new emphasis has been welcomed by teachers as it represents a much–needed appreciation of teachers' work, and also

in which it is implemented.

(f) Teacher-educators must know how to work in teams and collaborate in their work.

(g) Teacher-educators must enjoy teaching. This disposition will generate a positive attitude towards teaching their students.

It is possible to improve teacher education program in India because teachers seldom resign during their working tenure. But we must look at the type of challenges that have started emerging in the recent years. I do not come across any discussion on these challenges and certainly no efforts are being made by any university system in the country to face any of them.

The first challenge emanates from educational technology, for instance by the robotics. Honda has reportedly developed a robot Asimo to aid in the teaching of science to young students in areas like the centre of gravity, balancing and general advancement of teaching. This goes to show that it is the industry that has discovered new skills involved in classroom teaching and not the teachers.

At the end of the last century the advanced countries were already offering a teacher education curriculum comprising the basic components of Total Quality Management, Computer Literacy and Interactive Methods of Learning, Management and use of libraries for Human Resource Development, Lateral Thinking and Creativity, Entrepreneurship, Human Resource Employment as a Social Investment, Evaluation and Assessment Techniques and Public Relations.

In this connection I would like to make a reference to a paper written by Krishna Kumar, Chairman, NCERT (see, Sunday H.T. April, 10, 2005) that students are taught many things but not personal hygiene and at least no rural child seems to practice it. The evidence lies in rural children in recorded history are unaware of the advantages of paring their nails. The importance given to paring one's nails outshines the issues like why no one speaks truth whereas we never tire of preaching from the housetops the virtue of being truthful, or, why do we prefer drugs to leading simple addiction-free lives when everyone around us keeps telling the benefits that accrue from it. The chairman, NCERT should be congratulated for showing tremendous concern for the trivialities like paring nails but he overlooks the primary principle of learning, which seems to suggest that people learn more from their immediate neighbourhood and the company they keep than the books they must learn to pass an examination.

Recently not unlike advanced countries India too has mastered the skill of sending satellites into the orbit, therefore she too has successfully launched an educational satellite called EDUSAT. The technological advances achieved in the placing of the satellite in the orbit are decidedly not matched by the information and the uses to which this advancement could be utilized by teachers and the lay people alike. One may be asked to remember that technology is intended to assist the teacher and not replace her / him. But if the teachers let this development pass them by, what good does that do to the country? Unfortunately, this development is being used only for 'Distance Education' and that too is not being utilized for classroom instruction purposes. Teachers do not seem to realize that while for good teachers EDUSAT is a great aid, for the mediocrity it offers a challenge to their survival. The tragedy is that this innovation has failed to evoke any noticeably significant response anywhere, except in the private institutions, which were ahead of others anyway. In one of the latest issues of Television News – a monthly of the Consortium of Educational Communications (an Internet university centre of the UGC) Vol. 2. No. 3 April 2005 says in its editorial titled Director's desk," New Communication Technology, with the convergence of Video and Internet technologies are taking shape and it is going to have greater influence on preservation and retrieval of knowledge as well as teaching learning process in the universities. Before the advent of this technology knowledge was preserved in books and journals. One of the very significant places in the campus and source of information and knowledge was library. With the advent of this technology slowly the things are changing. The journals are now available on electronic mode. In India also UGC Infonet has been making these Electronic Journals available to many Indian universities." India has yet to launch electronic mode of the publication and journals. Already the source of learning has adopted the mode of video programmed texts and graphic based E-resources. Does our B.Ed programme reflect this development? How many teacher educators are aware of this?

Now I cite a book produced by the education's mafia that continues to rule the roost. The title of the book is Professionalization of Teacher Education by Mohammad Mian & Co. I cite from a write-up by C. Seshadri (pages 52-54). Read the lament of a man, who is otherwise thoughtful by training and logical by disposition and draw your own conclusion.

"Universalization of education in its true spirit as of now remains a pipedream. Making education a legally enforceable fundamental right and amending the Constitution to empower local bodies to assume responsibility for education are landmark achievements of course but the sheer magnitude of the task ahead is mind-boggling! Considering the number of additional teachers required alone, at one teacher—one classroom – forty children, we need 9.07 lakh additional teachers to take care of the 36.3 million in the age group 6-11 and another 7.35 lakh to bring the existing TPR (teacher pupil ratio) to 1:40, a total of 16.42 lakh teachers". (cited from A Paradigm for Making Education Indigenous and Contextual, by Maheshwari, A.N., mimeo.). Such is the overall scenario, which any vision statement of teacher education has to take a note of.

As to the growth in size, the launching of new projects and the amount of national regard it is enjoying teacher education never had it so good. India today has one of the largest teacher education systems in the world. Nearly 30,000 teacher educators are engaged in the preparation of school teachers. There are 1300 elementary teacher-training institutions, 430 DIETs and nearly 700 colleges of education and university departments of education. Also there are 5.98 lakh primary schools, 1.76 lakh elementary schools, 98,000 high/ higher secondary schools. Of these

4.52 m teachers are teaching at the primary elementary level. A sizeable number of these is untrained or under trained."

Here is the lament itself

"The spectacular developments, unfortunately, have not been accompanied by concurrent concern and reflection on issues relating to the state of teacher education, especially the capacity of teacher education institutions and the professional capability of teacher educators to address the tasks expected of them. Consider, for example, the case of the high profile DIETs, which came into being more than a decade ago. Although there was the usual euphoria and hype that goes along with the birth of new institutions the more material questions relating to their objectives, programmes, the nature and kind of educational support, which these institutions were expected to give at the district level and, more than all, the capacity of those who were appointed to the DIETs to carry out its omnibus terms of reference have not been discussed in depth. Besides DIETs several other schemes and programmes have been launched. Colleges of education (CTE), Institutes of Advanced Studies in Education (IASEs), Academic Staff Colleges, the pan-India Programmes of Mass-Orientation of School Teachers (PMOST), special Orientation of Primary Teachers and other distance education programmes and District Education Programmes (DPEP)

However, all this hurry of post-NPE activity has been mainly number-driven. But what matters ultimately, the bottom line as it were is the quality of the teacher performance in the classroom. On this indicator, one wonders whether and to what extent all these resource inputs have changed the track record of the teacher education for the better.

If he does not know, who would? At least, on one point he cannot plead 'not guilty'. He belongs to the inner circle of the ruling elite.

I do not think anything more could be added to the credit of the failed statutory body except to say its record of achievement hidden from public gaze stands concealed in the NCTE's archives viz. Anand Sarup committee report. It is one record, which explains why and how hundreds of self-financing teachers' colleges have been made to spring up almost overnight. A study conducted by me has brought out the real face of the organization called the NCTE and the people involved in the running of these institutions into the open. Since the Ministry has refused to bother itself with its working, everyone connected with it is making hey while the sun shines. Read what the founder Chairman of the NCTE — J.S. Rajput (p.31) writes: "Change is everywhere, progress is not. Not every change leads to progress." What does he wish to say? Defend what is happening or feel Socratic about it all?

In a recent National level Test I was amazed to find a peculiar near unanimity on one point among the examinees. They all stated unequivocally that the NCTE—the apex controller and guide of teachers' destiny, has failed to deliver. The examinees went on to add that they would have been much happier had this branch of professional training continued to remain with the University Grants Commission or if the creation of a separate body had become so essential, then it should have been mandated not to act in a hurry to implement half-baked, uninformed policies in such a slip-shod manner as has actually happened. Instead, the newly created body should have been asked to study the world trends in detail and offered couple of models to the Indian States and universities to choose from.

In a huge country like ours with all kinds of disparities no single model could ever hope to succeed and hence all the trouble. The change of guards in the apex system has also not contributed much. On the contrary what should have remained merely rumours are being considered ground-realities. If registrar of a university is issued two contradictory orders within a week on the question of affiliation of a self-financing college just because the apex body itself is unsure of its intentions, one needs no further proof that things are not right after all. There is no other statutory Government of India body like NCTE that has sunk so low in public esteem. I think the time is almost ripe that some one took note of the reasons why this should have happened, if it is really the case. It would be inappropriate for anyone even to suggest that the stories making rounds in the relevant quarters have even an iota of truth in them. It is possible that these stories have gained momentum only because the concerned organization has unfortunately cottoned its ears and has earned the sobriquet of being the most 'arrogant and rigid system' that any government ever devised.

It is quite legitimate to inquire into the reasons why must the UGC prepare syllabi for the B.Ed. programme when the NCTE claims it had done that exercise already? The details that have come to dominate private discussion are not covering anyone with glory. Why not make the details public. In fact, it is imperative to find out that why is the NCTE continuing to accord legal status to private centres for starting self-financing B.Ed. when enough number of proper colleges already exist? The interesting point that has not escaped anyone's notice is that academically advanced States have not been too keen to take benefit of this largesse. Someone therefore must answer the query: Has the Government of India mandated the NCTE to offer employment opportunities to its oldies in the economically starved States? And, why have these benefits been limited to those university departments of education that have only academic mediocrity as their sole criterion for existence?

I now come to a publication, which I am sure cannot be written in India for the simple reason we do not have focused thinkers in education. The title of the book is Educational Foundations (2004) edited by Alan S. Canestrari & Bruce A. Marlowe brought out by Sage. The chapter that should interest us here is: What makes a Good Teacher? The question that is raised and answered in this section of the book relates to: What should be done to improve the scenario?

Paulo Freire is the person cited by the editors who caricatures the teaching process followed in our classrooms. He calls it 'the banking concept of education', which means students come to the classroom with an empty mind, which has to be stuffed with the material available in the form of textbooks or teacher talk. This he calls banking process.

"Because banking education begins with a false understanding of men and women as objects, it cannot promote the development of what Fromm calls biophily, but instead produces its opposite: 'necrophily."

"While life is characterized by growth in a structured functional manner, the necrophilous person loves all that does not grow, all that is mechanical. The necrophilous person is driven by the desire to transform the organic into the inorganic, to approach life mechanically, as if all living persons were things... Memory, rather than experience; having, rather than being, is what counts. The necrophilous person can relate to an object— a flower or a person—— only if he possesses it; hence a threat to his possession is a threat to himself, if he loses possession he loses contact with the world... He loves control, and in the act of controlling he kills life.

Oppression— overwhelming control— is necrophilic; it is nourished by love of death, not life. The banking concept of education, which serves the interests of oppression, is also necrophilic."

The answer to the dehumanising process cited above lies in 'liberating education which, consists in acts of cognition, not transferrals of information. It is a learning situation in which the cognisable object (far from being the end of the cognitive act) intermediates the cognitive actors— teacher on the one hand and students on the other." Indeed, problem –posing education, which breaks with the vertical characteristics of banking education, can fulfil its functions of freedom only if it can overcome the above characteristics.

"Through dialogue, the teacher-of-the –situation and the student-of-the-teacher cease to exist and a new term emerges, teacher-students with students-teachers. The teacher is no longer merely the one-who-teaches, but one who is himself taught in dialogue with the students, who in turn while being taught also teach."

Of course by now we know the recommendations of Paulo Freire but let us hear what Neil Postman and Charles Weingartner have to say in their essay, titled, "So What Do You Do Now?" If the reader will recall these two are all for subversion of the classroom. Here is what they suggest:

1. Your first act of subversion might be conducted in the following way; write on a scrap of paper these questions: (a) What am I going to have my students do today? (b) What's it good for? (c) How do I know?

2. In class, try to avoid telling your students any answers. There are two books that relate the situation as to what happens when teachers refrain from telling students answers. These books are The Dynamics of Learning by Nathaniel Canters; and the other is Carl Rogers titled: On becoming a Person.

3. Try listening and not offering answers. Read in Rogers' book "Communication: Its Blocking and Facilitation"

4. If you feel it is important for your students to learn how to question, try this: Announce in the class that for the next two days, you will not permit them to make any utterances that are not in the form of questions.

5. Try finding out how much subjective you are. Think about it and undertake experiments.

6. Find out: What would you do if you discovered that students have the greatest potential and can achieve the inconceivable.

7. Try asking students to evolve their own syllabus. This is not done in India therefore, it will be little tricky to ask and expect results. May be you get some response.

8. The syllabi deal mostly with the past and nothing that relates to future. Therefore, one could help include questions that deal with the future. For instance, ask a question like; what impact would current technology have on our future?

9. Our future concerns media and communication. Therefore, media study should become an integral part of our classroom instruction. Marshall McLuhan's Understanding Media is to be made compulsory reading.

10. While conventional teaching and the methodologies in use are not taboo, but what is being suggested is fundamental change / shift in emphasis in the roles of teacher and the students. The concern is about the process

and not the product. Here both students and the teacher are one.

11. Ask the question: "Why am I a teacher?" Find an honest answer.

One should remember that teachers are transformative intellectuals. Therefore, the way we train them in India is definitively far removed from the world trend.

Address the problems teachers face in the classrooms.

Any good teacher education program for the country must address the following potential challenges.

1. The uses of technology in the classroom; be it, computer, EDUSAT, E-learning – today's teachers cannot be effective without it.

2. They should be enabled to feel committed to their students and be asked to take interest in their future. In brief, they must develop empathy with their wards.

3. Students should be made to develop skills of rationality. In fact, they may be encouraged to master language skills and develop a sense of discrimination between relevant and irrelevant information. Instead of acquiring a load of information they may be taught and trained to be selective. Therefore, it is much better if prospective teachers are taught logic in place of philosophy, which they will develop anyway.

4. Classroom instruction is a two-way process. Instead of teaching them how to deliver a lesson teachers should become familiar with 'dialogue mode'. A dialogue enables a child to use his brain and skills of communication. The function of education is to enable the learner to be intelligent and communicative. This is not possible if the child does not experience 'democracy' and 'freedom'. Only slaves are not free to talk.

5. Teach them to learn innovation and develop a sense of calculated risk-taking. The future being unpredictable and changes coming unannounced teaching has to enable a learner to be entrepreneurial in life. We need free citizenry with communicative skills and be assured to face future

boldly. For this end we have to change radically both the curriculum and teaching methods. Citing once again the ancient seer, I close with the hope that someday someone will listen.

A book edited by Philip G. Altbach titled: The Decline of the Guru (2002) brings out the fact that higher education in India has become highly politicised. The politics are also of two types: (a) institutional or academic and (b) societal. There is nothing wrong with the latter but everything is wrong with the former. In India right from the appointment of teachers, to their pay packets to working conditions and their consequences are politics-driven matters. The case of starting private universities, self-financing institutions and teacher absenteeism are all related issues. They cannot be seen independently of each other. The decline in the quality of teachers' academic performance is directly related to this reality. In the past single academic year (2004-5) Indian society has been a silent spectator to the non-academic persons getting appointed on crucial positions where their actions will have lasting impression on the future of teachers' classroom performance. But we as a nation have given two hoots to this serious consideration. It is not competence but issues that have nothing to do with academics. That have been allowed to hold sway over academic matters. The situation is becoming grave every passing day. Who would bell the cat? I see little hope that someone can or will tackle the problem in our polity.

Education in India is a political statement. With each change in the government a total overhaul takes place. The assumption for so doing invariably is that the outgoing government was misguided and all their actions must be taken to be suspect. Therefore, there is no surprise that these things happen, and heads roll.

Teacher preparation is likely to continue to be politically- dominated in India through politically favoured courtiers and henchmen fully reflecting policy changes in consonance with political changes. The NCTE –not unlike similar bodies within the Ministry of Human Resources Development will remain an ever-obliging body of sycophants, who will accord greater care to their success in keeping jobs rather than to applying their native academic acumen aimed at improving performance. A teacher by all norms is basically an interpreter of the text and communicator of knowledge. If teacher education program could accomplish even this much one would feel satisfied.

"When balanced scholars speak after due thought those that love education appreciate the relationship of words with their import, even as barley-meal is made blemish–free with the help of a sieve. Such teachers are fortunate because they receive blessings of goddess Laxmi."

Rigveda 10/71/2.

Reference

An international review of literature, 2003, International Institute for Educational Planning, UNESCO, ISBN- 92-803-1228-6, paperback, pp.198.

3

Professional Education of Teachers A Mirror Image

"Teachers should be subjected to rigorous training with rigid scrutiny of efficiency. This training needs to have greater relevance to the needs of the day. The ill trained teachers or substandard teacher would be detrimental to our educational system if not a punishment to our children. The government and the university must, therefore, take care to see that inadequacy in the training of teachers is not compounded by any extraneous consideration." Honourable *Supreme Court of India.*

Kohli's team has developed innovative methodologies using IT and computers to build a reading capability among the adult illiterates. The first experiment was conducted in Medak village near Hyderabad. *Without a trained teacher,* the women started reading the newspaper in Telugu in 8 to 10 weeks.

Any serious and inquisitive student of teacher education in India would find the University News (Vol. 43. no.18; May 02-08,2005)—a special number titled: *Teacher Education in the Knowledge Era: Issues, Trends and Challenges* both interesting and edifying. For me, as I browsed through it, I found it both very informative as well as revealing. Informative because it details all aspects of teacher education along with numerous suggestions for adoption (something no single nation-wide survey type research would have yielded as much), and edifying because it presents diagnostic report card of the current health of India's teachers' professional program. The added advantages are: the papers in the issue cover the entire spectrum of brotherhood, i.e., all types of teacher educators—the retired and the working; all levels of university departments of education, the NCERT, the DIET's, and the SCERT's etc. besides offering glimpses of what is happening in the four regions of the nation. I am sure these papers represent a whole range of political opinions too. Additionally, no one can fault a study based on this data as either inadequate or opinionated. In other words, the sample is fairly representative and the type of study—normative.

The questions the present study is expected to answer are as follows:

1. Does the teacher education program satisfy necessary requisites? One is not very sure about them either. How many define the requisites? (Teacher traits, classroom interaction, teaching methods in sync with changing times and the school curricula, differentiation between knowledge and information, the current goals of education, teaching skills—definition and methods of teaching the same etc.)

2. What is the focal point of the teacher education program that has attracted the attention of the scholars the most?

3. What is the frame of reference that teacher educators imply as they talk of the present scenario and the future prospects?

4. What are the adequacies that get pointed out as opposed to the inadequacies?

5. What are the suggested remedies, if any? How many of the teacher-scholars feel satisfied with the current provisions?

6. How many find the functioning of the NCTE acceptable and where do they fault the apex system and why?

7. Enlist lessons one can draw from the write-ups and also conjecture whether the NCTE will benefit from the efforts / suggestions? Do the authors find any hope in the system or are they disappointed and frustrated with what they find is happening all around them?

The Sample

As already stated the sample in question consists of 36 papers in all. It is possible that the Editorial board and the staff of the AIU may not have specifically commissioned the write-ups or given detailed guidelines (apart from the usual announcements a couple of issues before). Even if the advice were readily available, it is doubtful that authors would have benefited from it. I have therefore taken these papers as an exercise in design-vacuum because being a contributor myself I had no guideline to fall back upon.

I however take it that some care was taken to help the authors in as much as that the invitees were given a list of topics to choose from, which incidentally means that the editors did have some format or schemata in mind. As one tries to analyse the content of the issue, especially the editorial of the Guest Editor (in bold letters), the impression one gets is that the AIU did find the right man for the important job—a man who has seen teacher education from the vantage point – an insider both in the university system and the mentor of the present NCTE chief. Therefore, his each and every word or expression is quotable. It carries, to say the least, the hallmark of the most knowledgeable among the officially acceptable teacher educators and someone who serves as a bridge between the power seekers and the seat of power itself.

I cite the guest editorial, which defines the areas supposedly covered in the issue. These areas are: "development of teacher education in India; professionalization of teacher education, quality concerns in teacher education, policy perspectives and the role of the regulatory bodies, privatisation of teacher education, autonomy to teacher education institutions, evaluation and accreditation in teacher education, innovation and research in teacher education, in-service teacher education, distance mode in teacher education, ICT-enabled teacher education, inclusive teacher education and the challenges in teacher education in the 21st century." I think except for a few themes, all others have been covered.

The themes left uncovered are: (effective) teaching skills, the teacher and the changing school curricula, classroom practices—today and tomorrow, the SES of the school and training college teacher, learning habits both among teachers and their wards, teacher politics, selection of teachers, teacher-networking etc. One must accept the limitations of the publications. *University News* is not a research journal and with in the given format it cannot prevent heterogeneous entries. Ranging from the most casual of the write-ups to those that are a result of considerable thinking and research these papers also betray heterogeneity so characteristic of most educational writing. I have therefore tried to put some order into an otherwise chaotic situation. The first attempt in this direction is the background of the authors. However, this classification does not suggest that those that belong to the central government systems or are professors in rank are in any way superior or more quotable than others. In the joint papers the second author's background has been counted because it is common knowledge that the seniors exploit the situation to their own advantage.

The background analysis reveals that the lecturers (18) outnumber readers (5) and professors (13). The NCERT has around 4 contributors, and the central universities (5), Technical Teacher's Training Institute (1), state universities (4), and the rest come from colleges both private and government. There is one paper on self-financing teacher training under the column reserved for Communication and there is also a book review on the changing face of Distance Education. In sum, there is sufficient material to furnish a meaningful image of the state-of-the-art position of teacher education in India. If the themes listed in the guest editorial somehow do not match with the themes written on by the contributors no one needs to be blamed. The reader is advised to go through the list of the editorial and the titles of the papers contributed and draw one's own conclusions. That however does not take away the value of the efforts as most of the papers reveal professional commitment, at times 'vision' also but, in sum, their value judgments do make one sit up and read the stuff seriously.

There are two points that must be remembered before one wades through the papers. One, very few teachers have command on the language they employ in teaching. Researchers suggest that this is so because of the poor SES of these teachers. In this regard women fare much better than their male counterparts. The gender differences are clearly visible. And two, teachers in India are not very innovative in the classrooms. They set goals that are achievable. They consider teaching a textbook the real job on hand. The relevance of the content and the manner of its delivery are not always their major concerns. Teachers and their managers think alike on the issue of discipline. They prefer silence to discussion and there is hardly if ever a dialogue in the classrooms. Going to the class is a duty and not a mission and the function of a teacher is adjudged best in terms of examination results. These remarks were necessary because the possession of a teachers' training diploma / degree is a kind of license in India which is necessary for getting hired and beyond that it signifies nothing. Since all degrees are legally equal, institutions count for nothing at the time of selection. When one considers fine-tuned manipulations in the selection process the quality and standard of teacher training institutions fall by the wayside. The analysis given below should be found theoretically enough to measure the degree of competencies the teacher trainers and their trainees possess. Exceptions can always be accommodated.

The Analysis

For the convenience of the reader I have tried to classify the papers. The first three papers trace the history of teacher education. Except the first paper, i.e. , by Chandani Saxena, who tries to define teacher traits according to the ancient Indian scholars (rishis) and offers to relate the same with the developments in teacher education, the other two offer glimpses of the later day birth and regeneration of this branch almost totally independent of its indigenous moorings. The present day Indian teachers are inspired by Western practitioners of the trade and apparently have similar background and qualifications. Modern concept of subject-area specialization prevents them from acquiring a broad spectrum of knowledge with critical insights into other disciplines as well. Just as it is not possible to produce an Aristotle today, it has become impossible to have rishis either. At best we can have specialists with a smattering of other disciplines. But then it is understandable as well for the simple reason the knowledge is growing at a much faster speed than humans can learn. There are few areas in which both the sources of knowledge and its body have remained intact. Almost daily we find additions to the existing branches of knowledge. With each passing day the frontiers of knowledge get extended and the old knowledge finds only a few takers. It is difficult even to compute the rate of its obsolescence in the field. Kothari Commission had done it in 1966 but since then things have no longer been the same as they once were. Incidentally, not a single author has tried to give us an idea how the B.Ed. programme itself has moved in terms of its content and the borrowings. It would have been interesting had someone tried to inform the readers how teachers were trained in the early stages in India when classroom instruction was specific to teaching a given book. The total duration of the training did not extend beyond a week and teachers were trained for teaching Book 1 or Book 2 etc. Until the time Calcutta University came into being the teacher training program had not got standardized.

The next two papers deal with professionalization of teacher education. They discuss everything but not the criteria that entitles a vocation to be called a profession. The first paper in this category is by a Director, ASC, Rajkot. He merely distinguishes between two models—the administrative—bureaucratic model and the managerial – professional model and towards the end of his paper says, "One of the major criticisms of teacher education as a profession is the lack of an identifiable body of knowledge that is established by a consensus as a prerequisite to effective performance as a practicing teacher." Let me hope someone finds the true import of this observation. And, the second paper delivers some homilies and hopes, a teacher can become a professional in real sense if he fulfils all the obligations and remembers that a profession is above the professional and in no case he should allow his human instincts and feelings to come in the way of his profession." Does this read any better than the first paper?

These authors are reminded that teacher education is not a professional course of study, although we loosely say so. As a profession teaching community lacks two significant features that could have made them professionals like the doctors or lawyers are. It does not have a body of ethics for all to follow and is not either voluntarily or professionally regulated. I hope teachers will accept that teachers have no National registration numbers and without being a member of any professional Teachers, organization they can teach as long as they wish since they violate no social or criminal code. They are free to indulge in any habit that they so choose with impunity unless charged for a crime. The doctors and lawyers are more wary of their professional ethics than of the criminal law. Their names can be struck off the register once they violate the desirable and most essential moral or professional code. There is no such binding conditionality for teachers. An inefficient teacher with a temper cannot be removed from his / her position just like as an absentee teacher with a clout. With an enforceable code of conduct this behaviour would not be tolerated. The ancient Indians did have their codes but we have dispensed with them wholly. What regulate teachers today are criminal and civil laws and not professional ethics.

The next 7 papers relate to quality concerns.

What does one wishes to read in these papers? The benchmarks for quality, their sustained maintenance, their clearly defined reach, implementation and a mechanism to reward and penalize those that obstruct quality regime. Now let us see whether the authors of these papers view the theme as I do.

The first paper in the category defines quality: It "is not an act, but a habit. It generally signifies the degree of excellence." But then what is excellence? It is not defined for the obvious reason. The definition will not be universally acceptable. In the absence of a definition the twin authors restrict their effort to talking about the NCTE and the NAAC. It is the suggestion that I find useful. The skill development should match international benchmark. But then what is that? Where to discover and how? No help is offered. In the end there is a mention of some alternative models but we are not told where do they fit in.

The second paper in terms of its title is quite impressive. After a brief inconclusive discussion of 'quality' the authors suggest, "the application of industrial quality assurance system in the teacher education discipline may be possible by replacing the word 'teacher education' with' enterprise'. I do hope the reader got his message right. Follow the industrial model if quality is to be taken into account. The third paper holds" teacher educators need to be made conversant with various aspects of school experience." Besides doing several other things teacher education "should also aim to upgrade its standard"; but how does one do that the author throws no light. The fourth paper deals with quality concerns but ends up defining loss of quality, a suggestion to develop TQM and a concluding remark, "teachers have to acquire professional competencies, commitment and need to be empowered to perform their multiple tasks in the classroom, school and the community." I hope there is a lesson for all to learn from this author.

The next paper offers a list of quality concerns but ends up by suggesting, "in assuring the quality slant, the teachers have to seriously apply their mind to workout the paradigm shift where the focus of concern will be 'learning' as against 'teaching'." The sixth paper from two ladies from Goa is useful because it gives us figures about how many teachers' colleges we have and for what level. The paper discusses teacher education to prepare teachers for promoting Peace, upholding Human Rights, work for gender equality and suggests that future teacher education should be so designed that teachers look, "within for value and look beyond for perspective." It says nothing about teaching academic subjects—the real reason why teachers are hired. The last paper in this class is on quality improvement measures for teacher education. It would suffice if we were to read his concluding sentence. "Though we are really very much thinking about the quality first the teacher educators should develop the qualities on the above aspects because the trainees learn most by impression technique." I hope the reader will be able to guess the import of this concluding remark.

The next paper is by a professor and dean of a central university department of education in collaboration with a Reader from the same faculty. The theme is manpower planning for elementary teacher education. With the help of a brief write-up on the setting up of DIETs, the authors provide an introduction to the existing teacher education scenario and finally suggest a course structure "to prepare the human resource to respond effectively to the need of manning elementary education sector effectively." This suggestion is followed by two detailed diagrams—one, on the course structure and the other on the avenues for those who are equipped with these degrees. But the most significant part of the paper is a comment on the DIETs programs, which according to them, "leads to a mismatch between the expertise available and that required for managing DIETs' a condensed certificate /Diploma courses." Going through the bibliography one gets the impression that the authors are in possession of an unpublished report waiting to see the light of the day and have utilized the present forum for wider acceptance and publicity.

We have a paper on 'privatisation and / or commercialisation of teacher education: some consequences.' The author has listed various reasons why commercialisation has been encouraged and has suggested a few remedies too like grading of institutions and setting up a body called *Watchdog Panel* with the MHRD and has not shied away from saying that this panel should receive PILs against the NCTE's visiting teams that compromise with standards and norms for some undisclosed consideration. I am quite sure the author knows much more than has admitted about the functioning of the NCTE. This paper may be read along with the one published in Communication column, which details the misdeeds of the NCTE and portrays the health of teacher education in the privatised colleges—also called self-financing colleges. One gets the impression that since they are self-financed they can be allowed to function as they please and once the visiting panels have been duly entertained they have the license to anarchy. This is one place where someone should have written about Anand Sarup committee report as well that the NCTE has kept in its closet so that none comes to know of its complicity in criminal activities of being a party to the award of forged degrees from non-existent colleges in the thousands and for number of years. Incidentally, it was the NCTE with the approval of MHRD that had appointed the committee but due to political and personal reasons it couldn't be made public. Why should any one wonder that NCTE would, most certainly, forever continue to remain the favourite concubine of India's polity?

We have an author who considers that autonomous colleges of teacher education are the need of the hour. The author needs to answer what greater autonomy does he demand than the mushrooming privatised teacher education already enjoy?

The following paper is on Teachers' performance appraisal that deserves to be read seriously. A number of issues are involved in the process and product of an appraisal, but all the same, the principal function per se remains important. For the 21st century, i.e., for a 'knowledge-driven' economy, teacher education has been offered a model by an ex-vice-chancellor. He pleads for a re-definition of education, re-profiling of stakeholders, re-inventing education, besides restructuring and re-engineering it. These, he calls, the five-mantras for a new model. This paper is followed by a recount of innovations (in the one following it) in the area of teacher education with a concluding remark, " Indian teacher education institutions and teachers are full of novelty". Needless to say they need to be more widely propagated. **Inquiry Training Model** – with its definition, difficulties and possibilities of evolving an E-learning model have been considered in the ensuing paper. One is inclined to suggest that a detailed treatment of the same would have been widely acclaimed.

Three papers consider in-service teacher education program along with the challenges, points to ponder and its relationship with professional competence. Here one could easily learn from the world of business where newer challenges and complexities keep the professionals always on their tenterhooks. We must realize that all branches of education too are facing similar problems—finance, administration, techniques, saleability and the required technological skills. It is therefore in the fitness of things that we have three papers on ICT-related issues in the area of teacher education. The fact that ICT is knocking at our doors for quite a while needs no reminding because Edusat has posed the real questions already. It is too mild to acknowledge a reality that is likely to make instruction in the classrooms interesting and flexible, if not challenging in the real sense of the term.

The question of 'inclusive education' has attracted the attention of three scholars of special education. It is heartening to learn that we too have come to realize that education is much more than mere information gathering and its speed of acquisition. One learns more from the company and encouragement than from all the books put together. R.P. Singh in the following paper puts India's Teacher Education program in a world perspective. Here we are in excellent company with the sole distinction that those who should have been controlling the rot are themselves guilty of its mindless propagation. The rot in this sector is almost worldwide. The paper that follows, deals with the changes in teacher education program in the past five years. I find the placement of the paper unsuitable. It could have been placed along with those that deal with the history of teacher education.

In the paper "Malleability of Teacher Education Concerning early childhood care and education (ECCE)" pleads for going beyond the 68th Amendment of the Constitution, which merely talks of "The State shall endeavour to provide ECCE for all children until they complete the age of 6 years." Therefore, the paper records the urgency of taking meaningful action in this regard and proposes "qualitative and quantitative issues connected with teacher education of ECCE needs to be addressed without further lapse of time" Let me hope the NCTE wakes up from its feigned stupor and reacts positively to the necessary requirement.

Training in Creative Teaching is posed as a challenge for teacher education. The author also lists a few traits desirable for a creative teacher. But a few of these traits are not only undefined and vague, for instance, morality and spirituality, carrying of his work and conduct, it would be extremely difficult to even devise a program for 'originality in expression'. I do hope the author is not trying to be very original in this regard. On the whole there is little to disagree with him on the point of encouraging creative teaching.

The next paper deals with encountering emerging challenges in teacher education. The paper not only lists the major lacunae in the existing teacher education program but also suggests a whole lot of steps and directions it has to move in to become worthy of meeting emerging challenges. It would be difficult to go over the list of the lacunae because few would agree with him with the items given. All the same there is no harm to discuss a few of the lacunae.

"Challenges to Teacher Education in 21st century" and "Need for re-vamping teacher education program" are the last two papers that not only record their individual dissatisfaction with the existing program but suggest measures to improve the scenario. The interesting parts of the papers constitute the reasons for emergent challenges. For instance, in the first papers the reasons given are as follows:

Democratisation of the polity

Explosion of knowledge

Population explosion

Liberalization, privatisation and globalisation; and

Information technology revolution

If one desired one could easily pick up a bone or two with the lady author. India did not become democracy in 1947. It was always a democracy verging on anarchy with intervals of autocratic and dictatorial forms of governance thrown in during the past one thousand years or so. Secondly, it is information that has seen explosion and not knowledge. Information is only a means to knowledge but the two are not identical. I am quite sure the author knows both these points. Thus far no society has become knowledge society. One can dream of it but what shape this will take no one can be very sure. Such a concept is basically flawed because here one assumes that societies are homogeneous and all its citizens are equally gifted or silly. Therefore, all statements that we make in this regard are loose generalizations. Even when we talk of challenges we are talking of capacity building. We are capable of being democrats but one is not sure of which brand – the American or the British? Similarly, when we talk of information technology we talk vaguely of the possibilities and the individual's capacities and attitudes. No one can say exactly how many interests could one have and how much could one learn. There is nothing specific about it. Everyone wishes to have 'change' because we become quickly bored with the familiar and it is this familiarity that is likely to breed contempt. Ask anyone about anything. The likely reply is going to be on the expected lines. But the change desired by the teacher educators somehow does not seem to fall in this category. Everyone is dissatisfied with the present pace and the way NCTE is functioning. No one wishes that any system should suffer from the common malaise that every government system seems to suffer from. The criticism of the NCTE therefore is because we had lot many expectations from it. Also, in its earlier Avatar at the NCERT it had done quite a good job. Therefore, it was widely expected that things would immediately change the day a statutory body was constituted. The general expectations of the majority were that things would improve overnight. Nothing of the sort was either expected nor was it possible. Surprisingly, when the system was expected to take advantage of its newly created mechanism, the government's selections fell short both in imagination and human relations. Most of the ills teacher education programs suffer from today are neither political nor academic in nature. They lack vision and the will to act without prejudice. Unfortunately, visionaries are invariably selfless and basically reflective beings. They have messages to deliver but they are not good executioners.One does not need much imagination to reason out why the NCTE is a failed organization. It is not sufficient to flaunt the statutory status. One should also act accordingly.

To end this analysis, let me discuss a point or two raised by R.A.Mashelkar, Director-General, CSIR in a convocation address titled "Bridging the Development Divide through Science and Technology" also reported in the present issue of the University News. Like all men of science, Mashelkar is focused and relevant. He talks of gaps in the rich and the poor, which is explained as, the richest one percent of the world's people received as much income as the poorest 57%. In 1998, 29 OECD countries spent $520 billion on R&D- more than the combined economic output of the world's 30 poorest countries. So how does one make everyone literate in a poor country like India? And if the Governments fail to make everyone literate, individuals with ingenuity, missionary zeal and selfless devotion can. He cites the examples wherein scientific advances, (discoveries, inventions and innovations) have solved problems of the masses. If vaccines saved the majority from killer diseases, the technology can be used for making everyone literate and that too without the teachers produced under the supreme guidance of the NCTE. I now quote the text:

"We need to take advantage of these breathtaking advances to provide economic access of new technologies to the poor. We also need to focus more on creating technologies specially suited to the poor. As an example, look at the Indian development of 'simputer' done by Indian Institute of Science in Bangalore. It is handheld Internet appliance costing less than $200. It is based on the Linux open source operating system. The intellectual property rights have been transferred for free to the non-profit Simputer Trust, which is licensing the technology to manufacturers at a nominal fee. Simputer provides Internet and e-mail access in local languages with touch-screen functions and micro-banking applications. Speech recognition and text software for illiterate users has been provided. This is a technological advance that can reduce the divide."

The IIT, Madras has created low cost Internet access system that needs no modem and eliminates expensive copper lines. The technology is based on a wireless local system, which is ideal for providing access to low-income communities throughout India and beyond. Licensed manufacturers in India, Brazil, China and France, the technology is already in use internationally, in Fiji, Yemen, Nigeria, Tunisia, etc.

"There are two lessons to be drawn here. The first is, that public funding and incentives supported the cited initiatives. The second is, that they came from two of the most elite institutions, namely, IISc and the IITs. If modern technology can be used to reduce the development divide, it can equally be used for eliminating illiteracy. Here is what the Director-General has to say," Let us take the example of illiteracy. In India, we have about 200 million adults, who cannot read or write. There are huge constraints of trained teachers. The use of conventional methods of learning from alphabets to words requires 200 hours of instruction. This leads to a number of dropouts. India's illiteracy today is reducing at the rate of 1.3percent per annum. At this rate, India will need 20 years to attain a literacy level of 95percent. Can we do it in less than 5 years?

The great doyen of Indian IIT industry, F.C.Kohli believes that this can be done through his recent breakthrough. He has developed a unique Computer-Based Functional Literacy (CBFL) method. It is based on the theories of cognition, language and communication.

In this method, the scripted graphic patterns, icons and images are recognized through a combination of auditory and visual experiences by using computers. The method emphasizes on learning words rather than alphabets. While the method focuses on reading, it acts as a trigger for people to learn to write on their own. Based on this method, Kohli's team has developed innovative methodologies using IT and computers to build a reading capability among the adult illiterates. The first experiment was conducted in Medak village near Hyderabad. *Without a trained teacher, the women started reading the newspaper in Telugu in 8 to 10 weeks."*

Now this is something no teacher educator could have thought of and most certainly the NCTE would not have encouraged any research either, assuming as I do that some teacher educators had the talent for this kind of experimentation.

I find it very hard to conclude the essay without a comment on the book review. The book reviewed in the present issue is on Distance Education, apparently a collection of some essays by authors both Indian and foreign. The book as I gather deals with the innovative practices and technologies that have transformed the very nature and format of distance education. With a price tag of Rs. 2500/ someone has planned that the book never reaches its legitimate readers or the target audience, and the reviewer so improves upon the language that understanding it involves a grammar that has yet to be written. Read the concluding remark, "Certainly the book will be useful advantage (sic) to the open and distance libraries."

Now is the time when I can compare the objectives with which I undertook the exercise with the result my efforts have yielded. Let me recount a bit of what I originally set out to learn from the issue as a whole; everything I have covered included.

The reader is advised to go through the quotes given at the beginning of this analysis and ponder over them for a while. The message, if they can read it, is clear and fairly loud. It says 'either train teachers properly and responsibly or be prepared for becoming irrelevant because the technology will take it over wholly and throw the system, if it can be called so, into the dustbin of antiquity.

One is not very sure whether these essays enlighten anyone about the state of the health of teacher education. They somehow seem to suggest that working academics in the system are not too pleased with the present day dispensation. They do talk about the plans of the NCTE and perhaps think too that someday things shall improve. Being either ignoramuses or for want of courage few have been bold enough to take the bull (NCTE) by the horn. These essays also prove that teacher's training will forever remain backward looking and unsure of its moorings or of the sources of its inspiration. No one has gone into the problems of teacher absentees, or their delinquent behaviour, or their lack of command on language, or methods of teaching and assessing desirable teacher traits or their poor reading habits or their impoverished innovative practices or the reasons for their inadequate preparation before they take classes. At the same time no one has also thought of a theory of teacher education that Indians can fall back upon. The only people active in the field of theoretical formulations or model building come from either of the two places in India – Baroda or Indore. But this tribe of Abu Ben Adam is well known for a highly-specialized process called Dhanavantarikaran, something very unique to them. Incidentally, the late Professor M.B. Buch made me privy to the secret. They are, he told me, capable of the orizing where no theories are possible and can talk of a model, which they can adapt or adopt and propagate to an unsuspecting audience whose reading habits are inversely related to their sense of wonder.

They indeed are blessed souls who are not burdened with the load of knowledge, so says an Indian saint poet—Tulsidas.

4

Teaching
Its Nature and Functions

Teaching, like any other similar concept, is both complex and abstract. Teaching, in common parlance, gives rise to a mental image of a classroom teacher engaged in his task of making the class assigned to him to learn. Teaching, therefore, is a pre-condition of learning a body of knowledge that is already there. The teacher is not expected to question the information given to him. He is supposed to be performing his job well if his students learn what he has taught them to learn. Teaching in this case is not merely communication but comprises activities as well, which help him to communicate. However, this classroom activity isn't all that passes for "teaching". There are possibilities that a person may learn without any overt teaching. We become aware of becoming young or old with time. No one tells us that to be young is to feel youthful or otherwise.

Problems arise when one wants to be very specific and very definitive. "Teaching" is not "propaganda"; it is not "initiation", etc. But then what exactly is "teaching"? Teaching, as a concept, could not easily be visualised unless one took cognisance of learning. Could teaching take place in a vacuum or without any design? Certainly not. Similarly, learning cannot have any independent existence apart from teaching. We all know, however, that though teaching and learning are interdependent, they do not have a one-to-one correspondence. This again gives rise to a logical problem, i.e., of partial teaching or partial learning, or imperfect, overt teaching and inadequate, indifferent learning. Connected with this are the major problems of identification of the process of teaching. Does it constitute a single act or a series of activities until the implied purpose is attained? We have no definite answers to these problems. Indeed, the present work is an attempt to offer a few answers in resolving this tangle.

The Nature of Teaching Toward A Philosophy of Teaching

"Teaching" as distinguished from terms like "instruction", "initiation", "indoctrination", etc., lends itself to the possibility of being conceived as independent and distinct from the process and consequence of "learning". In itself this statement questions the validity of interchanging "teaching" with "instruction" or "indoctrination"[1] for the simple reason that "teaching" in this context has a built-in bias of incorporating within itself "purposes" purportedly added to it by society as a whole or a group of individuals. In other words the moment teaching takes on the shape of indoctrination it gets vitiated by an external agent (otherwise not included in the process of teaching). The major problem, therefore, constitutes in developing a theory of teaching, which could easily be discernible by those who have something to do with it. D.J. O'Connor raises the point of usefulness of a theory in the field of education: "But since education is not (and is not claimed to be) an exact science and does not even rely to any large extent upon the findings of such sciences, *the word 'theory' is used in educational context in a derivative* and *weakened sense.*"[2] Even so it is not futile to discuss the word "theory" in the context of education. Taking the cue from natural sciences where the word "theory" is used without any ambiguity we talk of theory as: (a) a hypothesis that has been verified by observation and, more commonly, (b) as a logically inter-connected set of such confirmed hypothesis.

Accepting this as the basis for proceeding without examination and formulation of a theory of "teaching" we may at first try to clear the ground by defining the distinction teaching has from words like *instruction* or *initiation* or *indoctrination*, etc.

As already suggested, instruction or initiation, *etc.* have a built-in purpose. One cannot think of instructing another unless one has: (a) a definite body of knowledge and (b) a strong reason for handing over this body of knowledge to another. In the case of initiation besides these two grounds, i.e., (a) and (b), *some kind of perpetuation of values also appears to be involved.* We could examine these words by citing two examples. For instances, a teacher instructs a child in

English language. There is thus a definite body of knowledge, i.e., English language. The strong reason or reasons to impart this instruction may be that: (a) English has a market value, (b) English holds the key to a vast ocean of knowledge, (c) it is the language of our former rulers and wields a charm of its own, (d) it helps us remain internationally aware and alert, etc. This sort of instruction could go on from generation to generation or terminate immediately after the first pupil or batch of pupils has acquired command over it. In the case of initiation the process must go on because it implies inheriting a value system besides a body of knowledge. *One is initiated* into *a profession which has a code of conduct all its own.* Therefore, unlike "instruction" which may or may not lead to this sort of a continuous process called initiation, the latter cannot be imagined of without a continuous process. If this "initiation" could be an initiation into the mystery of a honourable profession, it could equally be true of beggary, prostitution or thieving, etc.

The word "indoctrination" has generally been used to connote additionally certain political overtones. It does for that matter cover by implication that meaning which the word "instruction" and "initiation" carry within themselves. In all these terms a common link that runs through is that of "authority". *One has to have an authority to instruct, initiate or even indoctrinate.* It is quite irrelevant to say that the source of authority must always be external. In numerous cases indoctrination has the genesis in an individual "will". The authorisation for the exercise of this individual's "*will*" is a matter of time when the followers of that leader refuse to permit others to exercise their right to political choice.

The major difficulty in defining the term "teaching" and its parameters is, that it has hardly, if ever, been thought of without "learning". Not much work has been done in the West on its definition and none at all in India. Teaching seemingly overlaps several other concepts of the same genus with minor variations in their actual end products. At one place P.H. Hirst and R.S. Peters come quite close to the stand I should like to take:

Usually educational processes involved not only learning but teaching as well. There is, however, no logical connection in this case. *Education can go on without any teaching.* We can say it was a 'real education' for someone to take a boat out on his own implying that he learnt something desirable without anybody having been there to ram home the lesson. *There are many forms* of learning that go on without teaching, and 'educative' learning does not imply the additional criterion that *the learning must take place in teaching situation.* It may be a general empirical fact that most things are learnt more rapidly and more reliably if a teacher explicitly structures the situation. *But it certainly is not* a conceptual truth that either *'learning' or 'education' implies 'teaching'* (emphasis added).

Also they hold that whereas "learning" is logically necessary to "education", "teaching" is not. And while trying to answer the poser: what characterises teaching and how are we to distinguish its activities? They say: "It implies that the teacher intends to bring about learning. This necessity for teaching activities indicate or express to some extent, that pupils are intended to learn, serves to distinguish clearly those activities which are essentially teaching, from many which are not, however valuable they may be in the circumstances."[4] The second characteristic of teaching would, therefore, be that at least in terms of intention it has its end product as learning. Indeed, one of the major goals of education, which in several respects has been identified with "teaching", is to see that "character traits are internalised (as also) social rules such as honesty, punctuality, truthfulness and selfishness."[5]

The third characteristic, which comes up for consideration, is that teaching seeks to fill up a kind of void or perhaps meets a socially created need. Teaching may thus seek its goal somewhere outside its own process or activity identified as teaching. The quality and content of teaching would, however, depend on the method one follows—Plato or Locke. In other words, one was trying to be the other (child or adult) to discover or unfold what was already within, or add something that did not exist. True, in both cases the quality and processes of teaching would differ radically, but whatever happens either way it does add to the dimension of teaching.

Teaching has, however, to serve as an instrument for a specific object. The object in the present case is the meeting of a social requirement or a personal need. From whichever point of view we consider "teaching", for the person being taught, it might as well appear as though he were to inquire about the truth or be on a quest for further awareness about the nature of reality. It looks as though the student has certain queries and the teacher has to answer these. Of course, this sort of awareness in the student presupposes the identification of problems by the student. In reality nothing of the sort ever happens. In a formal school set-up the student does not put questions until he has reached a certain age. Answers to his possible questions are generally anticipated and answered. No one ever takes him (the student) into confidence, except while as a child he is at home where his parents and siblings attempt replies to his endless queries. Born into an unknown world the child is helpless. He has to be taught everything— ablutions, bowl-movements, food habits and gradually about the members of his household. The fact that the child is curious and wishes to be helped in everything he does, the need of a teacher whether of mother or father or siblings or peers, etc., is for survival— both physical and social. The structure of teaching, therefore, requires that irrespective of the form its base constitutes certain social obligations *vis-à-vis* a motivated, inquisitive mind.

It is here that we see certain subtle forms of teaching operations. We find the child at this age is being initiated, instructed, indoctrinated, etc., as he is gradually growing into a socially acceptable person. For example, he is being initiated into certain family "mores". He is taught to recognise persons and exhibit varying degrees of familiarity. His ablutions and bowl-movements and food habits and dress, etc., fall under the category of instruction. As the child grows up a little more and is ready for movement in social circles he is given sets of rules. These sets of rules are covered by the term "indoctrination". A child is warned not to mix with certain groups of children, or for instance, not to discuss internal matters concerning one's household. To be able to move about in an unknown world the child is protected by the shield of "do's" and "don'ts". The entire social fabric would crumble down if all the children started behaving the way they liked. The most well behaved child is regarded as a very well brought-up person. But the reality is that he has succumbed to certain tricks played by his family on him. True, he has thereby earned the "goodwill" of his family and approval of the society but at the same time he also betrays the deep impress of the social or family indoctrination.

When the society starts indoctrinating on given points it indulges in propaganda. Schools through their regular courses of study attach values to national behaviour. Such and such social system stands, approved or disapproved with a bias in logic in its favour or disfavour. On a national scale, for example, the USA condemned the political set-up in the USSR. People in the USSR held that they had a democracy in their country. As a people, therefore, they have come to agree with whatever they have been taught through their social system or political institutions. This means the logic advanced in favour of their institutions and disfavouring the others itself is such that a child grown into an adult has no rationality left in him to question what he has been taught or made to believe. It also means that besides the arguments for or against a certain system the propaganda undertaken in the classroom is the most well organised and sustained, resulting in the dulling of one's rational bases of independent thinking.

We come across a major difficulty in regarding teaching as one trying to meet a socially created need. Depending on the nature of society even indoctrination could pass as a socially created need. Teaching apparently does serve a useful purpose but this "use" is something one cannot anticipate and define. The quality and content of teaching could thus be determined by its end-result. Teaching, for instance, aims at transmitting a value system very close to helping maintain the *status quo.* The skills and the media of communication offered as "teaching" could never hope to be so revolutionary as may lead one to subvert the social order. "Teaching" in this sense when offered through socially acceptable institutions would always be "conformist".

What may interest us most is *the implied hierarchy of values attached to each of these terms.* Surely the value-attachment is relative and in another set-up all this defining may turn out to be a fruitless endeavour. For example, to a tribal inhabiting a dense forest all these concepts may appear irrelevant. For him what Peters suggests is degeneration, viz. "indoctrination" may itself be the only meaningful term. Questioning of authority or probing deep into some problem-area anticipates alternatives. For example, if the authority of the word of a priest is questioned, something quite common in modern urban world, there is another authority ready to take on that mantle. Similarly, one probes into scientific or philosophical problems for many reasons (i) there is reason to believe that an alternative may be in existence and finding or being conscious of the same may be worth one's while, (ii) that the confidence one reposed in the earlier teacher was misplaced, and/or (iii) that one has not enough knowledge or skill to test the word of an external authority against one's own which one may have acquired either experimentally or intuitively but in any case through one's own efforts. In other words, the hierarchy of values suggested by Peters and others is valid for a democratic country where questioning of authority by itself implies advancement of learning and acquisition of ability to compete internationally besides personal recognition and benefits that accrue from this recognition. No such conditions are imperative in the case of the hypothetical tribe we have been discussing. Also, this hierarchy of values expressed through these terms suggests the presence of a variety of knowledge. There is knowledge that may be questioned and there is that that one may not. For example, one does not question the birth of a child whether human or animal through a process and the need of father and mother in either case (even where artificial insemination is now possible). The same is not true in other cases, e.g., the birth of a day is not dependent on the periodic rise and setting of the sun in the arctic zones—something that has been accepted in other parts of the world as the gospel truth. A tribal would be horrified at the suggestion of questioning the authority of the word of the priest or the head of the family or even that of the head of the tribe. Firstly, for him, there is no point in seeking alternatives; secondly, the tradition is the law, and thirdly, the quality of life is not quite the same in the tribal and non-tribal settings.

The fourth and fairly important characteristic of teaching would thus be its variety in meaning and definition depending on the context it is used in. For a tribal initiation, instruction or even indoctrination may sound much the same but surely not for a non-tribal. In an urban-setting, however, "teaching" has quite a few shades of meaning. Where classed as "formal teaching" it generally means classroom instruction (curriculum? teacher, students, examination, etc. all thrown in under the broad term "instruction"), but in other cases such as in case of non-formal conditions "teaching" may mean anything ranging from mother's instructions regarding certain personal habits to being told to conform or not to conform by siblings, peers, posters and the other mass media. It is perhaps this loose usage of the term teaching, which has led to the confusion of "teaching" being used almost as a synonym for "education".

Whatever these terms may mean to a Westerner, for an Indian these two terms stand clearly distinguished by their end products. We distinguish between an "educated" and "learned" person. *A learned person is he who has been taught several standard works, but he cannot be regarded as an educated man unless learning accompanies wisdom, sobriety and a sense of discrimination.* This dilemma is evident in the case of Narada who approaches Sanat Kumar for attaining peace of mind. To Sanat Kumar's question, "What have you studied?" Narada replied that he had studied all the branches of learning—art, science, music, and philosophy, as well as sacred literature.[6] In other words, he explained the nature and quantum of this learning which Sanat Kumar qualified by saying: "Whatever you have read is only name." This "name" could be equated to Sartre's "words", i.e., Narada could pass as a learned man but he was not so learned that he could discriminate and distinguish between various terms like speech, mind, intellect, *etc.* This knowledge he received from Sanat Kumar who, while distinguishing between these terms, gave him the knowledge he sought. For Sanat Kumar the hierarchy of these terms in the ascending order would be: *name, speech, mind, will, discriminating will, concentration and insight.*

There is yet another way of looking at the activity, called "teaching". Assuming as we always do that "teaching" implies transmission of knowledge or skills however broad or specific these may be. Considering that teaching results in an educated man or is able to transform or bring about noticeable changes in the behaviour patterns of human beings the following possibilities of this transmission are suggested for consideration:

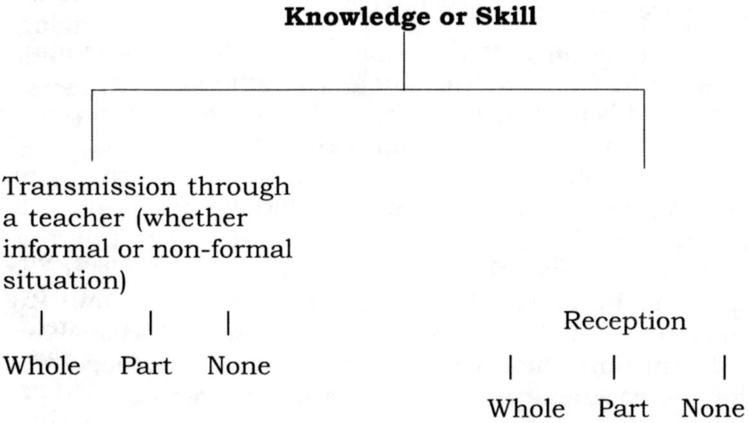

This diagram shows clearly that a teacher (whether in a formal or non-formal situation) could succeed in transmitting *all* that he knows of a piece of knowledge or skill or part thereof. The teacher could fail miserably as well in his attempt, which may be because, the taught is not ready for reception whether due to lack of maturity or motivation. There is a possibility that the teacher himself may not know all that he needs to know about the knowledge he was chosen to transmit. In fact he may not know anything at all and yet he be assigned the job of transmitting what he himself does not know. The possibilities would thus be like:

	Transmission	*Reception*
(i)	Whole	Whole
	Whole	Part
	Whole	None
(ii)	Part	Part (i.e., whole)

	Part	part (Part of a Part)
	Part	none
(iii)	None	none (i.e., whole)
	None?	Minus

OR

Confusion

The serious questions that one may like to consider here are: (i) Is teaching inter-personal or self-teaching? (ii) Is teaching static or dynamic? (iii) Does it get transmuted before it is transmitted? (iv) Is teaching unilinear? And (v) What are its specific attributes?

It would appear that there is an intermediate stage between learning and teaching. The term currently being used for this process is "internalisation" which implies that "teaching" appears to take time before it becomes "learning" and the period in between is covered by the term "internalisation" or "assimilation". Herbart came closest to describing this process.[7] I am, however, suggesting that teaching besides being interpersonal is essentially self or auto-teaching. The teacher may attempt transmitting knowledge but this knowledge would never be assimilated or learnt until the learner reduces it (this knowledge) to a familiar vocabulary or already learnt behaviour.

Conditions of Teaching

Teaching has pre-conditions the presence of a learner, whether motivated or otherwise, a teacher whether aware of his true role or ignorant of the same, and also a definite body of information whether defined or undefined, but ready to be transmitted all the same. In simple terms the process could be described as:

Figure 1

Teacher + A body of knowledge

|

Transmission

(The act of transfer)

|

Learner (The recipient)

On its own no knowledge could be transmitted because no matter in whichever form knowledge is present, it is inert. Dynamism is an additional attribute. In fact, this dynamism is what one may like to call an external agent. Unless one took pains or undertook the "effort", knowledge, irrespective of its form and content, would remain static. "Effort" is something common both to the learner and the teacher. Knowledge possesses no chemistry, which may make it self-propelling. Without "effort" knowledge would remain in the form of unknown phenomena or material not unlike the movement of galaxies which, on their own, do not ensure their conversion into awareness or knowledge.

Figure 2

Knowledge (Concepts materials and phenomena)	Knower (The existence of knower is essential for its transmission)

Knowledge exists whether or not there is a knower. The existence of knower does not determine the existence of knowledge. Knowledge exists in the form of material, phenomena or concepts even without being known and transmitted.

Referring to Figure I we may recapitulate that thus far we have attempted to learn a little about the nature of knowledge and the act of transfer called teaching activity. We have not considered critically the possibility of teacher knowing only imperfectly and also the student or the learner being ill equipped or over-equipped for this act.

In common parlance we use teaching as an equivalent of education. We assume that as we teach we communicate fully and that learning and teaching have one-to-one correspondence. We have already seen that this is not so. While education is a much broader term and comprises teaching as one of its important constituents, teaching is a specific activity, in which transfer of skill or information is the only significant component. *In a way we have also shown that the teacher, howsoever well equipped he may be for the job, knows only a part of knowledge. The true knowledge is as uncertain to learn, as its transfer is incomplete.*

The distinction pointed out by Schaffer between *believing in* and *knowing that* is quite interesting. Both, as he rightly suggests, are not quite the same. We may or may not *believe* in God but we *know* that the government functions for the common good of all. Both, however, are subject to certain conditions and the inferences in either case may assume significant proportions once we start going into the grounds of our belief or the knowledge.

We have moved away from the transitional standpoint, wherein it was believed "that knowing and believing are related forms of mental activity, the present idea leads us to differentiate sharply between them, in denying that knowing is simply a mental or psychological affair.[8]

To *know,* therefore, is not the same as to *believe in.* Austin holds that we ask, "*How* do you know?" and "*Why* do you believe?" and not vice-versa. R.M. Chisholm writes, "We must not think of knowing as being, in any sense, a 'species' of believing or accepting. A man can be said to believe firmly, or reluctantly, or hesitatingly, but no one can be said to *know* firmly, or reluctantly or hesitatingly." This should indicate very clearly that what we teach is not what we *believe in* or at time even *know.* For example, we need not believe that Alexander the Great was really Great. We are not sure of the truth that while teaching a problem in Geometry the solution given in the textbook is true. We assume it is, therefore, *although we teach both these facts, we neither know their truth nor do we believe in what we teach.*

While we are trying to understand the meaning and nature of the term *teaching* without its corresponding relationship with learning, Schaffer not unlike many others does not limit his area or inquiry in this sense. I would prefer to think of the activity before it tries to have a bearing on learning. This is one reason I am distinguishing between the pre-conditions and post-conditions. The intermediate stage is that of teaching learning, an activity in which the actual transfer takes place. If looked at in the context of education the intermediate stage is the most important one. If considered in terms of outcomes the post-condition should be as significant at it is measurable. But for a philosopher I think all are equally important, the first being a little more than the other two.

In my view the intermediate stage is of transfer of knowledge, skill or information. It would appear that nothing like transfer of items of furniture or goods takes place in teaching and learning.

Knowledge is also relative. We know a little less or more than the other person. Absolute and complete information is possible only to the Prime Mover who was and is the Beginning and the End. For everyone else partial knowledge like partial blindness is the only reality.

To the question, *"How does one know if one knows that knowledge is knowable?"* we may consider the Indian standpoint. In his work titled *Indian Theory of Knowledge,* Dr. C.D. Bijalwan has provided us with a readymade classification. The Indian philosophy differs on one major point with the Western philosophy. While the western philosophy accepts *only two* means of knowledge (a) perception and (*b*) inference, the Indian philosophy holds a divergent view on this matter. Different schools of Indian philosophy view the means of acquiring knowledge differently. It is thus quite logical to hold that under each of these schools acquiring of knowledge, the processes of both learning and teaching would have to be considered separately.

On one extreme we find the Charvaka who recognised only *one pramana* (evidence), viz., the *pratyaksha,* i.e., the direct perception and on the other extreme are the Pauranikas who accept *eight pramanas.* The Indians, unlike the Westerners, have a wide variety of available choices as far as evidence is concerned.

Before we describe the analysis of this classification we must make it clear that the role of the teacher is confined to being a catalytic agent in the process called learning. This act of being a catalytic agent is guided and purposive—guided in the sense that the goal is clear to one or the both and purposive in the sense that the selection of the tool of service is made carefully by weighing all pros and cons. The teacher is extremely careful in helping a child appreciate the value of *pramana* (evidence) and the purpose of utility to which this evidence is guided:

(1)	Carvaka	p
(2)	Vaisesika and Buddhist	p a
(3)	Samkhaya and Yoga	p a s
(4)	Nyaya	p a s u
(5)	Prabhakara	p a s u ar
(6)	Bhatta and Vedanta	p a s u ar an
(7)	Pauranika	p a s u ar an sam ai

CODE

P = Pratayksha u = Upmana Sam = Sambhava

(Comparison) (Conclusion)

a = Anumana ar = Arthapatti si = Aitihya

(Inference) (Presumption of an unperceived -object) (Succession of rumours)

S = Sabda (Verbal testimony) - an = Anupalabd h (Negation)

Incidentally, we have not questioned the validity of the need for a teacher in this process. One may tend to hold out that as knowledge could as well be self-evident one need not have a teacher. And once it is assumed or asserted that an external agent like a teacher (the knower) is needed, to that extent the abilities of the learner have been put under a doubt. Because the need has been caused as (i) the learner is inherently incompetent to learn himself, (ii) the knowledge exists in such a form that its logical and proper handling is possible by some other person alone, and (iii) the knowledge is not self-evident and is not readily comprehensible to all or to a few. Our premises are therefore different.

We accept the existing criteria or the means of knowledge, both the Indian and the Western. Indeed ours is a limited purpose, i.e., the examination of the relationship between condition of truth and the criteria of evidence. Involved in that it is the activity, which happens to be our principal concern.

We present definitions of each of the terms given in the code so that we could determine which one hopefully or possibly be involved in the process of teaching.

(a) *Prataykshа:* The terms are supposed to be equivalent of perception i.e., what could be seen is actually being shown to be seen. In Sanskrit it is a combination of *Prati* (*near* to or related to) and *aksa* (eye). In certain conditions "seeing may not be believing" as a stick in water though straight is perceived as crooked or bent. Here perception is regarded as illusion-free.

(b) *Anumana:* That is what could be inferred. According to Jayanta the process of *anumana* includes: (1) Perception of the reason, (2) The remembrance of the universal concomitance, (3) Judgement that the subject of inference contains the problems, (4) Knowledge of the consequence, and finally (5) Judgement that the consequence is worthy of being accepted or rejected.

(c) *Sabda:* Or the verbal testimony if based upon the statement of a trustworthy person or to perception if it is corresponding to a statement. Etymologically *sabda* (*sabdayati*) signifies sound (*dhvani*), literally it stands for word (*pada*) epistemologically it refers to a source so knowledge, namely "verbal testimony".

(d) *Upmana:* Or comparison is based on the well-known fact of resemblance between two cognitions wherein *Upmana* is a means and *upmati* the result.

(e) *Arthapatti:* Or presumption has been accepted as a distinct source of knowing more particularly when there is conflict it is resolved through the presumption of a fact and not of words.

(f) *Sambhava:* Is interpreted as the cognisance of a "part" from the knowledge of a "whole" with which is inseparably connected. For example, we tend to cognise number "hundred" from the number "thousand".

(g) *Aitihya:* It is held as a succession of rumours or the tradition spreading from generation to generation and emanating from unknown speakers. Ghost on a tree is one such example.

As the present paper does not seek to examine the viabilities of each of these sources of knowledge nor hold out any opinions for further examination, we would content ourselves by remarking that not all categories need always be taught. It would be interesting to observe that for each content area or what we call subject matter one or more sources and evidences of knowledge may be found necessary. Also, we have reached a stage of technological development in which most of these sources of knowledge are "impersonally" available.

We are considering here knowledge (*K*) or its variant k (the appearance of K) as that which exists outside of us and also that which needs to be cognised. This *need* may be spiritual or material but a need must surely exist as a precondition that something be cognised. In the absence of this "need" or "requirement" even the greatest object of beauty, valour or cognition would go absolutely unnoticed or at best indifferently or casually noticed.

We now come to another important stage of our discussion. *Teaching as an activity with precise goals must lead to a conclusion, not very different from the one that was intended.* Goals as we know could be self-elected or imposed/offered by society. There may or may not exist any choice on the part of the learner, still the outcome has to be judged in terms of the goals once set.

Conditions of Teaching (Goal Setting)

The Assumptions

Teaching being a purposive act, it has to be defined in terms of assumptions, goals, and conditions. Teaching *qua* teaching is an absurdity. If it did not meet certain requirements its need would be seriously jeopardised. The important fact to remember is that knowledge is seldom imparted to be an end in itself. As already indicated, teaching is intended to equip one to become rational. In turn rationality must enable one to discriminate and distinguish between good and bad. A rational person should be able to pick and choose his own information and content area, i.e.,

Knowledge, which means he begins to perceive the need for furthering knowledge. In this sense teaching activates a process, which terminates with one's final departure from this world. By itself teaching is a specific activity with a long-range goal called rationality. Teaching a skill in this sense is quite distinct from teaching knowledge.

If we assume that teaching leads to rationality—the imparting of a sense of discrimination, we could not be certain that rationality is an absolute value. To be rational is not *necessarily to be good.* There are several difficulties in this regard. For example, we all know our stay on this earth is brief and not always happy. People take birth, live for a spell of time and finally die. So death like birth is a small event and one should neither be depressed at the news of someone's death nor feel elated at the birth of a child. If this rationality were to be applied to news of the death of someone very close to us, society would condemn us for the callousness of our attitude and behaviour. In this case rationality would either invite criticism or equal indifference when a similar occasion came in one's life.

The problems of conscience are also dealt with at the same level. Society helps its citizens to develop a conscience, which is thoroughly conditioned to suit its own purpose.

What I am hinting at is that there is an inherent contradiction between *what we do* and *what we declare we are going in for.* These levels and shades of hypocrisy have their built-in mechanism or rationalisation to guide our action. *Over a period of time hypocrisy has been socially sanctified.*

It is commonly agreed that through education we do not insist on the transmission of knowledge alone but what we try is to equip the learner with a set of skills like reading, writing, etc., that may enable him to learn more.

This means that we ourselves do not attach any degree of finality about teaching any definite set of skills or knowledge for the simple reason that we know there cannot be any such finality. Reasons for this state of affairs could be: (a) knowledge itself is not final—it grows, changes and develops, (b) scholar's abilities and potentialities are so indefinite and /or (c) tomorrow's need cannot be easily anticipated. Besides, we doubt that any teacher could hopefully perform this job.

We have come to a point where we can state: (a) Teaching leads to learning, (b) Teaching, however, does not always lead to learning, and (c) Learning could take place without any conscious teaching as well. We could also say that a teacher may teach without believing in what he teaches and similarly a student may learn something without having any faith in it. In other words, teaching itself is value-free and deals with knowledge in a very noncommittal manner. Although in normal circumstances teaching as a process is helpful in educating a person, in others it may not be all that helpful. Indeed, teaching may help one to get de-educated, as well, therefore, terms like "progressive teaching" or even "progressive methods" of teaching are extremely inadequate and explain almost nothing. Indeed, Peters is right when he says, "it certainly is not a conceptual truth that either learning or education implies teaching".[9]

We thus have a negative definition of teaching. "Teaching" is not "propaganda", it is not "proselytization", and it is also not "indoctrination". There is some similarity between "teaching" and "initiation" but then the distinction between the two is also very clear. Whereas teaching could take place without being accompanied by learning, in the case of a student to be initiated this could not be so. A person being taught may be an unwilling participant in the learning activity but not the "initiate". Therefore, "teaching" and "initiation" are also not identical. Indeed, there is no other term, which comes close to "teaching" except "teachings". Teachings are crystallised forms of experiences handed down in terms of time by a person who comes to be accepted as a great teacher. Such teachers have followers or disciples. These teachers are not always physically present, only their recorded sentences are, which means, these teachers have extra-legal authority. The students of these teachers are generally highly motivated, informed and discriminating. They normally would not accept the authority of the teacher without any questions. These questions are, to use

Schaffer's terms, likely to be "radical questions".

Teaching is thus a unique concept, which does not resemble any other. From "teaching" to "indoctrination" is a range of activities, one being so distinctly different from the other not merely in purpose but in design and the layout as well. We could perhaps say that these terms are not so different after all except in the value-system attached to each. "Propaganda" is less subtle than "indoctrination" because the latter is perhaps more sinister than the former. "Training" is an "inferior" activity than "teaching" which in turn is value-free. These unspoken and at times unsuspected values come to distinguish these terms.

There are no easy answers to these questions. "Teaching" is an activity and also a series of activities that end up in attempting to help someone learn. It becomes a process when "teaching" is viewed in broader terms to cover "education" and towards achieving this end. Teaching must be conducted in consonance with the nobler and positive aspects of social behaviour. A master-cheat despite his university degree cannot be called an educated man or a person who has been well taught. *Education is a positive value.* A cheat like this one is obviously very "well-initiated" or "well-instructed" but not "educated". Education must reflect itself in the positive behaviour of an individual, which it does not in the cheat's case. A cheat like a professor of philosophy may be dependent on his wits to make his both ends meet but whereas one has no social sanction, the other one has. It is being suggested here is that the nominal resemblances do not necessarily make this action or concept alike.

There is yet another way of looking upon "teaching" as a concept. Though we call everybody teacher who meets the state regulations and takes classes, we call Gandhi, Tagore and Aurobindo also teachers knowing full well that they never qualified in the sense as the former do. In this respect what we *mean by teaching is instruction, which modifies our moral behaviour.* Whereas an ordinary classroom teacher deals with partial truths, half knowledge, resemblance and matter-of-fact information, the real teacher transcends these limitations.

References

(1) See: The concept of Indoctrination by Patricia Smart in the volume, *New Essays in the Philosophy of Education,* Editors Glenn Langford & D.J. O'Connor, R.K.P., 1973, pp. 33-46.

She holds the view that education and indoctrination overlay as concepts. 'Indoctrination' means teaching of beliefs but if they could be challenged, indoctrination would be eliminated.

(2) *An Introduction to the Philosophy of Education,* Rutledge & Kegan Paul, London, 1965, pp. 75-75.

(3) The Logic of Education, Rutledge and Kegan Paul, London 1970, pp. 70-71.

(4) *Ibid.* p. 80.

(5) *Education and Ethics, op.cit.* p. 57.

(6) *The Upanishads,* Trans, Swami Prabhavanand and Fredrick Manchester, A Mentor Religious Classic, 1957, pp. 70-74.

(7) J.S. Brubacher, *Modern Philosophies of Education,* McGraw-Hill Book Company, New York, 1950, p. 46.

"This view of mind leads to definitively different educational objectives. Judged by a theory of mental states the aim of educational psychology is to determine the structure of the mind by analysing the complex affair of consciousness into its various elements. Its parts explain the whole. On the side of learning, learning consists in putting parts together. It leans heavily on the psychological theory of associations. *Following this theory the teacher organises the lesson and presents it to the pupil so as to correlate and achieve the sequence of ideas or passing states of mind, which will ensure understanding and retention in memory.* This process is strongly reminiscent of Herbart and not a little mechanistic in spirit." (Emphasis added)

(8) *Op. cit.,* p. 25.

(9) *Ibid.* p. 77.

SECTION B
RESEARCH AND ITS STATUS

5

Research—Meaning, Functions and Progress

"The face of truth has been covered up by a golden pot. I, therefore, beseech you, O Sun, to kindly uncover it so that I may know what is true and righteous." Ishavasyopanishad, 15

Research is embedded in all human activity. It is almost instinctive. All that we know today is the cumulative findings of past countless centuries of human effort. Even before we learnt to formalize research activity, our ancestors had accumulated plenty of knowledge even without sophisticated tools or techniques. While in Europe first organized research started during French revolution, in India its history dates back to the Vedas themselves. Indian sastras are research treatises with all the necessary steps that characterize modern research. The fact that their findings have stood the test of time proves that their methods of conducting research, recording data and producing results were immaculate. This does not imply that the progress we have made or the tools we have evolved and the classifications with which we are familiar with do not amount to much. The truth is that each step forward is called progress. All around us we notice human advancement in a myriad ways. It can all be attributed to research. Indeed, modern achievements are the result of conscious and well-planned target-oriented research. Inventions, innovations and discoveries are possible because humans are willing to take pains to remain curious and inquisitive. It is in these efforts one notices the urge to progress. Sometimes progress and its ends are not very clear. We are not always very sure in our minds about the uses of progress. In the state of some confusion we tend to reject what we possess already. We forget that our possessions are a result of tremendous effort and sacrifice that our predecessors must have made. The value of the possession does not diminish only because we no longer propose to use it. This merely indicates that we are aspiring to get something different, more advanced, more appealing and eventually more useful. In a way this entire process of effort leading to a finding, innovation or invention results in making us happy and therefore we invariably welcome the fruits of our labour.

Two or three almost unrelated factors have forced me to share with you couple of challenges higher education faces today almost the world over. The first problem relates to the demands a competitive society places on higher education. Society is willing to share the cost of running and supporting the system so long as the system remains useful. No student is willing to opt for a course of study, which does not lead to a meaningful future. Between the two choices whether to support higher education or the sarva shiksha abhiyan, the government of India has already made a choice. The term used in this regard is 'non-merit' good. The second challenge emanates from foreign universities and systems already functioning in India. They claim to have more and better course offerings. Implicit in this category of challenge is the desire of a vast majority of students to go abroad and join institutions of their choice. Constant efforts are on to see that our universities become competitive. The only way they can advance and become competitive is to make their teaching faculties oriented to these challenges. Each year the Americans rank their universities and colleges on the strength of researches their faculties put out. Besides either 'publish or perish' slogan of yesteryears the latest is to research and innovate or invent or become an outcaste. And the other challenge comes from 'virtual classroom' technology. India's very own EDUSAT with immense possibilities is likely to become a threat to mediocrity in the system. Lastly, the WTO and IPR are no less a threat. India has on January 1, 2005 issued an Ordinance to formalize our stand.

Therefore, I am merely trying to remind my friends in the system to listen to these wake-up calls.

I shall restrict my discourse to the methods Indians evolved and used in the ancient times— long before the West offered us alternatives. The idea is not to praise the greatness of the times and the people long gone by but to present a record of the steps they followed to discover, innovate and create new knowledge. The point to note is that our forbears did not have the benefit of modern labs or tools and the methods to calculate and store and still they appear to have conducted proper research and evolved methods to record so neatly that their efforts continue to yield results even to this day.

There is additional reason why we ought to fall back on the treasure that was bequeathed to us and we in our cynicism have continued to ignore both – the treasure and the methods that helped our predecessors in their accumulation of knowledge. The obvious reference is to WTO and IPR. In number of ways we are uniquely placed. Like China we too are a *living* civilization. What we have is the envy of the world. We must protect our methods of study and also the treasure that is legitimately our very own. We can do it only if we are conscious of what is involved in all this. The time has come when we must compare our methods of research with the methods the West is offering. This does not imply that we should ignore what they have. In fact, like the Japanese and the Chinese we should also be pragmatic. Whatever is beneficial to us should be given top priority. Yet it is necessary to realize and remember that our own armory is not empty. Until we became victims of European exploitation India was far ahead of most nations in the world. Our contributions to human progress are not negligible. Historical documents exist to endorse this statement. For example, a study by Moreland *India at the death of Akbar* has recorded this fact. In historical terms this is not ancient. The idea is not to glorify our achievements. It is only stressing a given point.

Let me now come to the principle argument of my discourse. The point to underscore is that we too in India have methods of research. The purpose is to be clear in our minds why do we wish to invest labor, time and money in research. The research has its functions and uses. We conduct research either to enhance the efficiency of our system, increase the volume and quality of information to add on to what already exists or for creating material conditions of comfort. This also makes us become a class apart. In other words research has got to be meaningful. We do not conduct research only to while away our time. Research is purposive. It has definite goals.

All research is divided into two clusters. It is either basic (also called pure) or instrumental or applied. Basic research is mostly fundamental in nature. The findings of this kind of research are to be used by people in other fields. It yields principles, ideas, or clues to human understanding. Eventually it improves the quality of information in its relevant domain. For instance, the invention of wheel or the discovery of zero belongs to the area called *basic* research. They have their uses elsewhere. Our entire civilization stands on the invention of wheel. The applied nature of these acts of discovery/ invention or what have you comes into prominence by their users. It is not possible to plan for this branch of research. As we know research could either be planned or it can be accidental. We have all manner of records. But we do not know as yet who the inventors or discoverers of wheel or zero were.

Most of basic research is serendipity. The fundamental or basic research is not very common. It is also time consuming and very expensive. Examples in question are researches in the area of space, superconductivity or nano-technology. Poor Nations resort to thievery when it comes to undertaking researches in these areas. While they are quite unprepared / unable to invest in these areas they are willing to lend a helping hand in the application of these discoveries / inventions. In fact, it is much easier to steal the design or the formula than to create an infrastructure for having to start work anew. In a highly competitive world no nation is willing to share their discoveries or inventions. The application of research for commercial purposes is common knowledge. Almost everyday we find cases wherein someone or the other is caught stealing a secret. For instance, nuclear research or making of cryogenic engine or supercomputers etc. fall in this category. We all know the USA refused to help us out in these areas. Therefore, we took time to come up in these important areas.

The major problem that is staring into our face after the IPR comes into force is: What steps India will have to take to protect itself against the economic exploitation by advanced countries of the west. We are already facing numerous problems in tomorrow's agriculture and health-related researches. The mapping of genes, production of genetically modified seeds, cloning, robotics etc are a few such fields in which we are likely to face problems. The point is not how ill prepared we are to meet these challenges, the point is the speed with which we are able to anticipate challenges and get ready to enhance our capacities.

Applied research or the commercial exploitation of a research finding is yet another category that demands immediate solution. The UGC encourages universities to enter into MOUs with industry for basic / applied research. Numerous areas have been identified wherein scientists are being encouraged to enter into deals with the industry according to which industry funds a piece of research for an exclusive commercial use. Apparently these researches are undertaken for a social/ commercial good. In India agriculture universities have done a tremendous job in the area. All universities arguably can find areas where industry or business would be interested to co-operate in funding their projects. In the West such deals are very common. The days are long gone by when one could go like Lord Chesterton's son to Europe for cultivation of manners and broaden his mental horizon. Higher education today is supposed to yield results to everyone involved—the student, the institution and the society. In recent years we see the nature of funding and assigning of projects to capable individual scholars etc. has undergone a sea change. Institutions are known to specialize in certain areas and this brings them money and recognition both. For instance, IIT, Delhi has done a pioneering work in road-engineering, traffic-related matters and pollution (Transportation Research and Injury Prevention Program etc.) and BHU is doing work in developing a hydrogen-driven engine. If IIT Roorkee has its area specified the BITS, Pilani is developing benchmark staffing pattern, e-governance, virtual classes and a system of hiring faculty. Students are getting increasingly dissatisfied with the routine fare majority of Indian universities are still offering. All this has become necessary because of financial constraints and foreign competition. In both these areas challenges are likely to increase. Specialization has its own hazards. In a fast changing world no specialization is likely to resolve all problems or survive for long. The university faculty has to undergo a change in its character every time some new knowledge is created. I am nobody to predict what is likely to happen but I am quite sure wherever the staff is unwilling to change with times and refuses to remain in step with change that institution and its staff shall have to face unforeseen circumstances. Personally I feel a fresh challenge has already appeared on the Indian horizon via EDUSAT.

To continue with our story let us recall that ancient Indians defined knowledge to belong to two types: apara (lower knowledge) vidya and para (higher) vidya. Somehow these definitions continue to be valid for our discussion as well. Apara vidya is a kind of knowledge, which seeks to understand the apparent phenomenon of existence externally, by an approach from outside, through the senses and the intellect. This is how we acquire lower knowledge. The lower knowledge constitutes all human knowledge acquired through books or experiments. Even the Vedas fall in this category since they are not themselves the direct experience of the Self and of the eternal that is beyond all becomings.

The other form of knowledge is Para vidya. It is the knowledge, which seeks to know the truth of existence from within. This mystic knowledge does not follow any of the well-known steps of research. In an inexplicable manner it reaches out the truth. Although in terms of categories it is extremely difficult to place it, but the fact remains one does arrive at an undeniable Reality or Truth through indescribable means and methods. Indian mystics continue to talk of samadhi, the awakening of kundalini, yogic mudras etc. that yield definitive results. I have no personal knowledge of this branch of knowledge but I am no one either to affirm or deny its existence or validity either.

The ancient literature describes that avidya or non-knowledge is the knowledge of the multiplicity, while vidya is the knowledge of unity. So long as we pursue the knowledge of multiplicity to the complete exclusion of the knowledge of unity and oneness, we remain in the darkness. The same happens when we pursue the knowledge of oneness to the complete exclusion of avidya or knowledge of multiplicity we remain inadequate and incomplete. The plea is therefore for having – the vidya and avidya both, the knowledge of multiplicity and oneness keeping them both synthesized.

Let me briefly mention the *three types of knowledge* Indians have eventually developed. The *first* one is metaphysical or intuitive knowledge. We need not bother ourselves with this form of knowledge because it is a matter individual experience and consciousness. The *second* form of knowledge is rational or logical knowledge. India happens to have a vast body of literature in this field and interestingly it is far advanced of the West. We are the only people in the world who developed a logical method or reasoning called vitanda and our politicians have specialized in that form of logic.

The development of sastras or researched knowledge was the next. This was called rational knowledge. The development of logic in Nyaya or Mimansa philosophies is the typical product of that age and effort. It is this phase of development that came to its eventual fruition in the philosophical contributions of Nagarjuna and Dharmakirti. A glimpse of their logic can be witnessed in Milindapanha (the dialogue between King Menander / Mahendra and Nagsena). Then came the *third*, experimental sciences. This form of knowledge was no descent but a step toward progress. This gave us some of the greatest scientists and physicians. The astronomers, mathematicians, physicians, etc., are a product of this knowledge. William James recorded: " From the Vedas (ancient Indian scriptures) we learn a practical art of surgery, medicine, music, house building under which mechanized art is included. They are encyclopedia of every aspect of life, culture, religion, science, ethics, law, cosmology and meteorology." Read, D.P. Chattopadhyaya *Science and Socicty in Ancient India*, which goes into details of the rise and fall in physical sciences in that society.

It is now proved beyond any doubt that the West owes

its material progress to that knowledge. Albert Einstein wrote: "We owe a lot to the Indians who taught us how to count, without which no worthwhile scientific discovery could have been made." Let us not talk of specific formulas instead let us come straight to the methods of research the ancients evolved. I am now taking up the question of proof or evidence *that what is being said or demonstrated is true*. In this regards I shall take up first the methods our *sastris* or researchers followed and then discuss the grounds of establishing truth.

In the 7th century A.D. Kumaril Bhatt developed methods of research for discovering, creating and improving knowledge. He defined in the typical aphoristic style the steps one must follow in research. These steps are common to both social as well as physical sciences. The aphorism is: "Vishayo Vishaaschaiva purvapaksha stathotaram / Niranayaishchi panchang shastradhikarana smritam." In other words he declared that a researcher ought to remember five steps in writing a sastra.

The first step was doubt / identification of a problem. The second was review of existing literature or the establishing of the ground for conducting research or defining grounds why research had become imperative. Thereafter he, like Hegel, proposed dialectical method for arriving at the truth. The researcher has to propose purvapaksha or the arguments against the proposition. Then he must follow it up with uttarpaksha or offer answers to each of the grounds raised in the earlier proposition. The result has to be a synthesis or the final decision. It should be clear now that modern researchers too follow the same steps. Here is the latest version of the steps developed by an Italian researcher named Carlo Lastrucci. His steps are 1. Formulation of the Problem; 2. Surveying related literature; 3. Preparing research design; 4. Fixing the size of the sample; 5. Data collection; 6. Interpretation of the data; 7. Verification of the interpretation, or, the rejection of the hypothesis and lastly 8. Preparing research report. One could compare the steps and draw one's own conclusion. At least for conducting research we need not borrow all our tools from the West.

Since the purpose of conducting research is to either

Knowledge (Buddhi)

ANUBHAVA
(immediate experience

SMRITI
(Memory)
yathartha
(True) (unreal)

PRAMA
real
(valid knowledge)

APRAMA
(non-valid knowledge)

SAMASYA
(error)

VIPARYAYA
(doubt)

TARKA
(hypothetical
argument)

Pratyaksha
(perception)

anumiti
(Inference)

upamiti
(Comparison)

sabda or verbal testimony

confirm existing knowledge or creating some of our own. We must therefore know: what is Knowledge? A few thinkers in India took it to be an act; others thought it to be a relation, while some others declared it to be subsistent. A minority of scholars declared that knowledge was a quality in other words we are not quite sure about its nature and therefore we do not know like Bertrand Russell whether we are not dreaming when we are apparently awake. Knowledge like truth is not easy to cognize. Just as we are not very sure about the nature of Reality or about the First Cause our researches in the ultimate analysis give us merely a glimpse of Reality—nothing more. Without going into details we could agree with Jayanta—an Indian thinker of Nyaya School, that knowledge is a mode of buddhi, which transforms itself into the shape of the object it cognizes.

Knowledge has been classifies as valid and invalid knowledge. The invalid is an illusion and valid knowledge is just the opposite of the invalid knowledge.

Here is a frame of reference with which all branches of scientists will by and large agree. There does not seem to be much improvement or development in this regard. The Western scientists too believe in what they perceive. It is another matter that even perception per se could give us invalid knowledge. The experimental truth tested in the laboratories could also yield inaccurate or invalid results.

We may like to know a little more about non-valid knowledge. Memory is considered non-valid knowledge because the object remembered is different from the object memorized. Recognition is a qualified, real and direct perception of the object, whereas in the case of memory the object remembered is always absent. What may have been real once in the sense it existed at a given time and space but it has now ceased to exist therefore there can be no correspondence between the ceased object and its memory image. In practical terms autobiographies cannot be regarded as valid evidence.

There are three other forms of non-valid knowledge. They are samasys (doubt), tarka (hypothetical reasoning), and error / viparyaya. Doubt is of five types. 1. it usually arises when certain properties that are common create doubt in our mind. For instance, if in twilight we perceive a tall man he can be confused with a post because tallness is common to both. 2. When we cognize a unique property such as sound of koel, which may create doubt in our minds whether or not it is the same sound that is common to all koels or it was unique for one that I heard. 3. On the basis of conflicting testimony it is difficult to decide about the nature of the First Cause. 4. Irregularity of perception such as water in mirage and the water in a tank may create doubt in our mind whether water is perceived when it really exists or when it does not. 5. Irregularity of non-perception., e.g. we do not perceive water in a radish when it does exist and also on dry land where it really does not exist.

Hypothetical reasoning is an intellectual act, which contributes to the ascertainment of truth by means of adducing logical grounds in favor of one of the alternative possibilities when reality is not known in its actual character. This type of reasoning can or might not help resolve indecisiveness. This reasoning is also of five types. 1. Atmasraya is argument that is self-dependent in respect of genesis, subsistence and cognition, e.g., A is the cause of A. here A is must be different from itself, because the cause is different from effect. 2. Anyonyashraya is a mutually dependent argument. Such as A depends on B, and B depends on A. 3. Cakrak / circular. Here the argument is circular in nature, e.g., A requires B, and B requires C, and C requires A. 4. Anavastha is the regression ad infinitum. If we explain A by B, and B by C etc. we can go on doing so without explaining anything. 5. Reductio ad absurdum or tadanyabadhitaprasanga. It indirectly proves the validity of the argument by showing that the contradictory of its conclusion is absurd. This may be done by opposing the contradiction of the conclusion by means of some fact or by applying some universal law. If the contradictory be false the original conclusion must be true.

Error or viparyaya — when any object is presented in a form which does not belong to it, it is a case error or illusion. Sky-lotus is one such example.

The nature of Prama (Valid Knowledge)

Valid knowledge has two-fold characteristics of truth and novelty. In this regard all Indian philosophies are common. Perception, Inference, Comparison and verbal testimony are commonly accepted as four forms of valid knowledge.

Indian philosophies have accepted their own forms of valid knowledge. This might interest some to go through the following configuration and see how they are placed.

Lokayata	perception
Buddhism	perception, inference
Vaisesika	perception, inference,
Samkhya	perception, inference, word (sabda)
Nyaya	perception, inference, word comparison

Vedanta perception, inference, word, comparison, postulation (artha patti) and non-perception

(anupalabhadi)

Bhatta Mimansa perception, inference, word, comparison, postulation and non-perception.

Prabharaka Mimansa perception, inference, word, comparison, postulation.

One could easily select one or more of the methods for conducting research. I take it that nearly all these methods of testing truth or modes of knowing are currently used by scientists the world over.

Towards the end let me make a brief reference to Theories of False Cognition (Khyathivad). Each branch of Indian philosophy has its own theory of false cognition. It may be remembered that for a realist / scientist it is easy to have theory of truth since he believes in the mind-independent existence and nature of the objects of cognition but it is extremely difficult to have a theory of error wherein the objects of cognition are not mind-independent. Making a mistake in cognizing a rope as snake gives rise to numerous theories because here the snake is an illusion since the snake is not mind –independent. What exists is rope but what an individual perceives it as a snake, which is non-existent. For example, while for the materialists like the Carvakas snake is an illusion because a rope is mind-independent reality, but for a Yogachari Buddhist here a mental state is getting projected outside so the problem lies in the mental image being different from the real. Therefore, in their relevant context both are real—the non-existent, mental-image snake and the existing real rope. For a Vedanti the error consists in mistaking a part to be whole.

The real problem arises as we cognize, say K, the question one needs to answer is do the same causal conditions that give rise to K also give rise to the properties of the K? If the answer is yes, then K's truth, which is its property is intrinsic to K. Or does one learn the truth / properties of K after one knows K.? In the first case truth and falsity are inherent / intrinsic to K and in the latter they are extrinsic.

If we applied our arguments in the case of scientific

discovery or invention we are very clear in our mind that when we discover or come to know K we certainly do not cognize all its properties. Whether we like it or not knowing K can never automatically reveal to us all the properties of K. The truth in this case is extrinsic. This is not true for philosophy. Here we know K along with all its properties almost simultaneously.

The truth is that it is not within the powers of the humans to know the objective Reality the form in which it exists. All developments in knowledge are merely efforts to come very close to Reality. Therefore, even the best of researches in social or physical sciences are mere approximations and not the Truth itself. As Gunnar Myrdal said there is no objectivity in research. We see what we wish to see. In social sciences the truth gets colored the moment one tries to formulate a hypothesis. You eventually come to prove what you started to prove. The truth that we know is therefore relative, transitory and malleable.

We have seen in this small paper that while research is the innate function of all human minds, the purpose of research is to help humanity by creating tools of collecting quality information and revealing some aspect of the unknown. What we call advancement of civilization is in reality made up of knowledge created by innumerable scientists of all branches and hue. All progress is definable in terms of quality research alone with all other considerations constituting the very core of that effort.

Towards the end of the paper let me briefly touch upon the problem: Does research help us find knowledge or create it? If we 'find' it then we accept that it existed before we found it (i.e. knowledge is independent of cognition) and would have remained 'un-found' without our having made any effort. Here a couple of examples would help us explain this problem. Suppose in chemistry laboratory we discover a quantifiable relationship of one chemical with the other and make a useful product after making one react on the other in a certain proportion. This whole process thereafter helps us to create an equation, which enables every chemist to make the same product of identical quality as and when he or she so desired. The question is: Has this chemist created

Knowledge or merely discovered it? We could take another example from the field of Anthropology. Suppose on a journey in a tribal belt we discover a tribe about whose existence no one knew before and like Darwin we too find grounds to support the theory Darwin once proposed. The reinforcement of a theory in this case has then to be defined. What exactly does this finding amount to —an additional proof, supportive proof, an independent proof or the final proof? Or, it is just a serendipidity? The question that one must answer is: What is the function of research? — Is it to discover knowledge or to create it? Does knowledge pre-exist discovery or creation?

The best of the researchers have failed to support the thesis that research is always objective. Gunnar Myrdal had declared in his book *The Asian Drama* that even 'objectivity' itself is subjective. Wassily Leontief, Nobel Prize winner for modeling, said modeling has its own limitations. "We move from more or less plausible but really *arbitrary assumptions*, to elegantly demonstrated but irrelevant conclusions." It will be interesting to note that if a researcher cannot help having assumptions and if assumptions themselves are the reason for irrelevant conclusions all research findings become suspect.

Somehow these questions do not fall within the domain of epistemology but of ontology? Research may not be limited to this or that branch of knowledge but it does try to mostly enlighten its clientele and help life on the planet in general become more congenial than what it normally is. Seen in a certain context humans have failed to find a formula for peaceful existence. They have also not learnt how to be friendly with the forces of Nature. They have as yet to discover the meanings of terms, which they so commonly use. They apparently have no clue to the meaning of terms like— optimum levels of happiness, progress or advancement, etc. Let us hope our research efforts will some day bear reasonably appreciable fruits and help us out of the misery of living in a state wherein nothing is certain or definitive. To my mind this then is the principal function of research—an effort that helps us decide not merely the efficiency and effectiveness of research tools but also the grounds for selecting the validity of proof and the relevance of findings. Till then of necessity research findings must bear the brunt of remaining tentative, transitory, and trivialized Reality.

A last question: How do we define a 'good' research? The reality is only on two grounds quality could be defended or asserted. If the research is objective and the arguments built up for exposition of a finding are rational then alone we could say that this piece of research merits the qualifying adjective 'good'. In social sciences however we produce biased and motivated research. One cannot expect that certain universities in India are capable of producing unbiased and un-motivated research. In the recent controversy on NCERT's history books it came out very clearly that research is mostly subjected to political convenience and therefore it is extremely difficult to qualify this kind of research with an adjective 'GOOD' or even 'research'. In such cases the motives for the results are known even before the research has been undertaken. Research and 'closed' minds rarely go well together. In fact, researchers should not be identified with any given opinion.

6

Educational Research and Policy Decisions

Research is necessary to satisfy innate human curiosity. The cause and the urge to inquire into a phenomenon are basic to human advancement. Exploring into the unknown or unfamiliar comes naturally to all living beings be they human or animal. Human beings have fortunately recorded the steps followed in their methods of inquiry. Besides they have also classified various kinds of inquiry. All inquires are subject to the conditions of time, resources and the competence of the inquirer. For the results of the inquiry to be acceptable one ought to show demonstrable results. Regardless of the method one followed the study design should be easy to explain. For instance, one finds in the Vedas numerous scientific truths, (e.g., mathematical formulae) but there is nothing to show how the Rishis arrived at these equations. We have accepted by now that the method of inquiry they pursued was based on intuition. But intuition cannot help us everywhere without a solid base of knowledge. In India Kumaril Bhatt (7th century A.D.) was the first scholar to have given us steps to be followed in majority of cases. Surprisingly, these steps have withstood all advancements in the field. The ancient sastras follow these steps strictly. These steps are: 1. Statement of a problem, 2. Previous studies in the area including all the variables known concerning the problem, if any, 3. Objections—data that negates the statement made initially, 4. Answers to the objections emanating from the study undertaken, 5. Interpretation of the data and the presentation of results. Interestingly, Hegel's dialectics also follows the last three steps of Kumaril Bhatt. Carlo Lastrucci, an eminent research scientist recently detailed these steps on almost identical lines. According to him, the steps are: problem formulation, survey of related literature, research design, fixing the size of the sample, data collection, interpretation of the data, verification of the interpretation for the purpose of its acceptance or rejection, and lastly the report.

For our discussion, we have selected an important area for our discussion. We are going to discuss and see how educational policies are formulated. Generally it is believed that research has very rarely any bearing on policy making. May be the reason for so thinking lies in the fact that academics are not administrators. They can only conduct research and also teach their research findings to their captive audiences. The governments are run differently. It is not binding on any government to listen to a researcher, who in all probability may be far removed from the ground reality. Politics after all is a different kettle of fish. Here politicians and administrators have to please a wide spectrum of people. Their clientele is rarely well disposed to research. Be that as it may, research has its own value. We shall soon see how take benefit of research as compared with the advanced nations of the world.

In a recent publication (2003) titled *International Handbook of Educational Research in the Asia-Pacific Region*, Part 1& II, the relationship between educational research and policy-making has received a good deal of attention. Apparently, this area has largely remained ignored in India. Occasional questions apart no one seems to have seriously considered exploring the background of policy-making and recorded the exact sequence of events in their run up to a policy implementation and the eventual fall out of the same when stock is taken. Any serious student of Indian educational system will know that number of policy decisions have failed to yield positive results. In some cases like the 11+3 of the Mudaliar Commission ended up in creating a greater mess than the one it tried to address both at secondary and the higher education levels. We also have records of certain decisions made by Union Ministers of education in the past wherein failures of policies match successes in almost equal measure. During K.L. Srimali's regime his trip to Holland and Europe gave us Rural Institutes. Somehow these Institutes failed to achieve the goals set for them. On the other hand India's Agriculture universities that flaunt their America's land-grant colleges lineage proved to be overwhelmingly successful. It is one of those cases wherein a failure matches success. But the question is not what succeeded and what met with a disaster. The real point is the sequence of events in the background and also its level of success. The reason why such an exercise is necessary is because we seem to have a naïve belief that once a policy is made mandatory it should succeed. We do not realize that the success or a failure of a policy depends largely upon people's acceptance or rejection. Just as in life we discover that only a few of our efforts pay dividends, similarly all decisions are subject to the law of averages.

So far I have come across only one publication *(Educational Policies in India—Analysis and Review of Promise and Performance, 2002, NIEPA)* that has tried to address this problem. Earlier a Joint Secretary in the Planning Commission also came out with a book on how research and policies are correlated. The Education Policy Unit of the National Institute of Education Planning and Administration organized an in-depth discussion on the Analysis and Review of National Education Policy (NEP) and the Program of Action (POA) 1992 and toward that end developed a detailed paper. Sectorial analysis of the policy implementation yielded informed analytical papers. In my opinion this effort also fails to match the model I happen to have in my mind. For example, the first paper in the book cited above written by A.K. Sharma on the implementation of the Educational Policy (1986) gives the genesis of the recommendation for the start of Common School program along with the reasons for its inclusion in the policy but without assigning any reason for its failure declared it to be non-functional. I expected him to have at least referred to a debate on the question and mentioned the demand by several groups to be sincere in its implementation. But he did nothing of the sort. Similarly, he talks of the failure of MLL (Minimum Levels of Learning) but mentions nothing about an acrimonious debate between the two sponsors of the idea and a certain role the MHRD played. In the opinion of Sharma the NCTE – a doubtful starter, gets a green signal and is declared to be performing well because it has not allowed the sub-standard teacher education institutions to survive. Perhaps he did not read the Anand Sarup report (2001) or just forgot to tell the truth. The first condition of research study is to be truthful and objective.

I wish someone had prepared a paper on the exact sequence of events leading to the formulation of an educational policy. After that the same paper, I think, should also carry the record of the process of a policy implementation. The third stage is to make available some details about the manner the policy tries to resolve a given problem. Toward the end the paper one should also carry an assessment about the success or failure of the implemented policy and the next stage of the same must constitute to attempt to formulate or deduce a moral, if any.

There are several ways to trace the genesis of a problem-area, which demands the evolution of an immediate/ cautious approach for its eventual resolution. For example, it is the job of the Ministry of Agriculture to oversee the demand and supply scenario of agricultural production. Everyone knows that India's population is increasing therefore to meet its food requirements the Ministry has to prepare itself in advance. It is the responsibility of the Ministry of Agriculture to locate an agency that will calculate the demand and suggest ways and means to meet it. This obligation definitely falls within the Ministry's prerogatives. The agency that undertakes this job is actually doing so shall have to apply certain norms. These norms shall then constitute research design. In the present case the Indian Institute of Management, Ahmedabad has done the job. The decision the Ministry takes would form the basis of a policy. This then is one such example where the Ministry of Agriculture takes an advance action for a future demand. But it is possible that the problem at hand could demand an immediate solution. One will then have to look out for some quick-fix response. Could research help out in this situation too? For a quick answer too research can furnish a pilot design and its simultaneous replication on several fronts. These experiments also form a part of a policy formulation.

Put against this backdrop the issue, in its totality, does

deserve a close review. In that process firstly, we should take stock of the ground reality vis a vis educational research. For example, it is essential to find out who needs research evidence and why? Is it an institution or an individual? Is the demand for a long-range decision-making purpose or research is needed for a limited objective? Also, it is imperative to discover the nature of the query. For instance, if a private management is trying to find a solution to its financial problems one must assess the typologies of the parties involved. Before one decided to undertake research to help in resolving such a problem, number of questions would require straight answers. One should know how and which queries to make first. While there is no guarantee that a research can really help resolve problems, (because research takes time to show any result and also there is always a possibility that matters might get resolved even without any intervention) it is necessary to know whether there is a possibility that the findings / recommendations, as and when they do come, will be given a fair trail. Then there are questions like: who is undertaking research, who is financing it and how much time it will take to complete a project or exactly what does the researcher gain out of such a venture. Educational research is not like medical research where the gains are commensurate with the money and time involved in getting a drug patented. Secondly, we should examine the level and quality of research currently being done in this area. Surely we are not alone who get confronted with problems in education. Each and every nation today is faced with some intractable educational problem. Traditionally, we are used to finding answers for educational problems intuitively, if not according to our convenience.

It is also good to remember that the problems of private and public undertakings are different. Therefore, what succeeds in a private establishment may not necessarily succeed in a public undertaking. If some problems are poverty-related, there are others that might relate to learning, memory, student behavior, teacher training etc. Education like any other skill and information area is growing. True, it does not have comparably gifted members and serious workers (may be) because the chances of getting rewards are limited and also the one's who join it do not command the same levels of respect as people from other Disciplines do. But that should not dishearten us. Instead, it should inspire us to try achieving comparable heights that others now command. Thirdly, we must explore areas wherein some pioneering efforts are needed and which promise results.

There are a few additional considerations too that are involved here. We must make a distinction between basic and non-basic research. Basic or fundamental research in social sciences is mostly philosophical and is directed to yield results in the form of principles or theories. Ideologies impact in coloring decisions. Seldom do they come out boldly in the open. Political philosophies like that of Marx or Hegel merely furnish criteria for an analysis of social reality and may at times lead to some decisions. They could be motivated to reform society but it is not necessary that a philosophy must result in policy formulation. Policies are needed by societies to resolve their day-to-day problems. Here the idea is to suggest ways and means to the resolution of a problem. Here thinking is involved in first analyzing the precise nature of the problem, then weighing steps that measure up to its resolution and finally selecting one out of the several that normally crowd the scene. The nature of the steps that get suggested for the eventual application may come from some pilot projects, theory or a possible suggestion emanating out of a successful experiment.

The ground reality about institutions engaged in educational research is that besides institutions set up by the Government of India like the NCERT & NIEPA etc. that are supposed to work within the framework of the Ministry of Human Resources Development, Indian universities too have departments of education wherein some advance level research in various aspects of education is regularly undertaken. Directly or indirectly, therefore, the Government of India is apparently funding research. In other words, the Government is interested and also involved both in training and employing research workers. By implication therefore it is natural to assume that research, if meaningful and necessary, is welcome. Parallel to the Government there are numerous private agencies too that are involved in educational research. Besides few private-funded agencies, NGO's, etc., the most famous name involved is that of the Tatas. It would be quite revealing to discover and count the numbers involved. The Government of India has set up organizations like the Indian Council of Social Science Research, the Indian Council of Historical Research, and the Indian Council of Philosophical Research etc. to finance research in certain specific areas. Then there is an Indian Institute of Advanced Studies. Several State governments have also set up their own organizations to assist and fund research. The important point to note is that in Independent India research has come of age. Both private and public sectors have found to their pleasant surprise that research funding has paid dividends. Therefore, no one is averse to funding or conducting educational research.

Unlike several nations where the Government demand for any kind of research has to go to the universities only, in free India we have both the Government as well as private bodies to undertake all kinds of researches. One does not have to go far to find out reason for this. The Government of India does not seem to trust researchers very much and therefore appears quite unwilling to accept that researchers outside its own supervision could also provide meaningful and timely results. Universities on their part have done little to deserve this trust. But in this category too there are brilliant exceptions. Agriculture universities and the Indian Institutes of Technologies have paid back several times over the investments made in their setting up and support. But the general assumption seems to be that unlike Government's own employee's, university staff will not feel responsible enough to deliver on time. The dreamy professors might turn out to be a big bother. The Government's own employee cannot afford to be either irresponsible or else one is answerable to one's boss. In fact, it is the question of one's accountability. Theoretically the universities enjoy autonomy.

The other question one needs to answer is: Who wants research guidance? Uninformed decisions could prove to be national disasters. Civilizational advancement is impossible without research or critical evaluation of the existing scenario. No matter how trivial or ordinary looking decision one might be taking, a lot of critical thinking furnishes it necessary support systems. Success or failure of a decision is however another matter. Failures do not signify ignorance or lack of critical evaluation. While decisions are a projection of a dream, failures or successes signify the consequences of dreaming. Both help taking a determined step forward.

One question that has come up for repeated discussion on the theme relates to the point: How come educational researches do not seem to be informing decision –making? The write-up of T. Neville Postlethwaite in the *Handbook* referred to above holds out no promise for the either the researcher or the policy-maker. In his opinion the twins (the researcher and the user of research) are not likely to meet. This is so either because the policy maker was not taken initially into confidence; or, the researcher had a small or bad sample and hence the findings turn out to be of no consequence.

If only we were to delve a little deeply into the existing demand and supply situation in India of the said need the chances are that we would be in for a big surprise. For instance, if we looked around and tried to correlate research findings with the policy making we will be forced to concede that commissioned research has indeed been extremely useful. For instance, the location of primary school and the distance expected of a child to travel before reaching school was decided on the basis of a national survey. Each Census carries numerous questions prepared by Government's own institutions so that the furnished data could be used for policy implications. The setting up of National Institute of Open Schooling is the result of a Pilot project from where some useful facts and figures were collected and a policy evolved to implement. In fact, what we need is a proper impact study on the subject.

Numerous changes that occurred in Indian higher education after Teacher Commission Report (1984-85) are a testimony to the fact that research can contribute and indeed does in critical areas of decision-making. The setting up of Academic Staff Colleges, improvement in libraries and the working conditions of teachers, their grade revisions, increase in house allowances etc. were indeed the direct result of various researches conducted by NIEPAs Higher Education Unit. Similarly, the Kothari Commission had earlier received plenty of research input. Parallel to this we should notice that Institutes like Indian Council of Applies Manpower Research, Indian Council of Applied Economic Research continuously inform India's budget making. In the areas of Space, defense strategies, economic research, poverty alleviation etc. we find a positive correlation of research findings with policy making.

Meanwhile we should not forget that research findings need to be given wide publicity when they are found to have credible / authentic evidence. Mere reporting of research findings in the journals is seldom found to be either useful or sufficient. Research also needs wider and larger responsive audience. In the article printed in the *Handbook titled: Policy-Making, Planning and Change in Tertiary Education* the trend apparently is that while the State is unwilling to withdraw from policy making, it is in fact approaching this area through adopting market mechanism. The goals set for education to achieve are the pursuit of excellence, increased competitiveness and efficiency. One needs to ponder over one problem. For achieving excellence, one needs to define excellence. A definition like that will have to be contextual. There can hardly ever be a universally acceptable concept of excellence. This means that for a theoretical concept one needs a different kind of set up for conducting research than that of an applied type of research. Each research variant will need its own establishment. Therefore, one has to decide who will do fundamental research and who will take up some other type of research. This question also needs a policy input. Of late, one notices that numerous terms have become popular. We should look beyond the word and grapple with the reality that lies beyond it.

Under the major theme title: *Educational Research and National Development* the Handbook carries several articles such as: *Educational Research and Regional Development, Globalization and Education in Asia, Comparative Indicators in*

Education, Dissemination of the Findings of Educational Research and Donor Support for Educational Research. This section deals comprehensively with the definition, problems, donors, dissemination and relationship of educational research with regional and national development. Tuijnman records the way research in education has grown over the past couple of decades. For instance, during the 1980's educational research was treated less for how it informed policies but more for how it improved educational practice. In the 1990s there developed a strong emphasis on practice-oriented research that would immediately benefit teachers and school leaders. The 21st century is witness to yet another stage in research development wherein politics has started playing a direct role. The empowerment of practitioners and legitimacy of their knowledge base may well start impacting research funding. Pointing to a recent development educational research is currently being called upon to show a relationship between education and the raising of the quality of its workforce. The reason behind it all is to demonstrate that education does really contribute to a nation's economic growth. It has been argued that monitoring of student's achievement in science and mathematics in the region needs being paid attention.

Number of issues and weaknesses in educational research stand identified and some important suggestions too have been made. For instance, researchers should involve practitioners in both design and actual conduct of school innovation projects. Steps taken by New Zealand Ministry of Education in1999 for underpinning policy by sound research need to be paid attention by the concerned parties all over the Asian region. While we all know about the inadequacies of educational research vis a vis policy-making and classroom instruction, it is suggested that a good balance between basic research and applied development work will lead to research being accorded due respect. Unfortunately, in India we do not have many capable researchers to enter the area of basic research. The NCERT was the first institution that had in early 60s started with Foundations of Education for the purpose, but very soon the Government decided to close it down as the dividends seemingly failed to match investment. I am quite sure the organization must be ruing the day when it took such a negative stance.

Dissemination of the Findings of Educational Research is a useful area to explore. I have a feeling that so far no nation has succeeded in evolving a model worthy of being followed by others. The best model that a UNESCO group had come across was discovered in China. They had evolved a process through which the summaries of meaningful researches were disseminated on the national television channel during prime time viewing. Other than this there existed no model worthy of being cited. The usual method is only to have research reports published either in Journals or in books.

We have discussed in some detail the nature (research for what?), impact (its relationship with educational reform), needs and priorities of research in education, the areas being constantly ignored relate to training of research workers, regional co-operation in educational research and the challenges before research to inform reform-initiators. Perhaps the basic reason lies in semi-professionalism confronting this area. We, in India, do not have qualified and mature comparativists to undertake this job.

Currently the problems Education per se faces lie in swiftly changing times and the lack of identification of prospective skills that could be offered in advance. The ICT, globalization and the unpredictable nature of financing education are increasingly growing into areas of concern. We seem to have overstretched our demands on education and believe naively that the panacea for all our ills lies in it. Unfortunately, this is not true or else the developed countries will not face problems of unemployment, non-usable skills and irrelevant knowledge etc. As technology advances it brings cheer to some homes but utter destitution and misery to those of others. The unequal world is becoming even more sharply divided. We do not talk these days of only economic divide but of digital divide too. The more we train people, the less they appear to become equal to the task on hand.

There is a vast difference between the relevance and value of researches undertaken in Education and in other Disciplines. The most useful researches currently being undertaken in India fall in the fields of technology and agriculture. One finds their impact all around. For instance, the IITs and Agriculture universities have done more for the Indian economy and the common man than all other branches of academic areas put together. A single improvement in a seed strain yields more money to the nation than the total amount spent on the setting up of an agricultural university. These universities are responsible for making India self-sufficient in food. Even such academic subjects like sociology, political science, and economics etc. have made outstanding contributions to our knowledge and one notices their impact on informed decision-making every day. A recent study on the contributions of the Indian Institutes of Technology (*Times of India*, 25.01.04) to India's knowledge industry has attempted to prove that they are worth more than their structure in gold.

Unfortunately, this is not so apparent in Education. This is one question that needs some exploring. It might amaze some to note that in the fields of agriculture and technology the educational background of the users of highly sophisticated research is close to illiteracy. But no such luck seems to have come in the share of India's educational researchers, wherein the educational background of research users is as high as those of the researchers themselves.

There is some scope for discussing our Research compendia called *Surveys of Educational Research* the NCERT brings out every five-year. Studying the trend one will have noticed that the First Survey covered the years 1950-73 and brought out the titles of M.Ed. and Ph.D. theses (1939-61) with a supplement until 1966. The areas included numbered 16. The total number of researches reported was 342. While the number of non-Ph.D. researches was 269, the number of Ph.D. was a meager 78 The 16 areas included: Philosophy of Education, History of Education, Sociology, Personality, Learning and Motivation, Guidance, Tests and Measurement, Curriculum, Methods and Textbooks,

Programmed Learning, Correlates of Achievement, Educational Evaluation and Examinations, Teaching and Teaching Behavior, Teacher Administration, Economics of Education, Social and Adult Education and Educational Surveys. Since then 4 more Surveys have come and the Sixth is about to come out. Each survey has covered more areas than its predecessor. The *Second* survey added Comparative Education, Educational Technology, Higher Education and Non-Formal Education and its coverage increased to 806 of which 10% were research projects taken up by government employees. The Third Survey added to its list of areas covered: *Language Education, Researches in the USA and UK by Indians and Priorities in Educational Research.* Incidentally, it covered 158 NCERT projects plus 168 funded by other agencies. Decade-wise the Ph.D in Education were as follows: 1941-50=10, 51-60=63, 61-70=234, 71-80=850, 81-83=266. The trend is clear. Ph.D. in Education became increasingly numerous. But the non-Ph.D researchers remained many more (1017). The fourth Survey did not add anything new to the neglected areas, which included Theoretical Research, Case Studies, Law and Education, Politics of Education, Policy Research or Experimental researches, Curricular Changes, Educational Administration and Teacher Transfer Policies, etc. The *Fifth* Survey added Creativity and Innovations, Guidance Counseling, Curriculum Development, pre-Primary Education, Moral Art and Aesthetics, and Education of Girls and Women. Since then we notice the emergence of some more areas such as Education of the Challenged Children, Education of Minorities, Tribal Education etc. and currently the number of areas being covered might as well have exceeded 38. Still, the Indian effort comes nowhere near the work done elsewhere in the APR.

Compared with the Indian publications the above cited *Handbook* covers many more areas and with expected appropriateness. Somehow I have a feeling that there is a mismatch between the research efforts and the usability of research findings. Surprisingly, the best usable research in almost all academic fields in India is either coming from Foundations like that of the Tatas or Birlas or from the

Institutes and bodies like the NCERT, ICSSR, ICAMR, NIEPA, ISRO, and ICAR etc that work within the framework of the Governments' various Ministries. Somehow, the Indian universities have refused to take the bait of exploring into those areas that may someday help the Nation build a sound knowledge base. There is no reason to believe that prospective researchers from universities will continue to remain apathetic to their social obligations. This is more true for Education than for other Disciplines. It looks as though they do not know how to take into confidence policy-makers or the users of the research findings. I think this is one area that needs to be addressed on a priority basis. One also suspects that unlike agriculture scientists and the technologists, educational researchers have not learnt the art of exhibiting properly their wares. They have thus far failed to correlate their research findings with demonstrable success. Or, may be they have no rapport with the actual research users. Alternatively, either they think poorly of their products and consider them unworthy of being put on sale in the market; or, they lack confidence in their efforts. In either condition, educational researchers remain losers. Personally I would be interested to see that someone came forward to take up the gauntlet (of conducting usable educational research) and took the bull (of policy makers) by its horns.

We need to note that number of institutions both national and international is willing to finance educational research. I think it would be a good idea if a list of donor institutions along with their addresses and proformas etc. were made readily available.

7

Universities As Service Institutions

(Birth of high-tech Societies)

"May we associate with the learned and thus spread freely the system of education as propounded in the Vedic hymns. Just as my knowledge is valued by all, so should yours. The ignorant moving in the dark who are opposed to the learned, and whom the learned disapprove for their antagonism to knowledge, should be brought round to the path of virtue by hundreds of means available and let restriction on them be not removed till enlightenment. May the wicked be not blessed with prosperity, and pleasure of knowledge. O ye dutiful! May ye persistently follow the path of virtue." Yajurveda 1.26

"O Man under bondage! I loosen up that imperviously tight tie, which the mighty misery of ignorance hath bound round your neck for your life, vigor and strength so that you, when liberated, enjoy the ultra-mundane happiness.

Let there be weapons of knowledge against this misery of ignorance. May Divinity, endowed with sharp wisdom, loose these fastening fetters wrought of iron." Atharvaveda, LX111. 1 & 11

Universities the world over are under pressure to undergo major changes both in their teaching content as well as in their modes of content-delivery. The earlier definitions of higher education like the one Henry Cardinal Newman (The Idea of a University) in 19th century England, or Abraham Flexner gave in 1930s (Universities: American, English and German) came in for close scrutiny by American scholars like Clark Kerr in the 1950s who stigmatized them' as expression of ideal types' and declared them irrelevant in the modern context. Nearer home the UGC in one of its 1996 document stated: "As we move to the 21st century, it is country's policy opinion to decide whether the complex university system, built over five decades since India's independence with tremendous investment of both human and material resources, is to be adequately supported so that it is able to play a key role in the world institutions—educational, economic and professional—and be able to face the competition unleashed by a new world economic order, or, to decline for want of necessary support which has characterized it for over half of the last decade of this century."

Recent technological developments in advanced societies are forcing us Indians to ask our universities to lend a helping hand to meet the challenges we face everyday in all walks of life. It is not that this help has not been forthcoming. Our agriculture universities, our IITs, IIMs and medical and similar other institutions of higher learning have always been forthcoming in their ready help (see, Indian Universities—Towards Nation-building, UGC, 1998). They are immensely capable to meet all our requirements. What they are currently engaged in doing needs, however, to be accelerated. For instance, the universities have the means to enable vast numbers of our people to become knowledge-oriented and be able to master tools of learning. Today we also have the necessary technology to support these efforts in this direction. This blessing isn't entirely free from problems. Confronted, as we are, with the immense problems of equity and justice we have to supply on priority-basis vast numbers of humans the bare means of life and living besides tools of learning. The latest figures given by NCAER reveal that around 40% people in the rural India and 14.3% in urban India live on incomes below subsistence levels. The literacy figures given out by the Census are also not very encouraging. The abysmal rates of literacy among girls and none too encouraging reality among boys refuse to help us present a rosy overall picture. We are therefore witnessing all around us a very peculiar scenario of penury juxtaposed with plenty. We notice around us an ever-growing number of small islands of brilliant light and affluence comparable with the best in the world existing cheek by jowl with habitations of utter destitution and stark darkness. With air-conditioned schools dotting our metros we have to finance schools that have no teaching environment, or an infrastructure to boast of. The teachers in these schools leave much to be desired in terms of competence, fair play, humane behaviour, and devotion to duty. In majority of cases these schools do not have even usable toilets for girls and boys. The problems that we face are not merely definitional or semantic. They are real. Without resolving these problems anon all our efforts in other spheres will have little or no significance. Therefore, I plead that someone should address this problem on a priority basis and who would be better equipped than institutions of higher learning for preparing a roadmap for the nation in this regard. If prepared properly the Planning Commission might consider the same for adoption. And I sincerely hope that it does.

Education is a response to socio-political demands. Education's major functions too stand well defined. When India lived on the imported foodgrain her agricultural universities taught the illiterate farmers across the country modern techniques to usher in an era of plenty. The so-called *Green Revolution* was their response to the national demand. Universities today are no longer engaged in resolving problems in esoteric areas. They equip people with the wherewithal of earning one's livelihood and help acquire skills that make life meaningful. It is for nothing that society invariably chooses to use education as an instrument for undertaking these tasks. Since no society can either directly interact with or regulate education without the intervention of a proper mechanism, it willy-nilly assigns this job first to a government (irrespective of its form or ideology) and then expects that it in turn would express its 'will'. Governments by their very nature are merely interlocutors on behalf of the society. On their own they (governments) have neither the legitimacy nor the sense of direction to follow. Before the birth of secular societies the functions of the state were almost universally defined and controlled by priestly classes.

I propose to address two questions. The first one is: How do we offer education to all without prejudice to their class, faith, gender or avocation? And the second: What do we teach them? Could learning be differentiated and categorized? Masses rule over classes in democracies. We have to learn ways of selecting proper means/tools for interacting with our rulers. It should be interesting to learn that only those societies can maintain sustained growth and progress where the people and governments are in constant touch with each other and where both continue to engage themselves in a meaningful dialogue. Lack of such communication has its own hazards. In any case, in India it is not possible to dilly-dally for too long. We have to be both quick and efficient. And the only way open to us is to make right choices.

Indian constitution declared way back in 1951 that we ought to become fully literate and skilled citizenry. Despite several revisions in the target dates we are nowhere near the goal. Time seems to be asking us the question: When are we going to become a knowledge-society? The questions that beg immediate answers are: What is 'knowledge' and who should be its provider? Also: What is a knowledge society? The ancient Indians thought knowledge empowers. It liberates. Therefore, one must acquire it. So did the Greeks. In fact, if the Vedas were satisfied by merely defining the character and consequences of knowledge acquisition (tamaso ma jyotirgamaya) Plato went into details about the nature and functions of knowledge besides defining its socio-political ends.

In the West we find Plato pitted against Mill as they both defined the character and functions of education. Plato regarded education important because it "tries to cure the ills at the source while communism tries to prevent distractions that may corrupt the soul." He thought, "Virtue is knowledge" i.e. to know 'good' is to do 'good'. Plato's education reflected the demands of the Athenian society in contra-distinction to the one that Sparta offered. Plato's education followed the middle path drawing inspiration from Athens's values of creativity, excellence and individual achievement and from Sparta civic training. He was highly impressed by the results of state-controlled education. J. S. Mill almost two millennia later declared that a good society was one, which consisted of happy people, and happiness came out of self-reliance, rationality, tolerance, wide-ranging interests and a compassionate temper. For him "coercion is logically at odds with the creation of such a character."

He thought that state-controlled education was definitely not the best means of keeping people happy.

There are therefore two extremes on the issue. Who should be the provider of education— the state or the people? We have on the one hand Plato who preferred the state to censor knowledge before it was imparted. He consequently thought that state had a major role in its provision. On the other hand Mill would have none of it. Should the state desire to provide education it must abjure from controlling its provision. We are today aware of dangers inherent in permitting everyone and anyone to be able to offer education. Robson, J.M., Moir, M and Moir, J.; (1988, Collected Works of Mill, Routledge) write that for Mill "An educated citizenry was vital to the creation and perpetuation of a healthy body politic. The expansive ideal of citizenship inculcated by Mill put a premium on a widely diffused energy, virtue and intelligence. The achievement a higher politics required, among other things, opportunities for personal growth, which entailed bringing more and better schooling, more civic participation, and more benefits, and more beauty within the reach of more and more people." page LX.

While there is little doubt that state cannot always be trusted to become an ideal provider of education an individual too can be found wanting in the means of its provision and the honesty of purpose. Therefore, the so-called *totalitarian* versus *laissez faire* societies debate has its own brand of vocal votaries. The debate on the issue becomes at times acrimonious. We have therefore to devise ways and means to find a solution. Somewhere between the two extremes perhaps lies the middle path—an ideal for everyone to follow.

One must for a moment stop at the portals where a debate is in progress on the nature, functions and attributes of (institution-generated) knowledge and its providers. Instead, it would be in the interest of all to note that knowledge *per se* has been a valued product down the ages and evolutions of societies. If for the Indians knowledge is liberation (sa vidya ya vimuktaye), for the ancient Greeks it was the pleasantest element in human experience. Plato says, "Of the three types of pleasure, therefore, the pleasantest is that which belongs to the element in us which brings us knowledge, and the man in whom that element is in control will live the pleasantest life."

Towards Knowledge Society

Most of us associate knowledge with power. The nation that has the best form of knowledge as well as the most efficient system of its provision rules the roost. The reason why a country will be superpower and another the least powerful is adjudged in terms of its quality and types of knowledge-providers besides quality knowledge-products. It is no longer a question whether or not a nation has a system of education but whether or not she knows in advance that a 'Nation can be at Risk' if she fails to offer education that is at par with the best in the world. Knowledge does not merely signify ideas but it also lends muscle to a nation in the form of innovations, inventions and creating and building systems of efficient skill–providers that count. Such nations have goals to achieve and therefore they create means for such an achievement. It is here that we see clearly how education can be instrumental in raising the quality of a nation's life and make it a leader in highly competitive world. Nations that progress have thinkers with dreams and an infrastructure to fructify the same. While discussing the power-knowledge relationship Carrie Paechter in his paper titled Power, Gender and Curriculum (Knowledge, Power and Learning, edited by Carrie Paechter, Margaret Preedy, David Scott and Janet Soler, Sage, 2001) writes that Foucault himself talks of abandoning a tradition in which 'knowledge can exist only where the power relations are suspended.' He cites Walkerdine (1988) who says that decontextualized knowledge, such as 'pure' mathematics confers on the possessor power. Reason is seen as lying outside power relations and thus as having access to ultimate and unassailable truths, and it is this that confers power on those who are seen to have 'mastered' it. The interesting part of the tale is that it is only an illusion (of decontextualization of knowledge) but even' the illusion in itself confers power'.

In India too the higher form of knowledge is supposed

to be decontextualized. The moment one sees that knowledge is meant to serve some purpose such as an ideology, theory or a principle it stands transformed into a tool with an end in view. It assumes the garb of propaganda. Knowledge for an Indian has higher goals in view. It is not limited to pecuniary gains.

Education serves society but its relation with the state is not comparable to that of a slave with its master. Society is responsible for its birth and sustenance. At the same time society is also dependent on it for its 'intellectual and moral' survival. It is a bond that helps both to mutually sustain and help survive. Societies that are 'open' have a greater chance of being able to compete and excel than the ones that are less than 'open'. While open societies too have their faults but the closed ones are prone to getting ruled by the tyrants who are answerable to none. Knowledge needs fresh air and openness to prosper.

We have reached the stage when we ought to define knowledge. Knowledge is the cumulative store of what humans learn and propose to pass on to the posterity. Knowledge per se is neither backward nor progressive. These adjectives are applicable on societies and not on knowledge. Knowledge is always *contemporary*. Therefore it can be dated. The quality of knowledge can be assessed by its products. It evolves according to the changes in the nature of societal demands. The providers may change but the educational provision and its form generally remain unchanged. Schooling and education are commonly accepted as identical terms even as information is equated with knowledge. But information is not knowledge. Information helps in the process of acquiring knowledge. Surely, without information no knowledge is possible but information per se does not become knowledge. It has to go through a process to elevate itself. It is like vapor that arises out of water but to become rain other climatic conditions are imperative.

Since Time immemorial advancements in knowledge have originated either in human ingenuity or curiosity. Like food gathering, information gathering too is innate and instinctive. One of the major functions of education is to offer select information in appropriate dosages. The higher one goes the greater is the selectivity in quality and quantity of information, mode and time of its delivery. As one grows select information gradually crystallizes into knowledge, which in turn transforms itself into wisdom the moment one is able to coalesce all bits of knowledge through insight. Development of insight is the highest goal of life. It is a rare individual who is able to achieve it. Few teachers succeed in helping one develop an insight. But that rarely prevents individuals against moving in the direction. R.M. Hutchins dreamt in the early 1950's of transforming the USA into a *Learning Society*. When the Americans did not approach anywhere near their goal, they came out in 1980's with a document called *The Nation At Risk*. Nearly all societies imagine that one day they too will join the ranks of being a Learning Society or a Knowledge Society. Logically therefore achieving this dream is worth any effort.

The first reference to differentiating learning from wisdom in the Indian context is traceable to the Chhandogya Upanishad. Here we see Narada, a great scholar of his time, approaching Sanat Kumar with a request that he be made knowledgeable (mantra-vid). The teacher asks him about his existing level of knowledge. Narada says, "Sir, I know the Rigveda, the Yajurveda, the Samaveda, the Atharvaveda as the fourth legend and ancient lore as the fifth, the Veda of the Vedas (i.e. grammar), Biology, Mathematics, Augury, Chronology, Logic, Polity, the science of snake charming, and the Fine Arts. This, Sir, I know."

On hearing this long list of the subjects that his prospective pupil had mastered, the great teacher, Sanat Kumar remarked, that all that he had known thus far amounted to no more than mere 'words'. Since he had not acquired Atmagyan (the knowledge of the soul/self), he had not performed his duty as a scholar.

What is knowledge? What is its nature? When do we call a person knowledgeable? How do we impart knowledge? India's logicians have debated these questions for centuries on end and the debate is even now on. For us this discussion is both relevant and necessary, or else what is the meaning of our 'teaching' today— something beyond the mode of delivery. If we are not aware of the quality, level, or nature of what we intend giving to our students, teaching shall remain a string of vacuous words. These issues comprise the subject matter of epistemological queries that lead to the formulation of a theory of knowledge. Beyond the skeptics and the dogmatists — the two dominant schools of epistemology, there are a few who believe that this question can be answered. While some thinkers hold that knowledge is an act, some others regard it as a relation, and if according to some it is self-subsistent, for others it is a quality.

Gautama uses the terms jnana and uplabdhi as definitive synonyms of buddhi sufficient for understanding the nature of knowledge. This is neither the place nor the occasion to go into detail but according to most Indian thinkers of yore the term tattva stands for reality and the term jnana is considered a synonym to buddhi which means knowledge or awareness of objects. This ascertainment entails investigation, distinction, classification etc. and aims at giving everything a particular place in the scheme of things as a whole. The simplest test of the Nature of Reality is the type of evidence we can show to prove its validity/identifiable attributes.

Evidence or data per se does not carry much meaning. The important thing is to know how to present it and when to interpret what. A recent debate on population growth of Muslims in the census can be cited as an example of inapt presentation. There was nothing wrong with the collection of data or its classification. But the way it was reported in the press smelled of a deliberate attempt on someone's part to highlight and state a fact in a communal perspective. The explanations that followed in the newspapers both for and against the presentation proved to be even more ridiculous. One should have remembered that collection of data for census is a legitimate activity on the part of a state but it is another matter altogether how the data that the report must carry should be presented and interpreted. It is therefore important to remember that one must not only furnish correct data but equally important it is to interpret the same objectively. Here we can distinguish such terms like information and knowledge. The data constitutes information but its interpretation offers valid knowledge. Similarly, the subjects that we teach carry valid and reliable knowledge. They are only a means to help us arrive at the Ultimate Truth that we can cognize.

There are various ways to reach the goal. The goal is to be able to distinguish between the Truth and un-Truth. The Truth is not memory. Truth is 'experience' / 'anubhuti.' We become knowledgeable when we are able to distinguish between the information that we acquire from books, which constitutes memory, and the anubhuti / experience that we attain of the Truth through intuition. The Ultimate knowledge is anubhuti or experience. Learning subject matter is merely a path toward that goal.

In one sense Indians are lucky to have more than one source of knowledge. We have access both to the native ancient Indian sources as well as the contemporary Western. While the West witnessed a linear scientific and spiritual development (on the strength of their sources of knowledge dating back to ancient Greece) and peaked to become a dominant world power, the ancient indigenous wisdom of China and India is currently helping them to rise once again in a unique manner. They too are busy mastering tools of power— Western knowledge and modern industry, but additionally they have learnt to get back to the best of what was always theirs just for the asking— the ancient learning. In number of ways it would appear that in the days to come these two great nations are bound to reach the top. If one were to go by the areas of knowledge, which originated in the East and which have attracted the attention of the West, their number is staggering. Indian music, dance, yoga, indigenous herbal medicines, philology, grammar, Indian art and architecture, oriental languages and literature, philosophy, various schools of painting, Indian logic and linguistics, science of augury etc. have of late come to find a place in some of India's best universities. One hopes this would be India's answer to Intellectual Property Rights (IPR) in the WTO regime.

The Nature of Knowledge

Knowledge by its very nature is both hierarchical and

varied. It is not uncommon to use the terms like 'higher' and 'lower' knowledge. The division of knowledge into various categories, subject specializations etc. are also well known. This reality as it stands interpreted today suggests that while knowledge is indivisible and happens to have no boundaries, it is offered in bits and pieces for human consumption because it is the only convenient way for the ordinary mortals to learn and remember. In this respect knowledge has varied forms and divisions and can be put in a hierarchical manner.

The ancient Indians divided knowledge into two categories—higher (para) and lower (apara) vidya. The Chandogya Upanishad cited above talks of the lower and higher knowledge. Higher knowledge is an experience, which is indescribable in words. It is tantamount to acquiring an insight into Reality. The Reality is unreachable and difficult to cognize with senses. In this context higher knowledge deals with abstract ideas, intellectual exercises and reasoning. For example, when we teach a child how to wash mouth or learn to bathe we are training the child in a mechanical skill, which has implied hygienic value. This will hardly ever constitute higher knowledge. That is why we teach these skills either at home or school in the early stages of schooling. But when we start teaching theories of health and hygiene we immediately enter into the realm of research-based verifiable principles that require some level of maturity and understanding of both human body and its relations to social well being. Therefore, one must wait for some time before a child reaches higher classes where certain levels of knowledge acquisitions become imperative.

The difference between information and knowledge can be seen more clearly when we talk of a professional as compared with a skilled worker/labor. A professional has invariably to learn about the theory of the profession s/he belongs to apart from the ways of practicing it. No profession can survive without a specified code of conduct, i.e., the way a professional must interact with his/her clients. These distinctive features are hardly necessary for a skilled labor, at least no one teaches them a philosophy or economy of labor. If there are categories and classes of professions, there are several levels in the area of skills too. The last two categories in this class come pretty close to that of a profession. Because here also an expert does the job on the basis of an insight that s/he happens to acquire over a long period of time. In the paper titled Theories of Professional Expertise Michael Eraut cites the Dreyfus Model of Skill acquisition. As one goes through this model one can easily understand why and how information is not knowledge. But this model does suggest that it is possible for information to become one. Higher form of knowledge stands typified when in an inquiry intuitive and analytical approaches are combined for problem solving. This is the stage when an individual becomes an expert/professional.

Read the Dreyfus Model

Level1- **Novice**

Rigid adherence to taught rules or plans

Little situational perception

No discretionary judgement

Level 2-Advanced **beginner**

Guidelines for action based on attributes or aspects (aspects are global characteristics of situations recognizable only after some prior experience).

Situational perception still limited

All attributes and aspects are treated separately and given equal importance.

Level 3 *Competent*

Coping with crowdedness

Now sees actions at least partially in terms of longer-term goals

Conscious deliberate planning

Standardized and routinized procedures

Level 4 *Proficient*

Sees situations holistically rather than in terms of aspects

Sees what is important in the situation

Perceives deviations from the normal pattern

Decision-making less labored

Uses maxims for guidance, whose meaning varies according to situations.

Level 5 *Expert*

No longer relies on rules

Intuitive grasp of situations based on deep tacit understanding

Analytic approaches used in novel situation or when problems occur.

The Dreyfuses describe their model on depicting five stages of skill acquisition. Here the emphasis is on perception and decision-making rather routinized action. They therefore define skill as an integrative overarching approach to professional action, which incorporates both routines and the decisions to use them, while still maintaining that the term 'skilled behavior' connotes semi-automatic rather than deliberate processes.

What has come out by now clearly is the fact that knowledge and skills are categories and they stand apart from each other. However, when information reaches a certain level of achievement it acquires character that helps it to enter the realm of knowledge almost seamlessly.

Questions that need comprehensive answers

The premise that I started with was that recent technological developments are going to benefit Indians to grow into a knowledge society. Since I think my premise is correct there are number of questions that one must answer before the premise I present becomes acceptable to others. The first questions is: Is it not ridiculous to talk of a knowledge society when the literacy-rates are no more than 65 per cent out of which a substantial numbers, if examined properly, will not be able to either read or write?

I don't think that one can answer this question in the affirmative. Even without high percentages of literacy a society can be transformed into a highly developed modern knowledge society. What one needs to do is to examine the existing infra- structure and pinpoint areas that have in the past been obstructing the achievement of such a goal. For example, we assume that we have a homogeneous society and everyone is willing to become literate. We also assume that literacy and means of livelihood have one-to-one correspondence. The third assumption is that while infrastructure is ready we have failed to take benefit from it.

Sadly enough the reality is very different. If the availability of electricity were taken as an index of modernity or infra-structural homogeneity we have societal contrasts. Not only are the rural areas but urban areas too have either no electricity or its supply is erratic. Secondly, very few Indians have either the means or access to the high-tech gadgetry. Thirdly, India is home to numerous languages. Indian constitution acknowledges that we have 18 national languages of which Sanskrit is classical language. Besides these the 1981 census tabulated 87 languages outside the VIII Schedule. There are number of languages that have no script. (For details read Language Education in Multi-lingual India, editor, C.J. Daswani, UNESCO, 2001) One could go on offering examples from other areas as well. To be brief, we are not a homogeneous society.

It is not the geography or multiplicity of the languages alone that prevents us from becoming a cohesive, modern society but preparing teachers and textbooks in that many number of languages is by itself a Herculean task. And being a practicing democracy no coercion will be acceptable to anyone. Already we are faced with numerous political problems (geographical areas that are unwilling to be part of Indian union), making the medium of instruction an issue is likely to snowball into a calamity. In other words, we are stuck with *N*-number of problems with no end to it in view.

The composition of our society is such that to make it more homogeneous than what it already is, is unlikely to succeed. Even within a single community (like that of the Muslims, Sikhs, etc.,) there is no parity in desires, social goals, or expectations from education. Each class has different motivations. Therefore, becoming educated fails to meet any uniform law of the land. This is one reason why literacy programs seldom succeed.

However, we can take heart from certain examples that might show us the path to success. Higher education does yield results even in semi-illiterate or totally illiterate societies. India's agricultural universities proved that even in a country like ours with illiterate masses Green Revolution was possible. The most difficult technical terms in English language were understood and spoken by ordinary farmers in the villages. This happened because the farmers were not made to learn English language instead were offered tools and means to go up and become prosperous. Here learning technical terms was seen as a key to success and in the process this type of learning mattered. Without going into details of this success story we can come to the basics of the success. It all relates to interest of the farmers. It has everything to do with high motivational levels. The basic intelligence remains the same in most individuals. But it is the motivation that defines effort and the goals. If other systems too were able to raise the common / ordinary levels of expectations there is no reason why identical results cannot be achieved in other spheres as well.

The first step therefore is to be to prepare a *roadmap* for our prospective educational endeavors in future. We have all the data necessary for doing so. Only we have to redo the paradigm. Since technology is merely a ready tool to assist us one has to have the determination to get over the initial hesitation and doubt.

Indian Technology Today

Let me us recount the type of technology that is available with us that can be used with considerable acumen and economy for the benefit of our people. Let us not forget that we are the only country in the world, which has successfully placed an exclusive educational satellite (indigenously prepared and launched) in the orbit. The *Edusat* as it is being called is going to have 72 channels ready to be beamed from the height of 36,000 miles (i.e. from its geo-stationary orbit location). The entire program-preparation constituted three stages. When fully operational this satellite would offer connectivity to all levels and types of educational organizations. The second stage of the launch will cover deployment of hardware and the third or the final stage shall be reached when content-transmission starts. In fact, we are already in the game of providing education through our hub at IGNOU. The proposed satellite is going to give us far greater outreach and connectivity than hitherto possible. It is expected that this satellite would offer instructional facilities in the multi-media mode and video on demand service. We must not forget that numerous other agencies too are already providing similar services in India. They may not have educational channels like the DD at their command, but they are preparing course content in various formats and have a captive clientele too.

To cite ISRO Chairman, " Edusat is mainly intended to meet the demand for an interactive satellite–based distance education system through creating virtual classrooms at remote places in the country. It will provide connectivity to school, college and higher levels of education and also to support non-formal education including developmental communication. It is specially configured for audio-visual medium, employing digital interactive classroom and multi-media multi-centric system. Edusat will be ready for use in about two months (i.e. before Dec. 2004)."

He further explained, "Indian space programme has been tuned to meet the national requirements in a self-reliant manner." This statement has significance for us. This means we can place other satellites in the space if this one fails to meet all our requirements. The scope of the Edusat program will be fully operational in three phases.

There are several agencies both at the center and the states levels that are already generating content for transmission. For instance, the CEC, IGNOU, NCERT, NCTE etc., have for long been generating content ready for, transmission. In fact, 4 channels are already beaming educational programmes for their respective audiences through the national network. The educational hub at the IGNOU campus was beaming NCERT programmes for teachers and students, SITE programmes for primary schools and NIOS programmes for secondary levels. The 3 existing channels that are directed to address higher education clientele are called Gyan Darshan, Ek Lavya and Vyas. Thus far they have a captive audience. While the first channel telecasts 'enrichment' programmes, the second channel addresses engineering requirements and the third channel caters to the needs of higher education sector respectively. But these channels currently offer their services only to those who had access through a specially designed medium or through cables. Despite best efforts these channels have failed to generate much interest outside a limited geographical area and a highly select number of viewers. The major difference between the existing and proposed scenario is that under the proposed scheme programmes could be accessed anywhere and everywhere provided one had a DTH antenna, electricity and an ordinary Television set or even PC. For the first time ever the nation was going to be blessed with numerous educational channels that will meet all kinds of requirements—regional, linguistic and informational without any intermediary intervention.

It is quite obvious that for the first time content-generation has to be Gargantuan in proportion. Not only the existing content-generators both public and private have to redouble their efforts to meet national requirements, but also the variety in terms of languages, levels, and types was expected to be enormous. The challenges posed by the Edusat launch need to be addressed on top priority basis.

A given type of technology best suited for India has been selected. The principal objective is to reach out people both nationally and regionally almost simultaneously. Therefore, 2000 kg class satellite was selected, which could beam nationally as well as regionally. Since the idea was to impart instruction through this satellite, linking facilities had also to be kept in mind. The infrastructure for teaching–end had to be created and put in place. The reason why DTH was chosen is because it was thought that alternative to it was going to be both difficult and expensive. Considering future requirements, expansion of facilities and the cost of maintenance, etc., besides simple features for application and speed, KU-band was found to be most suitable. Firstly, it was an international band and secondly, its vendors were easily available. This band could provide national coverage.

It was a kind of extension of the existing facilities.

The basic elements of the satellite constitute a centralized Hub, various sub-Hubs and cost-wise having a receiving terminal (ROT), i.e., a passive classroom, would cost a mere Rs.20, 000/- only. The setting up of an inter-active terminal (SIT) would cost somewhere around Rs. 1.1 lakh only.

In the present case while the number of Hubs were limited, the ROTs could be as numerous as one desired. This means that signals with the help of DTH facility could be received anywhere across the country, irrespective of the terrain or the type of receiver one had – an ordinary PC or a television. The technology will suit any classroom with any number of students or the size of the classroom. In fact, for a country like India the cost of a technology mattered the most. The selected technology is most suited from this point of view as well.

One has to be introduced to two-way communication of interactive traffic, which is to be offered and explained how live programs would be transmitted and interactivity is likely to take place. This is one stage when any place could be converted into a virtual classroom. This technology offered the facility of both on-line and off-line accessing. One has to be explained the terms LMS and VOD. This technology could help create a library for future use, help administer institutions and conduct examination. During transmission one could use multi-media, organize television-conferencing or offer classroom interaction. It was possible to have constant rate or a dedicated facility or even offer free capacity.

While initially the network capacity will be to have a thousand terminals but later on when the Edusat is fully operational the number could be expanded to 5000 terminals. About 100-200 classrooms can be connected with a single beam. The facility could have forward link and also return link. One could send voice, text and image both individually and collectively. In other words, this technology was suitable for multi-media usage and transmission.

How one could attempt screen resolution, learn about the nature of delivery and be ready to prepare course content? One has to be ready to learn all this. One could also talk of learning content production system or LCPS and LCMS, i.e., learning content management system. One comes across terms like Metadata, which in one's understanding was comparable to index material.

For the benefit of those interested we should recall here that the UGC already has within its fold an organization called the CEC (Consortium of Educational Services – the one that runs Vyas channel) devoted exclusively for higher education.

As already referred to earlier the other current content-generators besides CEC are IGNOU and CIT-NCERT=IGNOU. Currently, IGNOU offers 90 programmes and the courses it covers number 904. It has about 1.1 million students on roll both within the country and without. The delivery mode it has adopted is Open Distance network. It broadcasts Gyan darshan 1 & 2 Channels, which are both interactive. The other channels it beams are Eklavya and Vyas. While Eklavya is meant for engineering students, the Vyas channel is addressed to higher education students residing in remote areas of the country. It currently has two studios and about 2000 programmes in its stock. The expectation is that Edusat would provide it deeper penetration in the country, i.e., into the areas un-reached or otherwise unreachable. It would offer facilities for multi-media transmission and that too in regional languages. In brief, the idea is to reach out all target groups.

The Times of India (21.10.2004) editorially commented, "A focused campaign to appraise educational benefits of using EDUSAT must be initiated. The potential to network the leading hubs of technical education in the country must also be actively utilized. Further, with the satellite, literacy levels could well take a quantum leap forward. The arithmetic is easy. In the fully operational phase, the EDUSAT network is expected to support up to 1.5 lakh reception terminals. With 50 students per terminal, that works out to a figure of 7.5 million. If five such satellites can be set up, then a staggering 37 million children in remote areas could benefit at a fraction of the cost it takes the government to set up primary schools. Obviously, there will be several hurdles in the implementation process. But here at last is an opportunity provided by technology for a complete paradigm shift in our approach to education for all is no longer a pie in the sky. The answer is actually up there."

The term 'countrywide classrooms' (CWCR) is widely known. Even before the Vyas channel became operational the CEC was running CWCR programme. The Vyas channel is currently being run by the CEC both making people knowledgeable— by offering opportunities to learn subjects (Disciplines), and also enriching the store what one already possesses, besides learning the correct methods to learn— thereby leading one to eventually realize one's potential, i.e., having anubhuti / experience, which is indescribable in words. 'enrich, educate and enlighten.' The Consortium is determined to achieving this goal with all the means at its disposal.

One can notice a paradigm shift in the way the new CWCR programmes are likely to take shape. On the one hand it is going to continue handling classroom situation with subject-wise approach (organizing courses in terms of lectures as granules, series of lectures as unit, and series of units as modules and finally series of modules as course ware), on the other it is thinking of introducing such programs that only few universities or institutions in the country have thus far thought of introducing. These are: -

- E-learning
- Up-gradation of technology
- W.T.O.
- Patenting
- Copyrights
- Women /gender issues
- Career watch
- Innovations in education, management and in other fields

The Roadmap

Our proposed road map will not consider the inclusion of middle class and the higher income groups. The reason for so doing is that either way these classes are focused on education. Even if a State had no desire whatsoever to impart education to any of its citizen, these twin classes will still manage to get a vestige of education for their children. On this premise we can see all around us that it is this class that currently monopolizes admissions in the best and most expensive schools. (See, Editorial, Times of India, Oct.15, 2004). As it is they have numerous options and choices. One must however not overlook the gender bias in the scheme of things.

In a democracy like ours we cannot afford to neglect planning and approach the problem of universal education carefully. In my view it is here that universities can step in and lend their most crucial help. They already have extremely qualified staff to deal with this problem. For instance, they already have departments of social welfare, rural economics, urban planning, health and nutrition, water resources, social engineering, environmental studies and similar other faculties that deal with different aspects of society and teach subjects that draw heavily upon their immediate neighbourhood for meaningful inputs. With a little incentive and motivation they can be mobilized to rendering excellent service to their society. I am suggesting this model on the strength of the socio-economic service agriculture universities have already rendered and continue rendering. If they can perform unimaginably so well as they have already done, while dealing with the illiterate farmers, why can't other traditional universities, which also have equally dedicated departments and competent faculty? These university departments have immense resources at their disposal and the same can be further strengthened and enhanced, if required.

For once while thinking of preparing plans for the future it would be advisable that nothing is left out for chance and no aspect of society remains uncovered. The major reason why best of the plans fail to achieve targets is that either they do not anticipate future scenario correctly or they leave out small details for chance. Let us prove that not only we can plan well but we can execute the same too.

Let us accept that Indian society is stratified in which a few live a rarefied life whereas others find it difficult even to survive. Complexities have grown because of the increasingly burgeoning middle class, whose presence makes us blind to the reality. The reality is that majority of Indians should discover latent meaning in education and teachers in institutions of higher learning start addressing problems beyond their theoretical frames. The latest Census suggests that things are on the move. In fact, all along the line people are discovering gradually a meaning in education, which they had not noticed thus far. There are indications that gender bias too is ceasing to be a great barrier. (Read, Sensing the Future by Ravinder Kaur, TOI, Oct.14, 2004).

Any comprehensive analysis of India's illiterate population would reveal that most of this segment constitutes rural population, migrant labour, street children, tribal people and the physically or mentally challenged. The means to reach them out either do not exist or society per se has accepted that they are unreachable therefore they are unteachable as well. Even in the urban areas where education that is seemingly being provided to the poor has little to commend itself. In fact, the infrastructure that makes education an enjoyable experience (notwithstanding Prof. Yash Pal) simply does not exist.

We have therefore to identify and target relevant groups where they exist and offer them an education, which is both relevant and meaningful.

The future plan should prepare a blueprint for identifying different segments of population that need to be approached for getting educated. While collecting and interpreting Census data it is possible to prepare a comprehensive plan for an all-out approach to access target groups. With the help of current levels of technology it is no longer a pipedream to be able to do so. For once the technology would help the teacher to reach the target group. Distances can be covered in no time and meaningful education can be offered at the time convenient to the learner. It is now possible to create multiple plans of varying levels of specialization and offer them simultaneously. This is where the intelligent use of technology can yield the best of the results.

Now let us consider what needs to be provided first, i.e., what kind of infrastructure is imperative for our gameplan to succeed. The entire modern technology is dependent on the process and availability of connectivity. If we are able to connect with our target groups / audience the first stage will be covered. All kinds of problems exist in the first stage itself. We are woefully short of electricity. States like Uttar Pradesh, Bihar, Rajasthan and Madhya Pradesh have very little electricity. The alternative sources of providing the same too are in a miserable state of development. The wind power, sun power and even atomic power have failed to reach people. How then do we connect? This is one area that demands our attention on a priority basis. There is no way to circumvent this stage of development. In fact, this question relates to a stark reality. We must continue to make efforts and keep thinking of tapping perennial energy sources. Indian scientists are perhaps already thinking on these lines. One isn't sure whether they are anywhere near a breakthrough.

The second part of the plan constitutes identification and bringing together of the target groups to a common point where they could access this technology at any point of time without interruption. This will require involvement of stakeholders in the process. The planning has to be at the grass-root levels. We have not only to provide connectivity but also to see that the process remains operative all the while. I think this is where we have to avoid taking risk. We cannot afford to overlook the NGOs, village elders, tribal chiefs etc. In case this is feasible one should involve social workers too but care be taken not to involve politicians. Once the plan starts succeeding the politicians will certainly like to join the bandwagon. Care may also be taken that money required for the purpose is either minimal or is routed through responsible hands who can be held accountable.

The third stage is to select target groups for specialized community-based learning. For instance, universities and colleges have necessarily to be selected for offering content learning. Here one visualizes the possibility of organizing virtual classroom conditions for two-way connectivity. At a given hour an entire state or the country as a whole can be covered. Of course, most of the places will have single-mode connectivity only, i.e., they merely receive a programme and for necessary guidance and question-answer sessions to be offered they wait for a while. Apart from the institutional arrangement of the type with which we are very familiar, we have to go out and interact and offer services that are beyond the ordinary work schedule. For instance, we can have programmes for the street children that vary in levels and content in different urban centers. For arranging a programme of this nature careful planning is imperative both for selecting content and organize target audience as and when the same can be assembled in groups. It is not only the content but also the ambience for learning is necessary. This is the most difficult part of the programme. The migrant labor, the casual worker and the like are difficult to gather together. One of the reasons for failure has precisely been this difficulty. These groups are neither easily identifiable and nor are they willing to listen. Lot of initial research into the psychology of these groups is imperative. The planning at this stage has to be delayed if it is not possible to organize classes for them or before any meaningful programme is feasible to chalk out. But we must also remember that this is the largest single group that needs essential educational service. This is one group, which has not been properly addressed thus far and therefore it has remained outside both the formal and the non-formal education orbit.

The reason why I am laying more emphasis on this aspect of planning is the common desire to overlook the inconvenient parts of any process. We must resist the temptation to neglect important sectors of a plan. This planning has to be bottom up and not the vice versa, which is the usual mode. I believe that for a plan to succeed the involvement of people on a large scale is always helpful. People refuse to involve themselves in any scheme if they find that it has no meaning to them. A meaningful scheme will automatically elicit a level of public involvement that will ensure a long and enduring relationship. By implication it is bound to be an insurance against possible difficulties and glitches. Thus far our planning has been top-down. For once let us reverse the process. This would also be a measure of our testing whether or not we can become good salesmen of ideas and schemes. Only a few decades back agriculture universities brought about a change in the age-old agricultural practices by involving farmers who were not even literate. If they sold better future the present technology is selling both – the present as well as future. Education empowers. It enriches. On top of it all it enables one to be creative. The universities are already aware of their own potential. All they need is a slight nudging and a push. And the path shall be traversed.

8

Indian Higher Education — Challenges in a Global Scenario

Mobility, competitiveness, innovation, relevance and technological superiority define contemporary higher education. Geographical boundaries in this context have become inconsequential. The most distinctive features of today's higher education are institutional mobility and the use of high-tech in the methods of instruction. Advance planning and keeping ahead of others appear to have become hallmarks of Western countries. They have used and are using research as a means and instrument of social progress. Western research has come to define every area of their social and material advancement. They are the ones who have shown how knowledge can be packaged and sold. In this system while teachers continue to retain their prime position but it is the content that has become both competitive and commercialized. While at the dawn of civilization *stationary* teachers and their institutions attracted students from far and wide (the ancient Indian institutions were known by the reputation of their teachers. To a large extent in the good old-world tradition the same practices continued cven during the medieval times. The Madarsahs too ran on the reputation of their teachers), today's institutions and the specialty have become both marketable and mobile. Unlike the past it is the institutions and their teams of experts that are eager to move out to reach their prospective clientele. Today's institutions boast of their highly skilled and informed teachers and institutional reputations are built around the areas that have maximum marketability. Education is no longer expected to merely enlighten. It has ceased to be an agent of broadening one's mental horizon. Education no longer enables one to become a humane, reflective being but a skilled, market savvy technocrat. It is not the quality of knowledge that sells but the skill that enables one to become marketable has a price tag. Educational entrepreneurs have transformed its product into a saleable commodity and a marketable 'good' and the process beginning with the admission policy to degree granting a business transaction. Today's education is like any other market ware that is bench-marked, standardized and branded before eventually made available across the trading counters. Advertising and packaging knowledge are the contemporary buzzword and its class is judged by its market valuation. Academic lexicons are getting replaced with commercial 'Market Informers'. In other words, the relationship between the teacher and the student is currently definable in terms of the relevance of one's area of specialization and the success to enabling one to become acceptable in a market to the highest bidder. A phenomenon unknown earlier, viz. "campus selections" is now considered commonplace. The higher the valuation of the commodity better are the chances for such institutions to get better and higher-class sponsors.

Gone are the days when Lord Chesterton would be writing a letter to his son, when the latter embarked on a European tour after his graduation, giving guidance to acquire some culture. Or, Alexander Flexner would write: Universities: American, English and German, which in the opinion of Clark Kerr (1930) was defining moment for the American universities to accept European model as a kind of "yardstick against which to measure the accomplishments of the present." Since then much water has flown in the American rivers. It is the American institutions like Harvard, Princeton, M.I.T., etc., who are currently benchmarking standards and courses offered in higher education institutions worldwide and the rest are merely trying to remain in step with them.

Higher education per se has the ability to define the prowess of the state. No matter which area of human activity one cared to investigate one would invariably find that the contribution of higher education is fairly noticeable. This being the reality we must understand the way higher education has gradually changed its preferences. The West first thought that " conservation of knowledge and ideas and their transmission to an elite body of under-graduate students" (Cardinal Newman); was the principal function of higher education, then it revised its opinion and suggested the 'Modern University' of Flexner, which was "consciously devoted to the pursuit of knowledge, the solutions of problems, the critical appreciation of achievement and the training of men at a really high level." Then we got the American model (currently in vogue) in which the service-function and under-graduate instruction have been interwoven with the advanced teaching and research functions. What we today have in fact is a pluralistic organization with many component parts, each of them capable of "highness and definiteness of aim, unity of spirit and purpose". For an Indian unfamiliar with the American model it is difficult to appreciate the variety in institutional arrangements, multiplicity of courses, heterogeneity in standards of individual evaluation, duration of the courses of study, and the freedom teachers enjoy in offering courses of their choice. The amazing thing about it all that they still manage and run excellent institutions rated as some of the best in the world. The reason for all their success perhaps lies in their accreditation policies. Our immediate concern is to see that our institutions are able not only to withstand the challenges from abroad but are able to put up a credible and creditable response. The idea is to devise strategies to meet the challenges.

Challenges to Indian universities are coming essentially from three sources. The first challenge constitutes our unpreparedness against increasing influx of foreign university campuses into this country. The danger gets further enhanced because of the WTO regime and the IPR, the serious implications of which have not as yet been properly understood. We find ourselves vulnerable in the extremes because of the compounded neglect of the responsible government bodies. I hope they are waking up now to tackling this problem on a priority basis after having issued an Ordinance recently endorsing commitment to the membership of WTO.

I am even more surprised by thc casual manner in which the university fraternity has responded to the twin challenges this institutional mobility and the WTO-IPR regime pose. They seem to believe that these global challenges can be wished away with as much as ease as we can some of the routine problems we face daily.

To my mind if we wish to be competitive what we ought to examine first is the way foreign universities run their programmes. We must also realize that we cannot continue to have the cumbersome procedures to update our courses of study. We should also provide for the freedom a teacher ought to enjoy while offering a programme. The evaluation procedures need drastic changes. The universities should not be seen as mere degree awarding and examining bodies. The confidentiality involved in all procedures must be dispensed forthwith. Freedom and innovation are the keywords for the university administration to learn. Only a free teacher who has the ability and freedom to make changes in the way he wishes to make while offering a course of study can improve the situation. There is no other way the mediocrity that is currently ruling the roost can stand challenged and made to leave the system. Similarly, the teacher accountability is the first condition that ought to be observed.

The half-hearted reforms and midway corrections that characterize our efforts and zeal require re-thinking. We should not only appear to be bold and demanding but in reality too the appearance must undergo a sea change in approach and design. We have seen in the past couple of years several reforms have been implemented by the UGC but they are not real either in essence or content. For example, there is a provision that colleges should become autonomous. Not only the number of autonomous colleges remains low, in reality they are not autonomous. They have no freedom either in changing the courses and curricula on their own but they have no freedom to award degrees. The question is: Why is the affiliation tag so necessary?

Numerous bodies that function in the name of helping administration need a re-look. Is this not the reason why the administrative machine remains so poor that for its proper functioning it needs artificial limbs? What is being suggested is to cut down expenses on unnecessary items and increase efficiency by off-loading garbage accumulated over the years in the name of tradition and heritage. The first and most important criterion that will decide what to consign to limbo and what to keep burnished and shining is the sole criterion of relevance. There is no need either to dump or adopt a practice the moment one comes to assess the real worth of an institution or practice. Only after due discussion must we take any important decision. Discussions are not supposed to be delaying tactics but the strategy to see that nothing is left to chance.

What I am trying to bring home is the point that we are still badly ridden with colonial legacy in which trust and encouragement are considered favours and where suggestions to improve is regarded equivalent of reprimand. In a free and progressive society dissent is a minor matter. We must accept disagreement with grace and forgiveness.

It is not only in terms of courses of study that we offer where we find ourselves lagging far behind the USA, in some other significant areas too we have consistently found it difficult to move forward. Compare the number of short-term courses most advanced nations allow to be offered and then think of the courses that we offer and one would immediately know the reasons for our backwardness. Look at the choices they offer and the speed with which they are willing to make amends—all this constitutes versatility. To get into the problem the statistics would help us in this regard. The USA offers several times over the number of courses that we offer. Out of these most of these are both relevant and demand – based. We have no such interaction procedure and then we have no contract system in hiring services of the experts. We have no such system according to which individual institutions granted degrees and they were considered as valid and acceptable as our university degrees. Our institutions do not compete because the degrees are uniformly awarded to all without institutional distinction differences. One could go on and on describing the lacunae in the way we are currently running our educational institutions.

We could look at the way we conduct our classroom instruction. Supposedly an advanced country in IT services but look at the way we Indians have continued to ignore this vastly potential field called educational technology – comprising internet services and the arrival of virtual classroom technology. While all other countries have adopted E-learning and virtual classrooms we who have the potential to be leaders in the field are still behaving like reluctant brides.

The EDUSAT technology is the other challenge that we face. In fact, it is not a threat but an opportunity that we should not ignore or fail to utilize. The day universities learnt to utilize the technology it will transform the teaching methods and raise standards of education. While this technology poses a serious threat to mediocrity in the teaching faculty, it is a tremendous help to brilliant students. The Consortium of Educational Communications (CEC) is as yet not been able to take full advantage of the technology and therefore it will be quite sometime before its impact is fully felt. Let me recount the type of technology that is available with us that can be used with considerable acumen and economy for the benefit of our people. Let us not forget that we are the only country in the world, which has successfully placed an exclusive educational satellite (indigenously prepared and launched) in the orbit. The *Edusat* as it is being called is going to have 72 channels ready to be beamed from the height of 36,000 miles, (i.e., from its geo-stationary orbit location). The entire programme-preparation constituted three stages. When fully operational this satellite would offer connectivity to all levels and types of educational organizations. The second stage of the launch will cover deployment of hardware and the third or the final stage shall be reached when content-transmission starts. In fact, we are already in the game of providing education through our hub at IGNOU. The proposed satellite is going to give us far greater outreach and connectivity than hitherto possible. It is expected that this satellite would offer instructional facilities in the multi-media mode and video on demand service. We must not forget that numerous other agencies too are already providing similar services in India. They may not have educational channels like the DD at their command, but they are preparing course content in various formats and have a captive clientele too.

To cite ISRO Chairman, "Edusat is mainly intended to meet the demand for an interactive satellite–based distance education system through creating virtual classrooms at remote places in the country. It will provide connectivity to school, college and higher levels of education and also to support non-formal education including developmental communication. It is specially configured for audio-visual medium, employing digital interactive classroom and multi-media multi-centric system. Edusat will be ready for use in about two months (i.e. before Dec. 2004)."

He further explained, "Indian space program has been tuned to meet the national requirements in a self-reliant manner." This statement has significance for us. This means we can place other satellites in the space if this one fails to meet all our requirements. The scope of the Edusat programme will be fully operational in three phases.

There are several agencies both at the center and the states levels that are already generating content for transmission. For instance, the CEC, IGNOU, NCERT, NCTE, etc., have for long been generating content ready for transmission. In fact, 4 channels are already beaming educational programmes for their respective audiences through the national network. The educational hub at the IGNOU campus was beaming NCERT programmes for teachers and students, SITE programmes for primary schools and NIOS programmes for secondary levels. The 3 existing channels that are directed to address higher education clientele are called Gyan Darshan, Ek Lavya and Vyas. Thus far they have a captive audience. While the first channel telecasts 'enrichment' programmes, the second channel addresses engineering requirements and the third channel caters to the needs of higher education sector respectively. But these channels currently offer their services only to those who had access through a specially designed medium or through cables. Despite best efforts these channels have failed to generate much interest outside a limited geographical area and a highly select number of viewers. The major difference between the existing and proposed scenario is that under the proposed scheme programs could be accessed anywhere and everywhere provided one had a

DTH antenna, electricity and an ordinary Television set or even PC. For the first time ever the nation was going to be blessed with numerous educational channels that will meet all kinds of requirements—regional, linguistic and informational without any intermediary intervention.

It is quite obvious that for the first time content-generation has to be Gargantuan in proportion. Not only the existing content-generators both public and private have to redouble their efforts to meet national requirements, but also the variety in terms of languages, levels, and types was expected to be enormous. The challenges posed by the Edusat launch need to be addressed on top priority basis.

A given type of technology best suited for India has been selected. The principal objective is to reach out people both nationally and regionally almost simultaneously. Therefore, 2000 kg class satellite was selected, which could beam nationally as well as regionally. Since the idea was to impart instruction through this satellite, linking facilities had also to be kept in mind. The infrastructure for teaching–end had to be created and put in place. The reason why DTH was chosen is because it was thought that alternative to it was going to be both difficult and expensive. Considering future requirements, expansion of facilities and the cost of maintenance etc. besides simple features for application and speed, KU-band was found to be most suitable. Firstly, it was an international band and secondly, its vendors were easily available. This band could provide national coverage. It was a kind of extension of the existing facilities.

The basic elements of the satellite constitute a centralized Hub, various sub-Hubs and cost-wise having a receiving terminal (ROT), i.e., a passive classroom, would cost a mere Rs. 20, 000/- only. The setting up of an interactive terminal (SIT) would cost somewhere around Rs. 1.1 lakh only.

In the present case while the number of Hubs are limited, the ROTs could be as numerous as one desired. This means that signals with the help of DTH facility could be received anywhere across the country, irrespective of the terrain or the type of receiver one had – an ordinary PC or a television. The technology will suit any classroom with any number of students or the size of the classroom. In fact, for a country like India the cost of a technology mattered the most. The selected technology is most suited from this point of view as well.

One has to be introduced to two-way communication of interactive traffic, which is to be offered and explained how live programs would be transmitted and interactivity is likely to take place. This is one stage when any place could be converted into a virtual classroom. This technology offered the facility of both on-line and off-line accessing. One has to be explained the terms LMS and VOD. This technology could help create a library for future use, help administer institutions and conduct examination. During transmission one could use multi-media, organize television-conferencing or offer classroom interaction. It was possible to have constant rate or a dedicated facility or even offer free capacity.

While initially the network capacity will be to have a thousand terminals but later on when the Edusat is fully operational the number could be expanded to 5000 terminals. About 100-200 classrooms can be connected with a single beam. The facility could have forward link and also return link. One could send voice, text and image both individually and collectively. In other words, this technology was suitable for multi-media usage and transmission.

How one could attempt screen resolution, learn about the nature of delivery and be ready to prepare course content? One has to be ready to learn all this. One could also talk of learning content production system or LCPS and LCMS, i.e., learning content management system. One comes across terms like Metadata, which in one's understanding is comparable to index material.

For the benefit of those interested we should recall here that the UGC already has within its fold an organization called the CEC (Consortium of Educational Communications – the one that runs Vyas channel) devoted exclusively for higher education.

As already referred to earlier the other current content-generators besides CEC are IGNOU and CIT-NCERT=IGNOU.

Currently, IGNOU offers 90 programmes and the courses it covers number 904. It has about 1.1 million students on roll both within the country and without. The delivery mode it has adopted is Open Distance network. It broadcasts Gyan darshan 1 & 2 Channels, which are both interactive. The other channels it beams are Eklavya and Vyas. While Eklavya is meant for engineering students, the Vyas channel is addressed to higher education students residing in remote areas of the country. It currently has two studios and about 2000 programmes in its stock. The expectation is that Edusat would provide it deeper penetration in the country i.e. into the areas un-reached or otherwise unreachable. It would offer facilities for multi-media transmission and that too in regional languages. In brief, the idea is to reach out all target groups.

The Times of India (21.X.2004) editorially commented, " A focused campaign to appraise educational of the benefits of using EDUSAT must be initiated. The potential to network the leading hubs of technical education in the country must also be actively utilized. Further, with the satellite, literacy levels could well take a quantum leap forward. The arithmetic is easy. In the fully operational phase, the EDUSAT network is expected to support up to 1.5 lakh reception terminals. With 50 students per terminal, that works out to a figure of 7.5 million. If five such satellites can be set up, then a staggering 37 million children in remote areas could benefit at a fraction of the cost it takes the government to set up primary schools. Obviously, there will be several hurdles in the implementation process. But here at last is an opportunity provided by technology for a complete paradigm shift in our approach to education for all is no longer a pie in the sky. The answer is actually up there."

The term 'countrywide classrooms' (CWCR) is widely known. Even before the Vyas channel became operational the CEC was running CWCR programme. The Vyas channel is currently being run by the CEC both making people knowledgeable— by offering opportunities to learn subjects (Disciplines), and also enriching the store what one already possesses, besides learning the correct methods to learn— thereby leading one to eventually realize one's potential, i.e., having anubhuti /experience, which is indescribable in words. 'enrich, educate and enlighten.' The Consortium is determined to achieving this goal with all the means at its disposal.

One can notice a paradigm shift in the way the new CWCR programmes are likely to take shape. On the one hand it is going to continue handling classroom situation with subject-wise approach (organizing courses in terms of lectures as granules, series of lectures as unit, and series of units as modules and finally series of modules as course ware), on the other it is thinking of introducing such programmes that only few universities or institutions in the country have thus far thought of introducing. These are: -

- E-learning
- Up-gradation of technology
- W.T.O.
- Patenting
- Copyrights
- Women /gender issues
- Career watch
- Innovations in education, management and in other fields

The universities and colleges must sit up and evaluate its impact once it is fully visible.

The only way out lies in improving the quality and focus of research. Institutional freedom and encouragement to innovations could help us come to international standards. Overtime created and accumulated flab has to be shed. Being lean and mean will help us not only survive but also outshine others. For once the target is clear. We no longer live in a country but in the world where no one is asking any quarters nor are they being given one.

To conclude, we are living in challenging times. Do we have the vision and grit to pick up the gauntlet?

The Chairman, University Grants Commission has attempted to answer most of the issues and the questions I have raised here. According to his formulation, "The Indian higher education system is facing all the issues, indeed *five* of them—access and equity, relevance, quality and excellence, governance and resources—that are faced by other nations." While discussing each of these issues individually he goes on to talk of the image Indians and their competencies have in Western countries. "However, there is one more interesting dimension to higher education. India, today, is recognized internationally as a nation, which is providing value-added trained human power at a premier level. Indian experts are now persons who generate wealth and also are the backbone in global science and technology revolution. Indians have made their presence felt, at the global level, in the field of information technology (software as well as hardware), electronics, biotechnology, pure sciences and economics; and even in financial management and in many fields related to humanities and social sciences. On the other hand, conversion of higher education of Indian graduates at a global level has led to rising aspirations among masses in the country. The student community in the rural, semi-urban and urban areas is craving to be part of new economic revolution. They do not want to be deprived of opportunities because of their social or economic background."

Everyone including the people at the UGC who are responsible for the management and supervision of higher education in the country realize that "in a way globalization in the higher education has triggered a churning process" the world over. Nations, particularly developing and emerging nations, are struggling to adjust themselves with this phenomenon of trade in higher education. "Everyone concerned seems to have realized the value of generating and possessing 'Knowledge'. The Chairman UGC mentioned categorically that everyone is aware of the linkage between knowledge and wealth, which in turn is linked with trade and this in turn has brought in substantial growth of trade in higher education. But somehow everyone is not agreed with this proposition. There is a school of thought, which believes that knowledge is not related to wealth and therefore is not a tradable commodity. This section of scholars holds the view knowledge primarily creates enriched minds and knowledge has its uses for the betterment of life style. Education is after all, culture specific, which defines a nation. To say that higher education is a commodity and is saleable is to say that national identities are commodities too and hence saleable. On the other hand the advent of ICT, education per se has become borderless therefore the above-mentioned proposition is untenable. This brings in the creation and existence of GATT (General Agreement in Tariff and Trade) and its implications for everyone.

Traditionally, trade has been limited to goods and services. But goods and merchandise have always formed the major part of bi-lateral and multi-lateral trade agreements. However, after the establishment of GATT under the rounds of negotiations between the years 1986-93 called Uruguay Round of International Trade Negotiations led to an agreement for establishing World Trade Organization. Since then the world has not remained the same as it used to be once upon a time. India being a signatory to the WTO has to observe the conditions as laid down in the GATT. The WTO Agreement clearly distinguishes goods and merchandise on the one hand and services on the other. Thereafter, Services also started forming a part of the economy of some of the countries. Nowadays they (Services) are an important segment of trade. Several rounds of ministerial talks (Doha in Nov. 9-13, 2001; preceded by Singapore in Dec. 1996; Geneva in May 1998; and Seattle in Dec. 1999) have resulted in an agreement in Doha in November 9-13, 2001. Now in March 2005 the Government of India has formalized its application. (See, Appendix)

Seen against this background the action taken by the UGC in this regard have their contextual significance. The UGC has clearly understood its significance and taken some actions too. To understand the various implications of these thought processes and the impending influence of GATT related matters one must appreciate the interrelationships between the ground realities and the growth of a developing nation in the context of the emerging scenario. The developing nations face problems that relate to size, access, equity, relevance, quality, and resource constraint. It would appear that the world as a whole is facing a knowledge revolution. The key principles, according to the Chairman, UGC, are: quality, access, equity and accountability. The problems one faces in India are: How and what is to be done for nearly 7 million students that join the traditional courses of study in social sciences, sciences, arts and humanities? The levels at which these subjects are taught in various institutions vary enormously. The rest of the courses of study and the number of the students in those areas have been taken care of by the institutions and the faculties concerned.

The ground on which the challenges of higher education offered by foreign institutions on the Indian soil have to be met remains an undecided terrain. Firstly, it is a new kind of invasion and no one seems to know what mechanisms can meet the challenges coming out from that reality. Secondly, until now it is the students who were mobile, but after the GATT it is the institutions that have become mobile. No definitive answer to this problem seems to have emerged.

As far as the question of equity is concerned the UGC has connected all institutions within its purview by creating an information flow network, called UGC- Infonet. The issue of relevance is being handled in a different way. The official view is that it has acknowledged the new reality of "the emergence of knowledge-linked societies". And for this reason the graduates are being required to have a sound base in the fundamentals of the core subjects. The knowledge base constitutes adding on 'appropriate utility oriented skills.' This is being done by providing, "an open and flexible education approach", wherein students can simultaneously pursue a degree course and add-on utility oriented certificate / diploma / advanced diploma programme". Open and flexible structural arrangements both for curriculum and framework can be arranged.

The Indian Higher Education is also addressing the question of quality and excellence. The National Assessment and Accreditation Council (NAAC) is made to look after that arrangement. Care is being taken to improve infra-structural facilities as well by giving block grants.

The UGC is aware that the sheer size of the Indian higher education system demands an extensive use of ICT in the management and organization of higher education, more so because of globalization. In the words of the Chairman, UGC, "India is carefully looking at the challenges of the globalization and the implications of Trade agreements." Besides trying to bridge the gaps between the old system and the new, "there is need to develop and follow specific normative standards and practices for running of higher education institutions of a particular nation on the soil of another. There is also the need for evolving healthy self-controlling mechanisms in the higher education trade so that it does not get drifted into 'sheer commercialization with profit motives."

In his perception there is a need to have an international authority to keep an eye on the entire provision playing the role of the 'third-eye'.

I think the UGC is still far behind in developing mechanisms and ideas to meet the challenges posed by advanced countries in the current scenario.

SECTION- C
TEXTBOOK AND THE GUIDING PRINCIPLES

9

Text books in Free India

"Publication of textbooks under the auspices of state-run bodies gained approval in this phase (posr-Kothari Commission report), and the responsibility to produce *model* textbooks fell upon the NCERT. The circumstances shaping the history textbooks were somewhat *fortuitous*." p.51 *Prejudice and Pride*, Krishna Kumar, (Viking, 2001).

Number of questions need to be answered first the moment one talks of textbooks and their production. Like so many areas the writing, production and sales of the textbooks have never been perceived to be a bed of roses. While the British were here the books projected their point of view. Clearly the textbooks defined the attitude of the rulers toward their subject people. After all, textbooks then and now continue to define the relationships in the governance of a polity and the attitude of the rulers toward their subject people. India is now a free and vibrant democracy but that does not take away the defining role of the government toward textbook production. Nothing could be more than clear in this regard than the heated debates in Indian Parliament over the question of modification of certain paragraphs of the existing textbooks by a government organization at the behest of Union Minister of the HRD. No government is willing to surrender its right to guide the conduct of its minions. The controversy that followed the fall of the NDA and the arguments advanced both for and against the so-called modifications / improvements in the History textbooks in Indian Parliament deserve some serious thinking. We should therefore raise a few questions and leave the learned to answer them. The questions are:

1. Who should write the textbooks? — The teachers who teach the subject or the ideologues, who are supposed to philosophize and project their political biases.

2. Who should publish the textbooks?

3. Besides fixing of prices, who decides the distribution

mechanism?

The present paper attempts to provide the backdrop against which the NCERT was asked to enter the field of textbook writing and their production. Prior to the founding of NCERT (1961) the Ministry of Education, Government of India already had a department called DCMT that looked after curriculum materials and textbooks. But somehow it did not produce textbooks itself, probably because majority of the State governments had their own departments/ bureaus of textbooks. There was no central agency/ organization for the production of textbooks. Also, it is for the first time with the setting up of the NCERT that research was brought to bear on the preparation and production of the textbooks in India. This research constituted writing/ preparing of textual material, testing the same in the actual classroom conditions for conceptual clarity and comprehensibility. Indeed, one of the things to be noted here is that the meeting of the State Ministers of Education with the Union Minister in the chair took a decision that the center should enter the field of textbook production in order to provide *model* textbooks for adoption or adaptation. It took time for the newly born organization, viz., NCERT, to start writing school textbooks. In the initial stages it had to depend on external assistance (mainly American) for learning the art and science of writing and producing textbooks but once it learnt the same, it set up two departments for the preparation and production of textbooks both in the area of science and mathematics, social sciences, besides humanities. The present day departments of education in science and mathematics (DESM) and of social sciences and humanities (DESSH) are the result of that vision.

Needless to say that these departments learnt to lead the nation in various ways and brought laurels to the organization to which they belonged. The staff of both these departments conducted classroom research examining the suitability of the content to be finalized for being including in the 'model' textbooks to be made available to the States. It is true that these *'models'* were meant for both—*adoption or adaptation* by the state bureaus of textbooks but studies have shown that the NCERT books *did* improve the quality of textbooks the State-textbook bureaus prepared. The impact of NCERT textbooks on the classroom practices has been tremendous. Though the precise number of NCERT textbooks users may be difficult to pinpoint there are states like the Arunachal Pradesh that have approached the NCERT to prepare its textbooks. Besides CBSE-affiliated schools the organizations like the KVS and the Navodaya Vidyalaya Sangathan use NCERT textbooks. Ever since India adopted 10+2 system her students have been able to compete successfully in the international arena largely because of the NCERT efforts in this area. Luckily the NCERT does not believe in resting on its past laurels. Instead, it has the vision to excel in climbing unconquered peaks. The production of good textbooks constitutes only part of a tale but this tale is born out of a dream and a vision.

One hopes and wishes that the NCERT's vision is spelt out soon through a policy decision /declaration in which all undefined aspects of textbook preparation and production are spelt out clearly. What is perhaps necessary is that the organization must evolve a proactive policy which defines clearly how a textbook will be accepted, royalty fixed and paid, its unmodified periodicity determined before revision/ rejection becomes technically imperative, the conduct of field research in determining its classroom suitability is transparently devised, etc. In the absence of such a policy statement the NCERT's work will continue to be trivialized by highly partisan criticism as is being done currently.

Recent continuing heated debate on the nature and the contents of NCERT textbooks has necessitated that a proper study on this subject be made. The fact that this issue was taken right up to the Supreme Court to decide and the Prime Minister of the country had to intervene to say that he is willing to take up the challenge of the Opposition and would not mind taking the issue forward to its logical end deserves a serious study. Such a study should cover the history of textbook writing in India and also how its content was viewed once they were brought out. Did the country have something like a censor board, or a body to supervise and see that only approved content was given in the school textbook. It would be interesting to consider how such controversies were resolved in the past when the need arose. In the following piece an attempt has been made to discuss objectively a few facts relating to this theme. In this regard one comes across a few passages in the proceedings of the CABE that throw some light on the decision making process. It would thus appear that the CABE did play some role in the event of a controversy on the issue. Here are a few extracts from those proceedings.

The first reference is from 13th meeting of the CABE held in Bombay in Jan.1947 with the Prime Minister and C. Rajagopalachari, the President of the CABE, in the chair. Item XIV—The Board proceeded to consider the question of exclusion from textbooks of statements derogatory to foreign countries and their Administration. The comments of the Inter-University Board on the subject were also before the Board. In agreement with the suggestion of the Inter-University Board it was recommended that books meant for educational institutions should as far as possible project an objective historical view and should not contain statements, which have not passed the test of critical judgment. The Board was also of the opinion that as far as possible school textbooks should avoid reference to current events of a controversial character.

In the very next item the Board recommended that suitable magazines for children should be published. The States may then be asked to buy such magazines in bulk and distribute within their jurisdiction.

Introduction

Textbooks as an area of research have escaped the notice of Indian scholars. Whatever information one laid one's hands on can answer questions only in parts. In reality one expects both comprehensive and definitive replies. For instance, what is a textbook? In what manner is it different from any other book in the same academic field? How does one choose an author for a textbook? Is a textbook writer practicing teacher or a researcher-scholar? Does one need to have some special qualifications for being a textbook writer? How does one evaluate the content in a textbook? Whom has the textbook to satisfy—the textbook consumer or his / her guardian? How should one fix the optimum periodicity / life of a textbook? In the ultimate analysis can State function as censor on the choice of textbooks? Of the several models already in existence which one suits which society? One could go on asking questions on the subject without getting satisfactory responses.

Plato's *Republic* gives us some idea of the problems one must confront if one were to read about the choices of content in textbooks or about the items in the syllabi. What goes into the making of a 'just' society and how does one prepare a citizen for such a society? There is a discussion about the subjects that must be taught and others avoided. For instance, Plato answered the question by highlighting the importance of education in such an undertaking. He went on to explain why must one teach mathematics and avoid teaching stories or fiction. The reasons are given for both. The results of a close examination of these arguments may not be to our liking but the arguments advanced do suggest that a textbook must conform to a philosophy or some theory of ethics that a particular society accepts as logically sound. In other words, *a textbook is an expression of a society's contemporary ideology and concerns* apart from other considerations, such as its comprehension by students, its general acceptability by the elite sections of society and its readability etc. There is yet another definition and this one is given by Krishna Kumar, "*Textbooks represent the grammar of a 'national ideology.*"(p.61) On a careful examination one would be hard put to defend an educational system that approves of the *laissez faire* approach to the prescription of the textbooks. No society, for example, would permit in the interest of its own survival teaching subversion in schools. It is another matter that a few decades back a school of thought emerged in the USA, which called for de-schooling the society because for these ideologues schools taught only consumerism being in cahoots with the big business. There is no need to look for further support to the argument that each society has the right to supervise and censor when necessary the content of the courses offered. What the erstwhile USSR had done through its Academy of Pedagogical Sciences, Japan is doing the same with its own version of the Institute of Educational Research—a wing of the Ministry of Education. Whether or not education is a subversive activity as Paulo Freire once called it, but the fact remains that the State has an obligation to see that in reality no subversion is able to flourish. Numerous examples exist when a prevalent fact has been thrown overboard by successor governments. If glorifying the Czars could be forbidden in the former USSR so is Communism getting a short shrift these days in Russia. If ideas change so do the practices.

A reference could be made here to a study undertaken by the NCERT in 1971 at the behest of Parliament that showed concern about teaching contents of certain textbooks found injurious to national integration. The details of the study are being discussed elsewhere in the paper but the findings endorsed the worst of the apprehensions. Duly approved and prescribed by their respective State Boards a few textbooks indeed taught material injurious to the concept of our Nationhood and national integration. A shadow is currently cast against certain type of institutions for the courses they are offering. All this merely goes to confirm what David W. Worley (1999) said, "future research would do well to focus upon an in-depth analysis of the theories, concepts, philosophical assumptions" textbooks betray. *(A Descriptive Analysis of Best-selling Basic Course Texts)* Probably this is one single reason why in democracies debates continue to erupt like rashes in and out of season.

It may be mentioned in passing that selection of a textbook depends largely upon the philosophy that the State proposes to uphold. Selection of authors or of textbooks would become impossible if the State did not pursue either its own ethical principles or a brand of philosophy. This explains why Communism could not be taught or allowed to flourish in the USA or concepts like freedom, democracy, and equality etc. have such great definitional variations in different countries.

We may now touch upon the tenets and organs of State and discuss who in the ultimate analysis is entitled to decide and declare policies. But before we do that it would be instructive to have a look at our colonial legacy—the one that continues to hang around us all the time. Indeed, one of the reasons why this must be done could be traced to having a look back at certain models we might like to consult for inspiration.

In the following few passages I am about to show that *our colonial masters used textbooks as a means of explaining their policies.* In other words, it would not be wrong to say that the potential of textbooks stands fully endorsed by now. Numerous examples on this point could be cited. For instance, the Communist Party of the USSR used textbooks to propagate its ideology just as the Chinese Red Army or the Japanese Meiji Regime did in their countries. Read this small paragraph from *Selections from Educational Records* by A. Sharp Vol.1 (1781-1839) p.176: -

"In the meantime the dangers to which we are exposed from the sensitive character of the religion of the natives, and the slippery foundations of our Government, owing to the total separation between us and our objects, require the adoption of some measures to counteract them, and the only one is to remove their prejudices and to communicate our principles and opinions by the diffusion of a rational education." The plan was to diffuse this new knowledge in the provinces through 'the *vernacular medium by the funding or assisting schools and by the preparation of textbooks* and a system of improved superintendence.'

In the Volume 2 of the selections by J.A.Richey (1840-1859) there is an extract, which speaks volumes on an important aspect of textbook preparation. The extract is from Committee's Report of 1840 item number V."To the preparation of a definite scheme of the several sets of books wanted for instruction through the vernacular language in the Seminaries of Ordinary Education, and by what means, and at what estimated cost, these books could be prepared."

In 1858 it was found (p.306) that textbooks were in short supply because of 1857 events. On p. 306 the Report says: 'The first thing to be done evidently was to *print new editions* of textbooks'. But there is also a mention in the body of the same text that *unsold copies* of the textbooks lay in plenty in Calcutta.

There is a mention of the name of one Ram Sharan Dass who had written four textbooks in Hindi as well as in Urdu.

The preparation of textbooks could be undertaken privately also by certain Societies like *Calcutta School Society* of which Raja Radha Kant Deb was a member. It may be mentioned in passing that Raja Ram Mohan Roy who was Deb's contemporary became more famous only because Roy was a progressive as contrasted with Deb who was dubbed a conservative Hindu. In terms of contribution Deb stands head and shoulders above Roy. The ineffectual angel that Roy really was has been discussed in a series of lectures that R.C. Majumdar delivered in Shantiniketan only a couple of decades back.

We have echoes of similar conflict in our times too. Hinduism has seldom been a popular religion among a particular brand of its followers. It would appear as though a few among the Hindus have always been ashamed of their beliefs. Self-flagellation characterizes their thought processes. Though all religions remain rooted in their Holy Books and honor their respective pantheons but somehow Hinduism must carry its Cross. What delights its co-religionists is that though it does not possess a commonly accepted Holy Book or a universally acceptable Code of Conduct yet a few commit the unforgivable folly of trying to define its parameters. The same continues to happen all the time. The hymn of the chanting dogs retains its historical validity.

Here we have a model worth consideration. This model has been appreciated in the First Report of William Adam. The extract runs thus:

"Printed, instead of manuscript schoolbooks are now in common use. The branches formerly taught are now taught more thoroughly; and instruction is extended to subjects formerly neglected, viz., the orthography of the Bengali language, geography and moral truths and obligations. The mode of instruction has been improved. Formerly, the pupils were arranged in different divisions according as they were learning to write on the ground with chalk, on the palm leaf, on the plantain leaf and on paper respectively; and each was taught separately by the schoolmaster in a distinct lesson. The system of teaching with the assistance of monitors, and of arranging the boys in the classes, formed with reference to similarity of ability or proficiency, has been adopted. and as in some instances it has enabled the teachers to increase the number of their pupils very considerably and thereby their own emoluments, it is hoped that it will ultimately have the effect of encouraging men of superior acquirements to undertake the duties of instructors of youth."

This quotation tells us vividly that before printed textbooks were prepared and given to children to learn from, there were *either* no textbooks *or* some textual material was prepared by local teachers in the form of a manuscript. One could only surmise about the quality or the quantum but there was definitely no policy as such about what to prepare and how to teach with the material available. The beginnings of the policy could be witnessed in Calcutta Book Society preparing textbooks for Calcutta School Society.

If one went into the actual mode of preparing textbooks we have witnessed two modes already. In a way these are the most modern systems in which local societies and practicing teachers play major roles. The preparation of textual material by the local teacher has tremendous possibilities. In some form the latter is practiced in numerous American schools. As for the other model represented by Calcutta Book Society the patronage of the colonial masters was forthcoming. This prevented any chance of playing mischief.

Now I present yet another model followed by the then rulers. This model carries two options. In the first option the authors could be commissioned. In the second one any book written by a well-known person could be accepted as a textbook by the appropriate authority. In the subsequent pages we will see that at one stage the NCERT followed both these options. It appointed its own subject panels and also got American books adapted to suit Indian requirements. In the case of British certain subjects like English language or literature they had no difficulty whatever. The books prescribed for the same level were just imported or reprinted. But the most common model adopted was the translation of textual material, into Indian vernaculars, already in existence in Great Britain. Local adaptations of certain books like that of English grammar was also quite popular. An observation on the policy of secularism may also be cited here. The reason the Colonial masters practiced it was because they had no intentions of hurting the religious sentiments of their subjects directly but if one opted to go to a government school teaching sermons was a part of their instructional strategy. One of the major grouse of the locals was that they indeed had a 'hidden agenda', which was to convert all Indians to Christianity. It is unnecessary to go into details about it all but once they opened their schools in Ajmer they declared this to be their intended policy. (Evolution of Official Policy in Education p.237 in *History of Vernacular Education in Bengal by N.L. Basak*).

Before we move any further it is necessary to remember that there were four types of educational institutions. For the traditional Hindus and Muslims there were the pathsalas and the maktabs at the lower levels and Sanskrit colleges and the madarasahs at the higher. The third type was grant-in aid institution in which rank the government schools constituted models of excellence. Each variety had its votaries and for each there were different policy perspective for handling. While the government schools offered an 'oasis in desert' model the grants-in-aid were regarded as the second best. In the other two types they made their own occasional forays of policy interferences.

As regards the contents of textbooks the history of Indian education records some of the most heated discussions in the well-known *Orientalists versus Anglicists* controversy and the now infamous *Minutes* of Macaulay. For our purpose this mention itself should suffice.

We will now take up the other two models of textbook writing. The first attempt to prepare textbooks in Bengali language was made by William Carey when he got appointed in 1801 in the Bengali Department of the Fort William College. For the first time a class of *teacher-authors* was created and textbooks commissioned to be written locally in vernacular languages.

There was no policy as such for doing so but the urgency of the requirement made this to meet the situation. At least this is the first time that a breed of teacher authors is recorded in India's educational history. These authors could be both – the ones who got appointed to teach what they had written or the ones whom fame got them to be commissioned to write a textbook too. Be that as it may there was definitely a scheme to reward authors for their labor. For instance, Ram Ram Basu who compiled a book entitled *Raja Pratapaditya Charitra* received a cash award of Rs. 300 and Pundit Mrityunjoy Vidyalankar received a cash prize of Rs. 200/- for his Bengali rendering of *Betal Pachisi.*

We may make here a reference in passing to yet another society engaged in the production of educational literature—the *Bethune Society of Calcutta* founded in 1851. As a policy they had banned discourses whether written or spoken on both – religion as well as politics.

There is an instance how one Ram Kamal Sen prepared Anglo-Bengali dictionary and how writers were invited through a newspaper advertisement to write a grammar book in English for Bengali readership. It is possible to evaluate by the content of courses the standard of proficiency expected to be attained in the three level examinations that were held then. But then this is a matter of detail. We have record of the prescribed textbooks but it is not possible to evaluate them. We do have incidentally a very important remark made in Vol. 1 (1859-71) prepared under the chairmanship of Sri Prem Kirpal which without going into details mentions on p. 277 item 341 "The publication, distribution and sale of educational books form a not unimportant portion of the educational system." It may sound like the concern of an educationist but as far as the policy makers were or are concerned the weightages could easily be different.

Long before India became free the question of nationalization of textbooks had been discussed. For this purpose one may go through all CABE proceedings especially the one of 1943 with profit. Of course, the concept of nationalization had colonial underpinnings. But as far as the issue had a vital component of political concern the British were not averse to include the same in their colonial agenda. The details given in this 1943 document of CABE cover the ground that has not been tread by any other subsequent committee. Indeed, even the Indian Education Commission's recommendations fall short of the insight shown by the then CABE. For instance, it gives procedures for an educational authority to oversee how textbooks are being supplied, how they are written, who are the authors, whether or not they are well-paid, how the books are to be printed, produced and distributed and how the cost of the books could be kept low. They went into the mechanism how matter prejudicial to communal harmony should be deleted. For the first time a definition of the textbook appears to have been attempted. I find it hard not to say that had this report been implemented both in spirit and details most of the problems that we face today concerning textbooks would have been easily prevented.

If one wished to go into the details how the world felt concerned about the appearance of some objectionable material into a nation's textbook that had no control over its prevention or deletion, the League of Nations adopted a Resolution in the early 1930's, i.e., before World War II that: -

A National Committee, finding an objectionable statement in a foreign textbook, might write to the National Committee of the offending country, pointing out what amendments it wished.

The League of Nations even developed criteria for the evaluation of textbooks for developing international understanding.

Textbooks in Free India – Policies and Practices

It is against this background that we enter 1947- the year of India's Independence with 8% literacy and a policy of promoting both British and Indian private publishers producing textbooks under the close supervision of the watchful eyes of the colonial masters. But by then number of things had already happened. For instance, most of the provinces had developed mechanisms to get textbooks written and evaluated. The import of textbooks from Great Britain had been reduced to a trickle and that too was limited to the area of English teaching. We must note here that unlike the British whose idea of promoting limited education among the natives was to share the economic burden of administering such a vast country and keeping it divided at the same time, the rulers of Free India wanted a fractured country to settle down and attain firm roots as a Nation. Schooling therefore received good deal of attention. *Also, the concept and practice of nationalization of textbooks took birth only after 1921* when diarchy was introduced in India. The main arguments advanced in its favor were: 1) there will be less profit making by private publishers; 2) the books will get standardized; 3) good books would be available well in time; and 4) the State would be able to prevent anti-democratic ideas from spreading. Following table will give an idea of what was happening in this regard

Year of Nationalization	*Name of the State*
1941-42	United Provinces
1948	Jammu and Kashmir
1949-50	West Bengal
1952	Punjab and Kerala
1953	Madhya Pradesh
1956	Rajasthan
1957	Andhra Pradesh
1958	Karnataka
1959	Tamil Nadu
1961	Delhi
1963	Nagaland and Assam
1964	Orissa

The above table shall give the reader an idea that

nationalization of textbooks does not have a long history. Still, the quality and content of a textbook had started to be matters of concern to the governments for a long time. The interesting part of the story is that the question of evaluating textbooks came up alongside their nationalization. Of all subjects History was identified as the most amenable to carry material prejudicial to national, international and religious sensitivities. The f irst committee that examined the textbooks in use in Indian schools was set up under the chairmanship of E.C. Bayley with R.M. Macdonald, Naraiyan B. Dandekar, R. Griffiths, and R.G.Oxenham. G.W. Leitner and Kristodas Pal as members and which submitted its report in 1877 on 10th October. For the first time it recorded dissatisfaction of the four committees "with the existing Histories of India and recommended the preparation of a new one." The committee also noted that one of its members; Dr. Leitner had found textbooks deficient in moral teaching. Therefore, it recommended that primary instruction should contain certain lessons on the following subjects:

(1) Reverence for God, parents, teachers, rulers and the aged.

(2) A simple sketch of the duties of a citizen.

(3) Cleanliness of habits, politeness of speech, kindness of conduct to other human beings and the brute creations.

(4) The dignity and usefulness of labour.

(5) The advantages of bodily exercise.

(6) The properties of plants, the uses of minerals and metals.

(7) The habits of various animals.

It should surprise many that emphasis on certain basic moral, hygienic and human values in education is not new and continues to occupy major contemporary educational concerns.

We may now consider a few criteria listed before 1947 to adjudge the qualities of History and Geography textbooks. Of these I am citing only a few and those too for the evaluation of History textbooks. These items continue to have their modern day relevance. Consider, for instance, the following: -

1. Are the books in accordance with the curriculum prescribed?

2. Is the language used in the books clear and easy?

3. Is the subject matter of the books correct and based on reliable data?

4. Have the religions and social conditions of different epochs of Indian history received due attention in the books of the series?

5. Has sufficient light been thrown on causes leading to wars and political changes?

6. Has a proper sense of proportion been exercised by the author in dealing with different events of the various reigns?

7. Do the exercises encourage the students to compare the present with the past conditions of life in India?

8. Is there anything in the books to offend religious susceptibilities or arouse communal, racial or class feelings?

9. Do the books contain objectionable references or undesirable political matters? In the event of the reply being in the affirmative, please mark the passage in the book and give details?

10. How do the books compare with other existing books?

In this section of the present paper we shall *first* consider the Secondary Education Commission's (1952-53) recommendations about improving the quality of textbooks and then the problem as perceived by the Indian Education Commission (1964-66), followed by an analysis of the policies of 1968 and 1986 along with the POA as revised in 1992. The *second* part of the paper will deal with the actual practices. After dealing with the *problems* towards the *end* I shall present a model arrangement for textbook production, distribution and copyright.

The Commissions and after

The Secondary Education Commission 1952-53 studied

the problem of school textbooks in historical perspectives and came to the conclusion that most of the systemic defects could easily be ascribed to the poor quality of textbooks. If the curriculum was unrelated to life, unscientific, narrow and bookish the quality of the textbooks left much to be desired. It therefore recommended: -

(b) A high power committee for selecting the textbooks for study at different stages should be constituted.

(c) This committee should lay down the criteria for the books.

(d) A fund should be maintained from the amount realized from the sale of books, which may be utilized for awarding and providing books and certain other amenities for school children.

(e) The Central Government should set up a new institution or help some existing art schools to develop training in the technique of preparing illustrations for textbooks.

(f) No single textbook should be prescribed for any subject of study but a reasonable number of books which satisfy the standards laid down, should be recommended.

No book prescribed as a textbook a book for general study should contain any passage or statement which might offend the religious or social susceptibility of any section of society of the community or might indoctrinate the minds of young students with a particular religious or political ideology. Compare this last recommendation with the criteria cited above and the similarities.

We must take note of what K.G. Saiyidain and J.P. Naik etc have said about the nationalized textbooks. They say

Although the practice of nationalization of textbooks has some advantages, it has often not succeeded in providing quality textbooks... but being Government sponsored, they are officially considered to be above criticism.

For the first time in the history of Indian education a *Commission like the one in 1964-66* was set up which did not leave any aspect or level of education untouched. It paid its attention on the state of textbooks as well. Here is what it found. The Indian Education Commission 1964-66 noted the following: -

Unfortunately, textbook writing and production have not received the attention they deserve. In most school subjects, there is a proliferation of low-quality, sub-standard and badly produced books, particularly in the regional languages. This has been due to a number of factors among which mention may be made of

1. The lack of interest shown by top ranking scholars so that the writing of textbooks has been generally undertaken by persons whose abilities are far from equal to the task,

2. The malpractices in the selection and prescription of textbooks, which defy control,

3. The unscrupulous tactics adopted by the publishers,

4. The lack of research in the preparation and production of textbooks; and

5. The almost total disregard by private publishers (who are interested only in profits) of the need to bring out ancillary books, such as teacher's guide to accompany textbooks.

9.15. State Production of Textbooks

The Commission found that 'textbook racket' has disappeared and some improvement in the quality of textbooks has occurred. (The reference is to activities undertaken by the central Ministry through NCERT) But in certain cases both in quality as well as in the production not much has improved "The main reason for this failure is that the Education Departments, which have taken over the responsibility of textbook production, have not adequately organized themselves for it." The Commission did not agree with those who wanted to close down the production work of State Departments of education. Instead, they wanted the State departments to organize themselves.

9.18. Programme at the National Level

(1) It is essential that the best talent available in the country should be brought together to produce the textbooks

and other literature needed, at the school and the university stages. This can only be done at the national level by agencies set by the Government of India.

(2) At the school level, we welcome the steps taken by the NCERT to produce textbooks with the help of scholars available in the country. Some books have already come out; and more will come out soon. These books are meant for use by State Governments who *can use them with or without changes.* We hope that the State Governments will make full use this pioneer venture to improve the quality of their books.

(3) *The production of textbooks and allied materials at the national level will be greatly facilitated if the Government of India were to establish, in the public sector, an organization, functioning on the commercial lines, for the production of textbooks...* We, therefore, feel that an organization of this type at the national level is urgently needed.

We recommend that the Ministry of Education should set up a small committee to work out the details of this project and take all the necessary steps to bring it into existence as early as possible.

9.19 Textbooks produced at the national level will have other advantages as well. One of the major recommendations is that *we should make an attempt to evolve national standards at the end of the primary, lower secondary and the higher secondary stages.* The definition of these standards as well as the organization of a programme for their practical implementation will be greatly facilitated by the production of textbooks at the national level. Such books can indicate the expected standard of attainment far more precisely than any curriculum or syllabi.

The Commission was conscious of the need to allow some elasticity or scope for local variations. It pointed out that in the teaching of mathematics, citizenship of the nation etc. variations may not be necessary but they acknowledged "teaching History from the point of social and national integration required well-written books on the subject."

However the most important recommendations from

our point of view were given in 9.21 (2) and (3). Consider the wording of the same. In the recommendation (2) it says, "Production of textbooks is a continuous process. For instance, it takes a year or even more to produce a textbook and a further year for the try out and revision. Within a year of its adoption on a large scale, a process of evaluation has to start; and very soon thereafter, it will be discovered that it needs revision. The machinery set up, therefore, should be adequate to follow all these steps for *every* textbook. It should be the objective of policy to see that a textbook is continuously revised and kept up-to-date, and that a *thorough revision takes place at least once in five years.* The need for frequent revisions is obvious.

In the next (3) recommendation the Commission said " No useful purpose is served by having only one textbook in a subject for a given class—this is almost invariably the position under the existing programmes of nationalization. *It should be an important objective of policy to have at least three or four books in each subject for each class and leave it open to the teachers to choose the book best suited to the school."* This is necessary even if there were to be a common syllabus for all the schools. It may be mentioned here that this particular recommendation is a repeat of the 1943 recommendation of CABE in which it was stated, " a textbook is a guide and an auxiliary and therefore the committee consider it desirable to ensure a certain measure of choice, for *this reason the number of textbooks in each class for each subject should not be less than two or more than six. The procedure recommended above should obviate the too frequent changes of textbooks* in schools..."

About the remuneration of authors for the textbook writing the rates were to be comparable with the private trade.

Kothari Commission was followed by 1968 policy. This policy did touch upon the core matters and avoided talking of peripheral issues. It recommended under the category.

Production of Textbooks

The quality of books should be improved by attracting

the best writing talent through a liberal policy of incentives and remuneration. Immediate steps should be taken for the production of high quality textbooks for schools and universities. Frequent changes of textbooks should be avoided and their prices should be low enough for students of ordinary means to buy them.

Most of what this recommendation says is a repeat of what has already been cited above. But the latter part of the recommendation somehow does not represent either the spirit or the actual import of the desire of the Commission. For instance, a textbook has to be reviewed regularly and the writing of the textbook is regarded a continuous process. It would be difficult to continue with an unmodified/or an unrevised textbook for a long time.

The Commission also recommended that "the possibility of establishing autonomous book corporation on commercial lines should be examined and efforts should be made to have a few basic textbooks common throughout the country. Special attention should be given to books for children and to university level books in regional languages.

Apart from this the 1968 policy document does not say anything more. Both the 1986 NPE and the POA as revised in 1992 fail to mention anything about textbook production. This is quite significant from the point of view of the importance attached to the preparation and production of nationalized textbooks. Anyone can assess the reality and distinguish the same from mere academic lip service.

We have with us an assessment of the situation around 1971 published in the form of *Fourth Yearbook.* B.N. Pal, a senior Reader in the then Department of Social Sciences and Humanities, wrote this paper. This paper carries figures of negligible progress of nationalization process in the States. Of the 13000 schools in the States only a thousand and odd had been nationalized for the sake of textbook adoption. Let us see what he says about the NCERT and its programme of producing textbooks, especially against the backdrop of Commission's recommendations cited above. If in the case of States the objectives had been specified nothing of the sort appears to have been done at the Center.

It would appear that the objectives would have been common both for the States and the Center. They were as under: -

1. To tackle the problem of non-availability of suitable textbooks, especially in regional languages;

2. To produce quality textbooks;

3. To put an end to unhealthy practices in the textbook trade;

4. To minimize the prevalent malpractices in the selection and prescription of textbooks;

5. To prevent private publishers from profiteering in school textbooks;

6. To ensure uniformity in the standards of attainments of pupils through good textbooks;

7. To reduce the price of textbooks as also to maintain a fair standard of textbook production;

8. To take all possible care in the selection of appropriate content and its presentation and of illustrations;

9. To rationalize the procedures for producing textbooks in order to effect further economy; and

10. To do justice to authors, reviewers, illustrators, etc. connected with the preparation of textbooks.

The observations of B.N.Pal should be seen in a perspective. It is fairly amusing to observe that even if all these objectives had been attained the benefits would have never extended beyond 1000 schools from among 13000. Today in the year 2003 the franchisees of NCERT's textbooks do not exceed beyond 3% of the total schools and even in the CBSE schools (KVS, Navodaya Vidyalayas etc.)—supposedly captive clients, no longer look upon NCERT with much respect and refuse to allow it any monopolistic rights.

In the context of the loftiness of the goals set for the State and the Center's organizations both by the Commission and other bodies, the achievements remain abysmally pitiable. Private publishers continue to fleece the public as merrily as ever before with the additional input from the ex-NCERT staff these publishers have reduced these days this Central Government organization to a mere shadow of the giant it ought to have been. With each passing day the publication industry is becoming stronger because of its political links. At least part of criticism NCERT publications face regularly originates from these quarters and at times with the connivance of its own staff. The NCERT finds itself helpless when viciousness in the remarks has political underpinnings. Today those that control the media have the cake and others with their hands tied to SRs and CRs can merely remain onlookers in a fast losing game.

One may like to put a question here. Why must then the NCERT publish textbooks when its mandate was clearly stated both by the Commission and also by its founding fathers in May 1961—a little before its actual birth. The reasons lie elsewhere. From its mandate and policies the NCERT since inception never enjoyed any autonomy. It is a body created to carry out the wishes of its masters. The deterministic character of the NCERT becomes explicit even before its birth. The State Chief Minister's Conference recommended even before its birth that it must produce *only specimen textbooks for adoption and adaptation* by the State Governments. In pursuance of this recommendation the NCERT at its own inception appointed the Central Committee on Educational Literature for Textbooks. The sub-committee was empowered among other things, to:

1. Appoint sub-committee or panels of experts;
2. Commission authors, illustrators and other experts for textbook preparation;
3. Arrange for the *printing and publishing of textbooks and other such materials;* and
4. *Arrange for their experimental tryouts.*

The first meeting of the Central Committee mentioned above was held on *11th, May1962* when five panels of experts in history, physics, general science, mathematics and Hindi were set up. The History panel had Dr. Tara Chand as the chairman and subsequently when the editorial board in History was constituted it had the following as its members: Dr.S.Gopal, Director, Historical Division, MEA, Professor Nurul Hasan, Head of the History Department, Aligarh Muslim University, Dr. Satish Chandra, Professor of History,

Rajasthan University, Jaipur and Romila Thapar, 19, Kautilya Marg, New Delhi. This team is deliberately mentioned. As far as the policy is concerned here is a quote from an autobiographical note of Romila Thapar to prove that there was none. Writes Krishna Kumar she recalls how the NCERT's history series was not really born out of a policy decision, but rather out of an initiative for which the ethos was just right:

"I may be autobiographical, in the early sixties some of us did a survey of the textbooks that were used in the schools of Delhi. We were appalled at how bad they were. We wrote a very passionate letter to the then education minister M.C. Chagla (1963-66) and said that something should be done to change this, at least start from the textbooks. Chagla promptly wrote back that since we were so concerned and we were a bunch of historians, we should write the new textbooks." (p. 52, Krishna Kumar)

In a way the history textbooks were prepared by a bunch of self-invited scholars and for whom Chagla's reply must have come as Divine blessing.

After Prof. Nurul Hasan became the Union Minister of Education he shared the largesse in various ways. The panels had been set up to prepare textbooks in their respective subject areas along with other instructional material. A little later a few more subjects were added to this list. These were: technologies, agriculture, fine arts and crafts for students studying in multipurpose schools. Until 1970 or so these panels in physics, biology, chemistry, commerce, geography, Hindi, history, mathematics, agriculture, technology and Sanskrit worked because they were abolished soon after. Some of us may like to know the methodology adopted by these panels to work.

A textbook panel usually drew up a detailed syllabus in the subject. The syllabus aimed at students' acquiring wider and deeper knowledge of the subject. After a long series of meetings syllabus was adopted, which got further spelt out in content matter, understandings and units. The units were then assigned to authors, selected on their teaching experience and expert knowledge in the subject area. The first drafts were sent to reviewers for suggestions and revision. The subject panels finally gave the seal of approval. The *Central Committee on Literature for Textbooks* assessed the working of each panel periodically. The *model* textbooks prepared by the NCERT under the care of editorial boards—the members of which had the Minister's approval. These textbooks were then *adopted or adapted or used* as *reference materials* by several State Governments. There are reasons to believe that the Minister who first bypassed the entire procedure and gave orders to delete the words 'experimental editions' from NCERT textbooks / textual materials to textbooks proper was Hon'able M.C. Chagla. And when Professor Nurul Hasan came to occupy this seat he glided through his tenure with even greater ease than any of his predecessors could have even imagined doing.

One should not miss a couple of points in this discussion. The State governments have always had the *final* authority in the choice of textbooks. They *were and are* free to adapt or adopt the model produced by the NCERT. Panels and the editorial boards did all the work before the books were sent for printing. These books should necessarily have gone through a field trial and review. But there is no record that it actually happened. The point to remember is *that at no point of time the NCERT itself took the decision to print or prepare or edit textbooks. The decisions/orders were invariably conveyed to it for execution.* And also the system of a single author writing a book had not emerged till then. Also, these books had to be tried out in the actual classrooms first both for their language difficulty and also for their conceptual clarity and acceptability and only after lengthy discussions could they be declared market worthy. The NCERT played the role of facilitator only. It never had the authority to force the acceptance or otherwise of a textbook. It did not involve its staff in the work of the panels beyond organizing meetings. The NCERT had a clearly defined role for itself. *It had to help in the tryout and finalization of the textual material.* Beyond research and printing it did not have much of a role. I doubt if this organization on its own wields even today either much power or influence. It has, for instance, no powers to prescribe a textbook anywhere in the country. It could not control the school system or even monitor it. *Its actual role is limited to merely trying to persuade those that have the real power to perform optimally, i.e., better than what they have been actually performing.* Any allegation against the NCERT could be in the region of transgression of its defined roles. Under the watchful eyes of the MHRD and the political leadership such an act would be tantamount to the commission of an unforgivable folly. These then are the parameters for operation for the NCERT.

To continue the story we have in the initial stages of the founding of the NCERT a comprehensive programme for the development of science education at the secondary level. The UNESCO under the United Nations Expanded Technical Assistance Programme offered the technical assistance for the same. The NIE and the four Regional Colleges of Education formulated their own pragramme for taking benefit from the offer. It was realized that for improving the quality of education, it is essential that the sequences of learning should be closely articulated for various stages of education and be adapted to the abilities, aptitudes and needs of the pupils. To cite a NCERT document, "this calls for a clear definition of objectives of each course of study and preparation of suitable textbooks and other materials for effective learning and teaching. The educational materials should be as up-to-date as possible, particularly in the areas of mathematics and science where the frontiers of knowledge are expanding at a rapid rate."

A high–powered Committee for the production of educational literature, with the Union Minister for Education as President was immediately constituted and panels (already mentioned) of experts appointed to lay down the objectives of study for different disciplines and to approach eminent scholars or groups of scholars for preparing textbooks which could serve as models for the whole country. *The Central Bureau of Textbook Research* continued to extend its assistance to the educational authorities of States for the preparation of textbooks for schools. It would be interesting to go into the details of the working of this organization called CBTR. But it appears that apart from organizing exhibitions and Seminars it also undertook jobs at the requests from the State governments. At times it trained scholars from third world countries in the preparation of curriculum and textbooks. At the request of the Punjab Government, the Bureau drew up the syllabus for classes 1 to V in Social Studies.

Meanwhile, the Council undertook reprinting of certain American school textbooks. The first one in this regard was *Physics* and *A Teachers' Guide* to it, by a special arrangement with the publishers, D.C. Heath and Company of the USA.

As early as on 9-1-1962 *the Governing body of the NCERT* resolved in terms of Rules 45 and 46 of the Council that a special committee to be called the *Central Committee on Educational Literature* should be set up to undertake this important task of updating textbooks for an effective educational process. It was realized even at that early stage that production of such textbooks entailed the application of applied educational research. The Committee members were as follows:

1. Dr. K.L. Srimali (Chairman).
2. Dr. D.S. Kothari
3. Sri P.N. Kirpal
4. Sri P.C. Bhattacharya
5. Dr. D.C. Pavate*
6. Dr. A.C. Joshi*
7. Dr. Tara Chand*
8. Dr. B.N. Ganguli*
9. Sri Raja Roy Singh
10. Prof. T.K.N. Menon
11. Dr. S.P.Chatterji*
12. And Dr. Hazari Prasad Dwivedi*

*Co-opted

This committee composition speaks volumes on the nature of competence that the Minister himself possessed and perceived in others. He himself came from a teacher's college therefore he knew Menon and Dr. Kothari came from his hometown. This does not mean that either of these two was not well known or was wrongly made member. It merely shows how the immediate friendly circle or the familiar persons of the Ministers tend to occupy seats of power. The rest come near them either because of their official designations or from their hard earned reputation. It is some kind of universal truth.

The Objectives of the Committee were

1. To prepare and publish or assist in the preparation and publication of books, manuals and *readers designed as textbooks* or supplementary educational material for use in educational institutions.

2. To organize conferences and seminars for writers, artists, illustrators, publishers, librarians, and others concerned with the production of educational literature for use in educational institutions.

3. To promote and conduct research in the production of textbooks and other educational literature.

4. To commission writers, illustrators and other experts for preparing specific books.

5. To prepare and bring out book lists, arrange exhibitions and organize effective dissemination of improved techniques of textbook production.

6. On behalf of the NCERT to advise the Government of India, the State Governments and other educational organizations and institutions on matters relating to the production of textbooks and educational literature and to collaborate with them in the furtherance of the objects for which the Committee is set up.

To implement the objectives, the Committee was vested with certain financial powers such as spending Council's money with the approval of its Finance Committee, to appoint sub-committees or panels of exerts for preparing instructional materials etc.

By 1963 the Committee had held three meetings and laid down the following general principles for the guidance of the authors who may be invited to write textbooks or other materials. These were:-

1. To begin with, the *textbooks may be prepared for the higher secondary classes;*

2. They should be prepared *co-operatively* by professors, teachers and other specialists;

3. They should be up-to-date in content and scientific in approach;

4. They should serve as *models* for authors, foster national integration, and be designed to serve the objectives of good education for the younger generations,

By August 1963 the Subject Panels had worked out the syllabus for the textbooks writers. In the course of less than five years from this date number of textbooks had been prepared. While some 18 textbooks were ready for use there is no mention of the procedure actually followed. We have no idea which particular type of research method had been followed to see that the levels of comprehension matched the age group for which they were actually intended. Each book however did indicate the methodology followed. Almost equal number of textbooks was under print. If one wanted to know the progress, it was good but surprisingly Textbooks Policy had to wait until 31st Jan.1970 when it got decided. On that date under the chairmanship of Dr.B.N.Ganguly, Sri T.R.Jayaraman, J.S and Prof. SVC Aiya, Director, NCERT Policy regarding textbooks was finalized and declared.

The Committee felt that in addition to dealing with the States of J&K, Rajasthan, Mysore and West Bengal as desired by the resolution of the Governing Body, it should not exclude considering the wider issue of the NCERT textbooks and their use in the States.

Item 3 discussed the issue why students do not purchase textbooks. Poverty and the habit of purchasing second –hand textbooks were the two main reasons enumerated. Additional reasons were given in the annexure 2. The general contention has been that these books do not conform to the State syllabus. Even the 70 % of the State requirement has to be culled from several books NCERT publishes. Herein lies the problem. When students are unwilling to buy a single textbook that conforms to their syllabus why would they buy several that NCERT publishes only to find that they cover only 70% of their syllabus?

A Conference organized by the NCERT on the 15th and 16th of January, 1970 recommended that if NCERT removed some of the drawbacks in their textbooks the situation might improve.

In reality the problem the new NCERT textbooks faced constituted the unsold stocks and their general classroom unacceptability. It was more than apparent that on both counts, i.e., absence of their actual tryout and excessive enthusiasm of authors in updating the textual materials; these books had failed in achieving the original objectives. Read the following item 11 of the policy: -

The NCERT Textbooks *may* by themselves be very good and a certain sections of the school population *may* buy them to enlarge their own knowledge, etc. but unfortunately, for such purposes, the required publicity for the NCERT does not exist. Similarly, no concerted attempt has ever been made to deal with the use of the NCERT textbooks on a person-to-person basis in the different States. This lacuna could be covered by the appointment of FIELD Advisors. They however made a very significant policy decision, which reflects to a large extent most of what had been thought earlier. Read the following: -

Item 12. In view of what is stated above, the NCERT is currently examining the question of the feasibility of publishing monographs, the question of furnishing readymade textual material to correspond to a syllabus, the question of appointing a Field Officer in each State and the question of improving the publicity for the NCERT textbooks.

Item 14. The Director informed the Committee that he impressed on the representatives of States at the last Conference on the 15th and 16th January that a syllabus by itself does not mean much. Even for a given syllabus, the method of presentation of the subject matter and the art of writing make a vital difference. He also pointed out that injecting what is latest in knowledge and injecting indirectly concepts on conservation of natural resources, national integration, population, nutrition and the inter-dependent economy of Indian States etc. together with guide-lines for evaluation to test the student could go a long way to make one book more important and useful than another even when both cover the same syllabus. A follow-up of these concepts more specifically could be useful.

Vide letter no.F.9-27/69-NCERT/School4 dated 7th march, 1970/ Phalguna, 1891(S) from Sri T.R. Jayaraman, JS, Ministry of Education and Youth Services, GOI.

Policy regarding the use of NCERT books by the State Governments.

Government has had under consideration the question of revising the policy with regard to the production of textbooks and other materials by the NCERT and their use by the State Governments. In view of the findings of the Governing body of the NCERT that the response from the State Governments has not been encouraging in accepting the Council's textbooks, a Sub-Committee was appointed by it with Dr. B.N.Ganguli. former VC, Delhi University, as Chairman to ascertain the reasons for non-acceptance of books for adoption or adaptation by the State Governments. The Education Minister as President of the NCERT has received the report of the Sub-Committee. Government have now examined all aspects of the problem and have decided as follows: -

1. The NCERT may, by and large, prepare in future *textbook materials* and make them available to all States and Union Territories. The name of the author (or authors) should not be displayed in the book to be published under this category. There may, however, be suitable acknowledgement of the assistance received from all persons connected with the preparation of the book. The State Governments and Union Territories can adapt the material for preparation of textbooks in their schools.

2. The NCERT may also undertake publication of outstanding books already available in the market or commission eminent writers to write textbooks. In such cases the author's name may be displayed in the book. However, the user Government should be informed that the publication is available for adoption only. In case any changes

are proposed, prior permission of the Council should be obtained. The Council, in turn, should consult the author and obtain his concurrence.

3. The Council may entrust the publication of such books to some organization *instead of itself* publishing them.

4. There should be a standard introduction to all NCERT books indicating the principles followed in the preparation of the book and the nature of adaptation, if any, normally permitted.

5. As regards books already published, the State Government may be informed that they can use the books without any changes. In case they desire any modifications or alternations to suit their syllabi, they should get prior clearance from the Council, which, in turn, may have to consult the authors in the light of the Copyright Act.

6. I shall be grateful if the above policy is brought into effect immediately.

This Annexure 6 was followed by yet another viz. Annexure 7 dated 7th March, 1970 which clarified rules guiding Adoption and Adaptation of NCERT Books by State Governments/Union Territories.

1. I am directed to state that in view of certain provisions of the Copyright Act and consequential legal implications, it is found that the recommendation of the National Board of School Textbooks for permitting the State Governments *to use material* from the NCERT books or *to adapt* the books as they desire without any specific prior permission from the Council can not be implemented for the books published so far. Under the circumstances, the State Governments / Union Territories are requested to obtain necessary clearance from the NCERT regarding changes, if any, to be effected in the books brought out by it before these are either printed or published as nationalized textbooks.

2. It has been decided that in future, as far as possible, *the NCERT will produce textual material, which can be used freely by State Governments* in the preparation of their textbooks. The publications concerned will clearly indicate this feature.

In between the evolution of policies the Government felt very concerned about complaints it received against certain prescribed textbooks in several States containing material prejudicial to the interests of national integration. In September 1966 the Ministry of Education appointed a Committee under the chairmanship of Dr. K.G. Saiyidain to examine the issue and advise the Government on the principles to be adopted in the preparation of textbooks suitable for a secular state. This Committee submitted its report covering mainly the points *concerning policies and principles* after it had examined several witnesses and studied the actual complaints.

In March 1970 the question was raised whether *all textbooks* likely to contain material harmful to the interests of national integration could be scrutinized and the States concerned advised in the matter. By this time the *National Board of School Textbooks* with all state Ministers of education as its members had already been established. Its real work was done by the department of Textbooks in the NCERT. At its *first* meeting held in *April 1969* it *had* recommended that the evaluation of school textbooks should be conducted by the State itself. Therefore in its *second* meeting this came up as an item on agenda for discussion and decision. The unanimous decision was that *all* books prescribed or recommended for use in the schools in *all* States should be evaluated from the standpoint of national integration.

Under orders (issued on May 27, 1970) from Ministry the NCERT was asked to take this up as a crash programme to be completed within 6 months. The response of the States was not encouraging therefore even within numerous constraints the NCERT examined some 3000 textbooks relating to subjects like languages, history, civics, moral sciences and social studies.

The Crash programme brought the Council for the first time into intimate contact with Education Ministers, Education Secretaries, Directors of Education and others. This programme got slated to be over by July 1972. In fact, the real work took some more time to be over. By 1977 the report on the evaluation had been prepared in which it was found that more than 65% books were perfectly above board from the national integration point of view. The other books needed partial or more changes to suit the national requirements.

Meanwhile by 1974 the school pattern had changed to 10+2+3 and accordingly newer sets of books ad to be prepared by the NCERT. By 1977 the emphasis on vocationalization of education had become the focus of secondary education. Once again the NCERT had to prepare itself for the challenge. What is being laid stress on is the fact policy change is the domain of the Government of India and the primary duties of the include carrying out the orders of the Government. On its own it can exercise little freedom.

I cite now from a document prepared by the NCERT that got printed and circulated in 1986. This document declared"these guidelines in the form of a booklet are addressed to those who are interested in improving the quality of textbooks from the standpoint of national integration." The present booklet, the Foreword said, "contains guidelines in the subject areas of Languages, History, Geography, Civics and Sociology". In other words by the time these guidelines came the national concerns included casteism, communalism and regionalism besides national integration. I am citing the guidelines regarding History only since I have already given above pre-Independence criteria. The 1986 document on the subject defined the parameters: (a) To see that the content does not foster communal, caste, racial and regional prejudices, and (b) To see that the presentation of the past is authentic and is also free from myths and factual inaccuracies.

Under Communalism it was suggested that religious books, personalities and tenets should not therefore be derided. The idea was to avoid fostering intolerance. Caste and untouchability in the post Mandal era had become even more taboo than ever before. The tragedy was that politics had already vitiated the atmosphere and the NCERT was asked to counter the scourge in the classrooms through good textbooks. Similarly, the other concerns like regionalism and linguism that were created by various interest groups were sought to be met head on by the NCERT through quality textbooks. The guidelines wanted glaring inaccuracies to be avoided. Other than these vague and highly generalized statements these guidelines were in reality not much of a use. They lacked focus, clarity in definitions, objective criteria to judge deficiencies. To that extent a big time suave politician might as well have prepared these guidelines. Their relevance lay in their vagueness and easy maneuverability.

Problems

The reason why the NCERT is unable to avoid embarrassments is that in its mandate there is no mention of the words 'publication of textbooks' except a clause 10, which reads as follows: -

11. To undertake the publication of such books, periodicals and other literature as may be necessary for the furtherance of its objectives.

It may be stressed here that the major functions of the NCERT as defined in the Memorandum of Associations are to undertake, aid and promote research in all branches of education. This by implication covers textbooks but does not name it. Surprisingly, the Council has neither ever produced on its own a single piece of original empirical research in this area or nor was it ever asked to do so. To its credit it does have a volume titled *A Study of the Evolution of the Textbooks* published in 1987, which too unfortunately suffers from innumerable drawbacks. To name some it does not cover any empirical research may be because it is a historical survey and does not have an index too for some inexplicable reasons, which would have otherwise revealed the ease with which the survey moves forwards and backwards without any consideration for its readability or coherence.

I also have with me yet another document which purportedly presents an *Appraisal and Guidelines* on the subject declared as the title *NCERT Textbooks*. This document has been prepared by R. Joshi and submitted in its draft form in May 2000. This document covers almost the same ground as I have but in greater detail and some criticism laced with highly reluctant praise. It would be interesting to read the draft document and see whether I have left out any point worth notice. Dr. Joshi presents his document in four sections. Section 1 is on Establishing An Identity. Section 2 is titled Textbooks for a New Pattern of Education; Section 3 titled Textbook Development under NPE-1986 has four sub-sections such as, rationale and the development of textbooks for primary stage, upper primary and the secondary stage etc. He has also separately discussed the development of these books subject wise. The last section that is section IV deals with *Guidelines for the Preparation and Production of Textbooks.*

In my paper I have not talked of the guidelines and neither have I given any definition of the textbooks. I shall deal with this issue separately but before I do that I should like to present a summary of the content that Joshi deals with. The idea is that the reader may like to see that the same matter can be presented differently as well. The following is the content of Joshi's draft presentation.

Section1 starts with the section titled *Establishing Identity* in which Joshi defines "textbooks provide the vital link between the policy makers and curriculum developers on the one hand and the teachers who undertake the responsibility of its transaction on the other". He goes on to answer the query why NCERT started writing and publishing textbooks as opposed to the earlier practice when experts selected books written by others and declared them as being suitable textbooks for a given subject and given class. All this changed after the establishment of the NCERT. In the initial stages the NCERT undertook the following projects/ programs: -

1. A survey of school textbooks in the country (1969-1970).

2. Development of a theoretical framework for preparation and evaluation of textbooks in different school subjects.

3. Development of textbooks in different disciplines that may serve as model/pacesetters for State and UT's agencies.

The first stage (1961-1975) was the "most innovative and productive eras of the Council as far as research and development in the area of instructional materials including textbooks is concerned." In the first stage brochures were produced giving details of the principles and procedures for the preparation and evaluation of textbooks in general science, biology, geography, history, mother tongue, mathematics and social studies. Thereafter, science syllabus for classes 1-VIII was prepared in which spiral approach was adopted. Joshi deals with the major defects in the set of science books prepared on page 12. Similar syllabi were prepared in all other subject areas and for all classes from I to VIII.

In the second section Joshi has dealt with the development of textbooks for the new pattern of 10+2+3 declared in 1975. Until then only the KVS institutions had adopted the model textbooks produced by the NCERT for classes I to VIII with help of UNESCO. In the opinion of Joshi "as such the Council had no formal commitment to provide textbooks in all subjects and for all stages of school education."(P.18)

According to the Council's decision two important points became noticeable, one, with the help of experts from universities and elsewhere-instructional materials be developed within the Council and gradually for all classes from I to VIII spread over three sessions starting from 1977-78 to 1979-80. Also, this is the time when the NCERT came out with "The Curriculum for the Ten Years of schooling—Framework." In the session 1975-76 the KVS was the first system to switch over to the new pattern and therefore logically these schools were the first institutions to have accepted NCERT textbooks. At this time science and social science textbooks were introduced in the classes IX and X in the year 1976 and the students their first public examination in 1977. It is during these times the NCERT curricula and textbooks for the first time came under severe criticism and had to face review committees. The Review Committee recommended major changes in the framework besides several deletions. Accordingly the NCERT was forced to make the requisite changes in their textbooks.

The third section deals with textbook development under NPE-1986. This again was a historic period when a political party in power used the NCERT to define its own goals and programs. The NPE-1986 defined and identified national goals which got stated in the form of a document called "The National Curriculum for Primary and Secondary Education—A Framework." This National Curriculum Framework thus gave the nation detailed guidelines for the organization of curriculum for primary, upper primary and secondary stages of school education.

It is this period when the NCERT prepared textbooks for Arunachal Pradesh and for Navodaya Vidyalayas too. Also, the NCERT took help from CIFL for preparing its English textbooks and History textbooks from a section of well-known historians and science books under the leadership of the famous scientist C.N.R.Rao.

Now the NCERT has entered its fourth phase. Since this phase has just started its analysis is not possible but it has also started with a bang like the previous phases. It has its own National Curriculum Framework for school education—2000 and its textbooks prepared accordingly. This also means that NCERT faces once again problems with which it is already familiar. Joshi goes into some of the details of the framework as also of the problems. But beyond that there is neither any scope nor a possibility.

This appraisal ends with the guidelines with which one could not be concerned at this stage because everything that the NCERT does now will attract adverse comments and observations. In his appraisal Joshi has not tried to explain the reasons why the NCERT had to produce textbooks. He does however mention clearly that in the initial stages the textbooks were actually tried out in the actual classes and reactions recorded for future revisions. This is how a research organization should behave and actually function. But all of a sudden this practice was abandoned. He mentions this fact but not the reasons behind such a major decision. Interestingly, Joshi emphasizes on the fact that the NCERT books *were always adapted / adopted or modified and it's actual clientele remained highly restricted.* Special efforts had to be made to sell its books on the market. The production of books by the NCERT has always been in the eyes of mini-storms. If at times the criticism constituted delays in their marketability at another a few raised questions about their content or approach. For instance, at one point the switch over to new mathematics appeared non-acceptable. Similarly, the delay in mentioning the break-up of the USSR came in for adverse comments. This position in itself does not seem to have changed in any appreciable measure. Also, while Joshi is all praise for the achievements of the Council in its textbook production he does not hesitate to record the opprobrium such a production must bring in its trail.

The most unacceptable part of R. Joshi's study is the premise, which he states in these terms (p.91):

"The preparation of instructional materials for all stages of school education as a part of the implementation of the National Policy on Education within the stipulated time helped the Council to further establish its *credential as an apex organization* in the school education."

The point is that the NCERT did not have to establish its credentials as an apex organization because it came into existence as one. Just as there is no official body in the country to compete with the UGC in higher education, there is none to compare with the NCERT in school education. Whether it published any instructional material or not the NCERT shall always remain an apex body / system in school education. The publication of instructional materials was also not its own choice because it was not around when its functions were decided. The day NCERT prepared any material of its own choice in response to its own policy decision it would be logical to make an assessment of this nature.

In his book *Prejudice and Pride* cited above Krishna Kumar is quite critical of NCERT's history textbooks. This reference is deliberate because of late these books have been at the center of an unnecessary controversy. Here is the opinion / judgment of one who has himself been critical of NCERT's books. On page 52 he says, "These textbooks were undoubtedly far superior to the ones in use at the time (by implication *not now*), marking a significant departure in perspective and content, but in terms of style and the ability to communicate with children, they were not particularly distinguishable from earlier texts." If these books were not particularly appropriate in style and communicability, they did not rank very high in conceptual clarity either. For instance, he talks of both the secular-minded Left and the Hindu revivalists for whom"the Partition (as a concept) represented an event that had injured the idea of India. From the secular perspective, Partition was a blow to the pluralist character of Indian society and its composite culture. The opponents of secular historians also saw Partition as a blow—to the continuity and territorial integrity of the Hindu civilization—engineered by Muslims whose ancestry was said to lie among medieval invaders. British manipulation to ensure India's division was a prominent component of both interpretations of Partition. So long as the text did not encourage children to think about the nature of injury that Partition had caused, rival interpretations would stay buried. The NCERT text fulfilled this condition as happily as any other schoolbook written on the freedom struggle, because *none of them were designed to make children think."(P.54)*

Krishna Kumar's feels legitimately concerned about explaining certain concepts to children in the history textbooks for enabling them to think for themselves. When he finds that both in India as well as in Pakistan certain facts are either kept hidden from them or distorted he feels a little frustrated. For instance, while no Indian school textbook mentions Moplah riots but all Pakistani textbooks do. "It needs little imagination to appreciate why no Indian textbook mentions the Moplah riots, and why every Pakistani textbook does. The mention of the Moplah violence would seem to spoil the web of Hindu-Muslim unity that Indian textbooks weave against the background of Gandhi's first experiment of Satyagraha." (p.145) He gives yet another example to get his point of view across. Gandhi's representation in the context of the early 1920's offers an example of this problem. Gandhi is denied all honor and stature in the portrayal of Khilafat and Non-Cooperation in all Pakistani textbooks. In India, he is cleverly portrayed to ensure that the politician in him is left out, only the Mahatma remains. As captive audiences, children of neither country are allowed the opportunity to appreciate the enormous challenge he faced in bringing Hindus and Muslims closer together.(P.147) This is not all. He cites from a class VIII textbook of NCERT written by Arjun Dev and Indira Arjun Dev to show how hiding facts and giving an acceptable definition is quite common in India too especially if the textbook is produced for the state. The authors mention in detail the large number of communal riots that took place across the country during 1923-39 period. They write,"For some years after the withdrawal of Non-Cooperation movement there was no nation-wide struggle. For sometime,there was a widespread feeling of disappointment and frustration in the country. There were communal riots and Hindu-Muslim unity – achieved before and during the Non-Cooperation struggle—seemed to weakening. 'Within the next two statements, however, the narrative retrieves its uplifting tone,' The struggle for freedom had apparently suffered a setback. These years, however, were also the years of preparation for a more powerful struggle.' From here onwards the text focuses on the activities of the Swaraj party, which was formed in 1923 ... and this choice of focus makes the Dev couple ignore the divisive consequences that the working of democracy, especially the provision for separate electorate, had in the functioning of local level institutions of democracy. The focus also enables the narrative to ignore the significant role that religious revivalism played among both Hindus and Muslims in encouraging separatist tendencies." In the next paragraph Kumar takes up a senior-level textbook written by Bipan Chandra and finds him getting 'amazingly convoluted while interpreting the events that followed the formal withdrawal of Non-cooperation and the end of Khilafat on account of developments in Turkey'" (P.149)

In yet another analysis of Chandra's book Krishna Kumar finds discrepancies between the reality and its description. For instance, " most Indian textbooks maintain a complete silence on the fact that the formation of the Congress ministry in the United Provinces was not a smooth affair. There was considerable tension on the question of Leagues participation. The functioning of the Congress government, particularly its programme of educational reform, which was based on Gandhi's Wardha scheme, aroused a controversy and caused a rift between Hindu and Muslim politicians." And still Bipan Chandra persists with his contention that 'people felt as if they were breathing the air of victory and self-government.' (p.177) There upon Krishna Kumar remarks, "One wonders what the Indian school historians gain by presenting the 1937-39 period in so sketchy and inaccurate a manner. The only answer is that by eliminating the record of controversy, the textbooks sustain the young reader's impression that the *Congress was a moral force, not merely a political party."*

The above critique cited from Krishna Kumar's book should be enough to show that with so much of selectivity and elimination of records in school history textbooks deliberate, pre-planned distortions in statements are always possible that may influence individual readers' perceptions. If this is what *can* and *does* really happen it remains a mystery why should the NCERT produce textbooks at all when at best it should prepare only textual materials or model textbooks for adoption / adaptation through actual classroom research and at worst merely recommend *number* of authenticated textbooks—something, which the *1968 Educational Policy* laid down specifically. The discrepancies and inconsistencies in its policies and practices have proved to be NCERT's major bane. Since this organization never built any mechanisms to defend itself independently of the Ministry it has been subjected to pressures and pulls the epicenters of which lie elsewhere.

The second and the major shortcoming of the NCERT constitute provisions in its Constitution, which currently gives it very little autonomy in functions or in decision - making. Technically, it cannot even defend itself. It is an autonomous organization *within* the Ministry of Human Resources Development. The parent has to protect its baby since it has neither grown teeth or muscles of its own. The policies that could have defined its exact status and the nature of its working cannot therefore be evolved within the Council. They must invariably come from above. Still, it need not be all that helpless provided it learns to function as a professional body, which it really is.

The nature of Indian society is yet another dimension of the problems the NCERT has to contend with. The vote bank politics has complicated the problem even further. On this count the NCERT is a sitting duck.

In brief, it has problems but does not know how to

overcome them either through research or professionalism. It has no capability to defend itself against the imposition of political decisions of those in power.

Still, there are ways to overcome difficulties. The wise know them and opt for them too, the rest merely keep on watching helplessly.

Concluding Remarks

The NCERT can also come out of its present state of uncertainties if it follows standard procedure. The criticism that the NCERT faces today relate to procedures, policies and practices in textbook production. No one has accused the organization that it is not competent to take its own decisions even with regard to textbook production. Also, no one said that it has not helped the nation to produce better class of students comparable with the best in the world. It continues to remain an apex system in several ways. There is no reason why it cannot retain the heights it has already reached. What it requires most is initiative and a proactive policy. And for that one has to be a little imaginative. It remains to be seen what this leadership would do to come out of the morass in which it has got stuck.

The present paper argues that there is need to be clearheaded about all the stages starting from the word *go* in writing a textbook until it reaches the class-teacher and her students. It is not the textbook alone that one must produce. The textbook is the result of a curriculum that a given school and a class must follow. A textbook is its mirror image. At the same time a textbook must also accompany teachers' guide/ handbook, students' exercise material, proper questions, list of graded concepts to be explained and learnt etc. The textbook author should have a blueprint of the parameters for its preparation / production. The breakup of the curriculum into graded bits of syllabi and the terms to be used and explained is a cumbersome job. Ordinary practicing teachers or even great scholars may find preparing a school textbook a tough job. *What* and *how* of a textbook writing requires patience which everyone may not be gifted with. Therefore, the choice of an author by itself is also not free from customary problems / hazards.

As I write in the summer of 2005 I am given the impression that the textbooks prepared by the NCERT continue to be admired by the practicing teachers and few are willing to accept the ones prepared so caringly by teacher-ideologues of the group that supervised the preparation of textbooks by Delhi SCERT. I gathered this impression in an interaction with Delhi's secondary school teachers. Let me add, since I have neither written nor produced a textbook therefore I am unwilling to act as a judge.

10
Values Education in Indian Democracy

In the past couple of years I have had the occasion to read several studies on values education and have come to the conclusion that Indian educators are obsessed with the word 'value'/ 'values' perhaps much more than with any other term used in the context of education. It would appear as though all other concerns in education in this country have suddenly been subordinated to this single requirement. Interestingly, this term seems to be used by them as an adjective to qualify the noun 'education' and not as a noun in its plural form. A book that I read recently used the term 'values' only to highlight their distinctive role and character in education, i.e., an education whose core content relates to values that can be identified, prioritized and also ranked. That they require some specific methodology to teach has also been researched and reported. For the first time I have stumbled upon a publication that distinguishes values so very neatly and packages each one of them with appropriate labels in terms of their priorities in twelve nation-states. The book that I am referring to is *Values Education for Dynamic Societies: Individualism or Collectivism* edited by William K. Cummings, *et al* brought out by The University of Hong Kong. Since India did not figure in this particular study I thought I might as well offer my views on the subject.

I firmly believe that no living being is devoid of values. It is another matter that the values upheld by one may be injurious to the life or property of another. But the fact remains that each individual lives by the values s/he cherishes. Similarly, each community or religious or political group can have its distinctive values. These values are given different names according to the area of their concern. For instance, one can have religious, moral or political values according to one's education, tradition or belief. When a value is stretched too far to enable one to justify one's actions, it would be rare that such a definition of a given value becomes socially acceptable. It is all right, for instance, to follow and practice one's religious values but if this act turns into a kind of crusade, then surely it would be unacceptable to many including those that have faith in that particular religion. Not many Hindus, for example, hold the activities of the VHP in high esteem just as all Muslims do not subscribe to the Jehadi viewpoint. Religious or political extremism has been with us since times immemorial. Some have suffered it, while others have staked their lives to fight against its pernicious consequences. Modern liberalism carries a history of human endeavor to give all an equal regard and give others a right to present their points of view.

The objective of the above-cited book was to describe recent developments and debates on values. Also the idea was to outline the new directions that emerge from the study. They had some very specific reasons for undertaking this study, for instance because:

1. The region is rapidly rising in importance in the new international order.

2. The region is exceptionally diverse in terms of traditions and history.

3. In many Pacific Basin settings past traditions are undergoing intensive review.

4. Much of our understanding of the region comes from research on macro issues and processes with less attention to the views of leaders, either past or contemporary.

5. Values education is a prominent part of education in most of the Pacific Basin countries. There may be lessons in all this to learn.

The 12 countries included in the present study were Thailand, Malaysia, Singapore, China, Taiwan, Korea, Japan, Russia, USA, Hawaii and Mexico. In terms of civilizations these represent European, Chinese, and the Mayan. The reported studies cover a very wide representation of elites from each country reported. For example, the study on Russia includes elites from as far distant regions as Moscow, Kemerovo and Vladivostok and in the case of the USA elites from New York, Michigan,

California and Hawaii.

I believe India too qualified for the study. This was one good reason why I have paid attention to this lacuna. I started thinking that had India been included in the present study how would have one prepared the write-up. Against the backdrop of the 2004 elections an American journalist in NYT wrote: "In a turn of events seemingly tailor-made to demonstrate India's diversity and capacity for co-existence, Mrs. Gandhi, raised a Roman Catholic, is making way for a Sikh prime minister who will be sworn in by a Muslim President A.P.J. Abdul Kalam." (TOI, May 23, 2004)

One would be hard put to discover pan-Indian values because the values Indians cherish are neatly classified as Buddhist, Jain, Hindu, Sikh, Christian or Islamic values. Differences apart, these values rarely create insurmountable problems. I made a hurried collection of some of these values to collate and compare whether or not they lead one to live a peaceful living. In the Gita, XVI / 1-3 / 17. Lord Krishna lists some as, "fearlessness, purity of heart, steadfastness in Karma yoga, austerity, uprightness, non-injury, truth, absence of anger, compassion, modesty, forgiveness, fortitude, renunciation, tranquility, absence of fickleness / hatred / pride / covetousness etc." The Vedas had earlier defined proper values as purity of body and mind, self-restraint, non-attachment, truth and non-violence. Besides these, we have Buddhist values as avoidance of two-extremes, i.e., following the theory of golden mean. And the Jains hold compassion, ahimsa, discipline in thought and action, and the pursuit of ten-fold morality and righteousness, asceticism, continence, and voluntary purity. If one went through this list of values one would discover the emphasis is on renunciation, and leading a peaceful life of co-existence. In essence, one can take it that Islam, Christianity or Sikhism would also not preach any differently. The tragedy is that what one religion preaches and practices are seldom identical with what others follow. We do not have to select any elite group in India to reach this sad conclusion.

The current loss and dissensions in the domain of values across the world is reflected in the present study. The study therefore seeks to find out values that political / social leaders believe in and the specific approaches that they have in mind for their spread and communication.

Each country sampling constitutes thirty leaders with a record of accomplishment in the field of values education. To carry out interviews expert teams were formed with at least one senior researcher and the other a junior one. At times even 'outsiders' were included. In the Pacific Basin region the thrust of the values has been to foster collective values and to de-emphasize individual values. In the European / mainstream Western thinking about modernization, primacy of individual over collective values is stressed. This then is one of the major contentious areas in the contemporary discussion on values, hence the raison d' etre for the study. If collectivism over individualism is getting defended in the North America and Western Europe the Asian side of the Pacific Basin is developing a more favorable attitude toward individualistic values. One can easily compare the recent political turmoil in India over the hegemonic ideology of a section of society over an unwilling mass of people who too had an equally strong political and social worldview. The struggle isn't over yet. What goes on constitutes contemporary history.

In the earlier times when leaders thought of new values they chose schools to promote them. But overtime most of the high raking leaders are asking schools to intensify its contribution to other forms of socialization, notably a strengthening of the academic curriculum and an increasing stress on the development of vocational skills. The curricular challenges have led to the diminution of the time and attention devoted to value education. The present publication therefore addresses this issue. I think that this conclusion too is arbitrary. No one is sure whether schools alone can do much or they are the right place to firmly implant any given idea or ideology. One could however concede the ground that schools do provide a very good platform for the propagation of certain values provided the teachers who teach them also have identical commitment and a desirable amount of missionary spirit.

In the book under reference during the course of

interviews with the elites *four* core questions were discussed:

1.Why should there be improvement in values education?

2.What values should receive greatest attention?

3.Who should be the focus of the values?

4.How should these values be developed and transmitted?

An early decision of the combined group responsible for the book was to develop a research approach that would help highlight points of divergence in the thinking of elites rather than areas of agreement. The group had concluded that diverse tendencies in values education of the region were a reflection of the emerging complexity of the contemporary life. The methodology for highlighting differences required a new survey approach, *the Sigma International Elite Survey*, complemented by careful investigations of the socio-political context in each of the Elite Survey. The special features of this Survey might interest Indian researchers; therefore, they are being reported here;

1.The intentional selection of an elite sample from each setting that represents important points of variation in terms of political / ideological affiliation, social position, gender, and regional location;

2.The development of questions that reflect the particular concerns of each setting;

3.The use of a question format that requires respondents to clarify where they stand, (e.g., rank-ordering from a list with many options); and

4.Follow-up questions to selected respondents who take exceptional positions on particular responses.

If the findings of the research suggest that different nation-states have differing value scales, even within the same nation-state also they vary with each change in the government. For instance, if the INC-governed India purportedly declares to have one type of ideology, the BJP-governed India reportedly opted for very different values. The political ideologues tend to define their group values in the hope that their values would help them remain in power for a long duration of time. In the case of India unfortunately it does not happen that way. This type of discussion has been going on in other nations as well like Russia and China. In fact, it would be interesting to discern the subtle differences in the use of terms like secular, democratic, people-oriented policies and so on. If approached all political parties would like to swear by their commitment to any or all of these together. The truth is that American democracy is nowhere near the democracy Great Britain happens to practice or the absolute anarchic democracy that India boasts of. But no one will say that each of these countries cited are not democratic. What I am trying to say is that the use of common terms and concepts can be very deceptive. One can discover the meaning of a concept in relation to the context in which it is used. There is a very old story commonly heard in Indian villages. Once a Brahmin was stumped when a butcher asked him whether he had seen his runaway cow. If he said yes the religion did not allow him, if he said no his personal ethics would be jeopardized. I suspect all of us face this dilemma when asked to be precise and specific. As long as we are vague and deal in generalities we are safe. The moment we come out of our individual grooves we stand exposed.

We should not forget that over a period of time values change even within individual societies. For instance, the Vedas talk of a democracy where leaders were elected. Beyond this notional or terminological similarity there is nothing in common between today's Indian democracy and the one that was practiced some three millennia before. Historically the causes for change may be political, social or predatory. But societies are seen to change dramatically. For instance, Indian society has historically witnessed numerous changes. The Vedas defined one type of society and the Buddhists defined another. If revivalist Hindu defines it one way, the Islam and Christianity surely have their own definitions and those too may be very different. Each definition thus bears the characteristic features of the religion they preach or practice. Political definitions too come to add their political views and values. For instance, if the

BJP swore by the Hindtuva of their dreams, the Left never forgot to respond to the call of their proletariat.

Let us assume that I also had an occasion to follow the same technique that this study has adopted and I too could cover the same type of sample in this country. What would be the result of that study? I have hypothesized while presenting the following picture as I think it shall emerge. Let me therefore take up each question seriatim.

The first question is: Why should there be improvement in values education?

In India answers to this question would come according to the group one queried. For instance, today the INC – dominated Alliance would say that because the earlier government distorted the Indian values, which regard everyone equal and wherein all religions have to be accorded equal respect. This did not happen therefore some improvement in the contemporary situation has become absolutely necessary. This is only one set of a political reply. The social response would depend upon the region and the community one put this question to. In brief, the responses can be very varied. In terms of social responses the answers region-wise would be enchantingly colorful. For instance, a Meghalaya youth would differ markedly from a Bihari youth or a Keralite youth. It is impossible in India to have any pan-Indian response. Only, people will agree on the values as defined in the Constitution of India. There is no possibility that on any other ground could one across a wide consensus.

2. What values should receive the greatest attention?

All honest Indians would like to be free to pursue their own life without too much State interference. Indian society is basically freedom loving. Its concept of freedom verges close to anarchy. Indians by nature abhor discipline. This may sound strange, but the truth is that Indian diversity alone is a living testimony to this innate desire. Conformism may be a choice but its option cannot be made obligatory.

But let us look at what the book under reference has to say on this point. To some extent I tend to agree with the rank order given on p. 255. It says according to its survey the rank order was

Civic values 1

Democracy 2

Work values 3

National Identity and Patriotism 4

Moral values 5

Personal autonomy 6,

And so on.

I do not think many will differ with this rank order. Except for the hypocrites all would prefer to place moral values several notches down below other listed values. No one knows what these moral values are. One can use terms like truth, justice, peace etc. as moral values but then there can be no agreement on their definition. There is nothing like absolute truth or absolute justice. All these terms are contextual and explainable in terms of some immediate reference. There is nothing universal or eternal about them. While the terms may remain the same, one the context is changed their usage are bound to differ. If we forget this we forget everything else.

Interestingly the book also furnishes a list of controversial issues in the Thailand's Values Education, i.e., on, which there is, no general agreement. They too have their rank order. For instance, the first rank is given to the issue

Schools should foster values supporting the family, such as respect for the parents, fidelity, and taking care of children and elders.

The next rank is given to the point:

Girls have essentially the same talents as boys and should be given equal opportunities and encouragement in schools.

Then we have: Schools should promote a truly global view of the world, or Schools should help young people appreciate the essential role of unions in guaranteeing safe work conditions and fair wages, etc.

3. Who should be the focus of the values?

The answer would have to be "the growing child." But as we answer the question we should realize that in a country like India where school–going population is around 65% only, of which girls are much less than the boys, and where higher education is limited to less than 10% of the college–going population, the answer is both incomplete and considerably vague and irrelevant. Let us see what the Chinese response is like.

Who should receive civic education?

1. Pre-school children and toddlers	1. College students
2. Working teachers	2. High school students

The following table is interesting, which tells about

Greatest and the Least Need for Values Education

Top 3 groups	Bottom 3 groups
1. Working teachers	**1. High School students**
2. Toddlers	**2. Students in teachers colleges**
3. Pre-school children	**3. Middle school children**

I am quite sure this cannot be the case in India. It would be unwise not to say that those who preach the values the most also need them too. Being what we are, we love to pontificate but seldom practice what we preach.

4. How should these values be developed and transmitted?

The Indian answer would be: that values need to be taught through all social, political and religious institutions.

Let me cite an example from the book where a particular response to the query Why should there be Values Education? is summarized on p.286.

Develop reflective/autonomous personalities. The Nation-wise response according to rank order is as follows:

Russia 2, Japan 1, Taiwan 1, Mexico 1. USA 6, Singapore 9, Thailand 10,Korea 1, China 6

To try explaining this response will require going into the cultural and political history of each country. This is what makes the values education at once important and ridiculously simplistic.

Let us stop pontificating. Instead, let us think of what is important for the generations that would come to follow us. Also, let us remember that there is nothing eternal in the world, and that there is no society that is happy with the values it cherishes or follows.

11

The Central Advisory Board of Education (CABE)

The Origin

Indian history has neither ever known nor experienced the existence of a body like the one, which the Calcutta Commission proposed for the first time in 1919. During its life time, i.e., as and when it has been allowed to function, it has been responsible for many an important academic decision and has also been witness to numerous serious debates on varied topics concerning educational content, structure, stages, policies and efficient governance. In one way the history of Central Advisory Board of Education is also the history of the progress of Indian education as such, both during the British regime and after India attained her Independence in 1947. The CABE has been a most remarkable institution having remained forever a beacon of light to those that went to it for guidance in the wilderness of conflicting opinions. If it served the interests of contemporary leadership by upstaging their opinions, it never allowed itself to be a party to any sales promotion for what it considered unworthy of public attention and always spurned the overtures of market forces. In the following few paragraphs I have attempted an outline of the history of CABE since its inception for the reader to arrive at his / her own independent decision.

The Calcutta University Commission (1917-1919) headed by Sir Michael Sadler recommended "that the Government of India can perform an invaluable function by defining the general aims of educational policy, by giving advice and assistance to local governments and to universities, by acting as an impartial arbiter in cases of dispute, by helping to obtain the service of scholars from other countries, by co-coordinating the work of various universities, and by guarding against needless duplication and overlapping in the provision of the more costly forms of education." *Ch. XXVIII, Para 27*

"The Government of India accepted these recommendations because it realized that a central organization was neededfor coordinating the policies of different provincial governments as the first step toward evolving a common national policy. While this recommendation by itself was meant to resolving problems concerning uniformity in policy making and for taking a comprehensive, homogeneous view of education per se but numerous complications arose because of the Government of India Act of 1919. Firstly, because Education was given to the Provinces to manage therefore it fell under transferred category. The main question that logically arose was whether the Government of India now really needed a body like the one recommended by the Sadler Commission. After a very close examination of the issues involved in the matter the *Secretariat Procedure Committee* of the Government suggested that such a body when created would have only a limited power in reality. In place of executive powers such a body will have to exercise its powers through moral persuasion. "It will or should tend more and more to become *a center of the best information, research and advice.*" The committee also felt that, " in the new set up, the creation of a central organization for the purpose was absolutely necessary, in fact even more necessary than in the past." (Silver Jubilee Souvenir, 1960; p.1)

As we go through the historical reasons for the creation of the CABE, we must *firstly*, remember that we are talking of British India in the first quarter of the twentieth century when the administrative noose around its weak neck was fairly tight and when more than 600 Indian princes shared their powers with the colonial masters in such geographical regions where the latter did not directly govern. The British India then included Burma as well, which is now a separate country. *Secondly,* the colonial powers were not so much interested in providing education for all *but in its control* with whatever existed or got provided in the name of education. Many an Indian educationists have committed the mistake of regarding the British as an enlightened people who had come to India for giving this country light and education. The fact is contrary to this assumption. These alien rulers were business people and whatever benefited their business alone received top priority. Their CABE was intended to oversee

Indian education as a whole and try to prevent all attempts to subvert the foreign rule. The potential of education to subvert a political system is an acknowledged reality and no government whether colonial or otherwise could possibly overlook this reality. What I am saying is that the functions of the bodies like the one the British created and the body that functioned after Independence are two radically different organizations with very distinctly different functions and objectives, the similarities in the names notwithstanding. I would also like to make clear that the urgency shown and the need for such an organization to be revived then and the need to do so now also have very distinctly different objectives. To differentiate between the motives of the two most dissimilar realities is not very difficult to see.

With this small though necessary digression let us continue with our story.

Consequent upon this recommendation of the Secretariat Procedure Committee the Government of India constituted a "Central Advisory Board of Education" in the year 1920. In a Government of India letter no.1060 dated August 21, 1920 its functions were described and defined thus: -

5. "The Government of India desire that it should be clearly understood that this body would possess purely advisory functions. It will be open to the Governor –General, should he desire to make a visitation of any university with reference to which he is empowered by statute to make such visitation, to utilize the proposed Board or certain members of the Board for purposes of inspection. But, apart from its use by the Governor- General for such statutory purposes, the Board will have no administrative functions. Nor will it in any sense interfere with the control of education, which will be a provincial transferred subject. It is possible that the Government of India may entrust to it the conduct of certain examinations, which they will control, but this question has not yet been decided.

6. Apart therefore from its position as an agency for the exercise by the Governor-General of his visitorial powers mentioned above, the function of the Board will, as regards

local governments be restricted to the giving of advice whenever they ask for advice and, as regards the Government of India to the assistance of the Department of Education in such educational questions as will still come within the purview of the Imperial Government and may be referred to the Board by the Member-in- Charge of Education. The precise duties, which it will be convenient to attach to it, will become clearer after it gets to work.

Following functions were suggested out of which the Board was expected to make its choice for performance:

1. The visitation of universities on behalf of the Governor-General as Visitor.

2. The giving of advice regarding the equivalence of examination standards.

3. The scrutiny of any points of university legislation which is either subject to Indian legislation or reserved, when the Government of India refer such points to it.

4. The giving of advice regarding the management of Imperial institutions.

5. The production of occasional reports, monographs on special forms of education, etc.

6. The conduct of educational surveys whenever required, and

7. The conduct of such examinations may be entrusted to it.

For the due performance of most of these functions, it will be necessary to collect a body of authorities who are not merely experts in educational matters but will have knowledge of the conditions in different provinces and whose names will carry weight and influence. The intention of the Board, in fact, is to link the Department of Education more closely with the various official and non-official educational authorities and institutions throughout India.

It was stipulated that the constitution of the Board would be largely non-official. Its composition was to have:

1. The Educational Commissioner with the Government of India as Chairman.

2. An expert member from the U.K. whenever required.

3. Two Vice-Chancellors of universities in India, one of them will be a whole time officer.

4. Two Principals of privately managed colleges,

5. Four D.P.I.'S

6. Four non-officials who, though not immediately engaged in education, are interested in the subject.

With the exception of 1,who is appointed by the Governor General in Council, the others members of the Board will be appointed by the Member-in Charge of Education with the approval of the Governor–General. In addition to the above, departments dealing with technical education in any of its branches will be invited to send representatives to take part in the deliberations regarding any technical matter that may be included in the agenda of a meeting. It is clearly necessary that a permanent official of the Government of India should hold the Chairmanship of the Board. The Educational Commissioner will also be able to conduct correspondence with members of the Board on questions, which have been referred to the Board but cannot conveniently be postponed to the next meeting.

The tenure of office of the two vice-chancellors (who will be selected as members) will be two years and the tenure of the rest of the members (except the first two) will be three years each.

The meetings of the Board will be held quarterly—the first being in February next at Delhi—and agenda of each meeting, as approved by the Member- in-Charge of Education, will be circulated sufficiently in advance of the date thereof to enable members to come prepared with their opinions. It will be necessary and desirable to conduct some of the business of the Board by correspondence.

This in brief is the story of the birth of CABE but before we deal with its actual performance it is necessary for us to interpret everything related to its inceptions, regulations and the functions. We must bear in mind that the CABE of 1920 was meant to perform the functions for the benefit of a colonial power. The purpose of their administration was to control and regulate education in such a manner that people came to learn and realize that they were welcome to be free only within a given frame.

The proposed functions of CABE underwent changes several times right from the conception until its actual birth. For example, the Calcutta University Commission had conceived of it as a policy-defining body, a body that would render advice and offer assistance to both local bodies as well as to the universities—in brief, to the entire system of education, and also function as an arbiter in cases of disputes while protecting disregarded interests. They also thought of it as a coordinating body for the universities and help save money by avoiding unnecessary duplication. To me it appears to have been conceived as a very powerful body, only if it could have been allowed to take birth.

But in reality what did finally take shape under the British was a pale shadow of the real with its powerful wings having been clipped and the sharp beak muzzled. The Proceedings of the Department of Education, August 1920, Nos. 15-16 allowed the CABE to emerge as a purely advisory body with no executive powers whatsoever. It was expected to perform most of the functions, which today are routinely performed by the Association of Indian Universities, the UGC and the statistical division of the MHRD. The rest is done in the Executive Councils / Committees of bodies like the NCERT, NIEPA, AICTE etc. This body originally was expected to offer advice only when asked. On its own it was not to perform anything more. For all governments at New Delhi both foreign as well as native the temptation has always been to centralize power and give the country a national system. But the reality has always defied this expectation. The pulls and pressures of the regional groups and cultures have rarely allowed a national perspective to emerge. This was true then (1920's) as it is true even now in the Lord's year 2003 when we are an Independent nation.

The socio-political conditions were such that a body like the one that the alien rulers had created did not go well with all sectors of Indian populace. The reasons why the Indian intelligentsia did not uniformly welcome a body like the CABE lay in India's contemporary political and socio-economic scenario. For a detailed discussion one has to go through the history of National Council of Education and the Swadeshi Movement that ran self-supporting institutions, which flourished outside the purview of the Government control and supervision. For instance, Tagore had already opened his school at Bolpur and the Indian National Congress wanted to promote a self-financing educational system that would be particularly useful to the Indian masses and while in action would also remain outside both the control and supervision of the alien governance. There were numerous other unresolved problems like the medium of instruction, its script and textbooks etc. People like Mahatma Gandhi, Aurobindo Ghose, and Tagore etc. had their own opinion on all these issues. Politically too the INC and The Muslim League were not expected to be unanimous or agree to co-operate. It was not possible for any alien government to resolve these problems amicably. Considering that education had the potential to be an explosive affair the Government wanted to rope in as many native intellectuals as possible to provide semblance of trying to govern by consensus. The CABE could supposedly provide that forum.

There appear to be two very different reasons why this body was created. One of the two reasons has already been referred to. The other one is clearly implied since it happens to be universal. No Government is— be it national or alien, interested in providing any facility/service to any public let alone education, which is an investment unless it brought in some direct or indirect benefit. The central government in India has always been interested in an educational policy that it could dictate and supervise. Before the British the Mughals wanted to do so and later the East India Company and its successors wished to pursue the same very logical endgame.

It would be pertinent to refer to the address delivered by Sir Girija at the time of the revival of the CABE in 1935. It would also be instructive to go through some of the criticisms, which the Board had to meet at its revival. As is well known the Board functioned only for a brief period of about two years and could manage to hold only five meetings.

In the year 1923 due to financial stringencies it was abolished and remained frozen until 1935 when it was revived once again and this time with the single handed efforts of Sir Girija Shankar Bajpai. Considering the political turmoil the country was already going through it was only natural that all political parties were not expected to hold identical views on matters educational. One has only to consider the agitating mood in which as a political party the Indian National Party already was. The various pulls and pressures within this party only added to the woes of the rulers. In his inaugural address as the Chairman of CABE Sir Girija defined the powers of the Board and met its criticism on its own turf. "A very dear and distinguished friend, who will remain nameless, told me the other day that the Board had been criticized as the superfluous revival of the lifeless piece of machinery; a body without executive power, and, therefore, without utility. "The Chairman's response was" to the extent that this criticism alludes to the educational autonomy of the provinces and states it is true, but nothing new or disheartening. None of us would, even if we could, centralize educational initiative or control; one might as well attempt an educational Pan- Europa, and with equal chances of success."

The reasons given against centralization are valid even today. Not only is centralization politically unthinkable, administratively too it was impracticable. Therefore the then Chairman defined "the main function of the Board as ' to sift and cohere the current educational thoughts of the day and to impart to what may result from such creative effort the lasting impulse of a progressive policy." He further stated, "If we fail in making the Board useful... it will be either the advice we give is unsound or the springs of action in the provinces fail to move. Either may happen, but it is a singularly barren form of pessimism to make that possibility the basis of a condemnation of the Board in advance." Then he delivered the severest of the blows to the critics when he said " Destructive perfection is not difficult of attainment; constructive effort, however, imperfect, is frequently of greater value. "(Souvenir Volume, p.15) Evaluated against the backdrop of today's performances of different states in the area of education it would appear that the springs of action in most cases have either dried up or been politically blocked.

However, the revival of the CABE in 1935 did meet as expected with a stiff opposition from the Indian National Congress. The grounds offered were "purely political." In the Standing Finance Committee when the proposal for the revival of the CABE came up for approval the three members of the Congress (Pandit Govind Ballabh Pant, Sri Srikrishna Sinha and Sri T.S. Avinashlingam Chettiar) in the Committee opposed it saying that they were unable to accept it since "it was based, to some extent, on a recommendation made in the report of the Joint Parliamentary Committee." In fact what they were objecting to was not the expenditure on the CABE or the need for such a body, but the source of the suggestion, which lay in the British Parliament. Also because in the very same year, i.e., 1935 education as a subject had been transferred to the provinces through Government of India Act. The INC was currently not interested that the center should continue to supervise an area of governance, which was their exclusive preserve as they were in power in most of the British India.

Whether or not a body like the present one was needed read the following quote from a contemporary newspaper. The Hindu reported on 23-6-1934.

Questioned if the objects in contra-distinction to producing self-supporting national minded workers, Mr. Gandhi said that the attention of workers should be directed to the creation of village workers as opposed to city workers. That should be the primary object of national education. Mr. Gandhi opined that primary education was most needed in the system of national education. He approved of the ideal of an All-India National Education Board, but said that the time was not yet ripe for such measures, but it depended on workers to prove its utility and for bringing such a proposal before the next Working Committee meeting. Mr. Gandhi emphasized the need for public education as part of national education.

If critically examined this press coverage explains that although a Central organization to deal with education was necessary but there ought to be some kind of consensus on the aims and the level of education needed for the country. Secondly, the area of education that needed to be addressed first was to be primary education and the clientele the village youth as opposed to urban kids who could somehow fend for themselves. Since the vast majority came from villages, education, in order to be national in outlook and self- supporting in its mode of operation, must be imbued with the spirit of nationalism, which without doubt had to be its principal goal. The education being provided by the then government served none of these objectives. Hence, his opposition.

But then Gandhi was not the only one to oppose there were others – equally condemning and distrustful of the Government and its policies. The string of Gurukulas was yet another manifestation of disagreement. The Indian Muslim League did not lag very much behind in their disagreement although the ground in their case were distinctly different both in content and tenor.

Going through the Government of India Act of 1935 one can understand that the Act could not satisfy the nationalist aspiration for both political and economic power. The INC found to its dismay that through a series of special powers the Governor General continued to retain lots of administrative powers. Therefore, the Congress declared the Act itself as "totally disappointing". If there were supposedly valid reasons to winding up the CABE in 1920, there were reasons galore to let that body to have been kept in animated suspension for a much longer time until the Indian's themselves controlled their destiny.

It is necessary to recall the reasons why the Board had to be wound up. It was said:

"In view of the essential modification of the position of the Central Government vis-à-vis the Provinces under the Reform Scheme in respect of education and medical administration, which are now transferred subjects over which the Government of India exercise a very limited control, we do not consider that there is any justification for the retention of the Educational Commissioner, the Bureau of Education, or the Central Board, costing about Rs. 100,000/- or indeed, for the continuance of the department as a separate entity."

We have already gone through the reasons for opposition from the side of the INC let us in brief recount now the unhappiness expressed at this rather 'unfortunate' decision for its discontinuance. As early as 1925, the revival of the CABE was discussed in the Government of India "The need for a central agency" was an item of Agenda of the Conference of Ministers, which got convened in Delhi in January 1927. Somehow the item never came up for discussion. In 1928 the Hartog Committee, which reported in 1928, dealt with the role of the Government of India in education at some length, and recommended very strongly that the CABE be revived at the earliest.

These were the days of world economic depression and any proposal that had anything to do with additional expenditure was resisted by the Finance Department. Though for activating the CABE a meager Rs.43, 000/- was needed in the first year and Rs. 58, 800/ in the subsequent years. The Department of Education, Health and Lands however didn't take the refusal kindly and the Member-in-Charge returned the case to Finance Committee observing: "We must proceed with the scheme. I wanted to set up the organization in 1931. That would involve expenditure for 4 months only. If the Finance Department would rather, we did not do so in November 1931, we might put it off till1st January 1932—thus needing funds for two months only. If the Finance Department insists upon shelving the scheme, I am afraid the case will have to be taken to His Excellency the Governor-General." The Finance Department was not only adamant but stuck to its guns: "The Finance Department is concerned with the practical question of the provision of funds to finance the scheme and it certainly cannot commit itself to the expenditure of money, which it has not got and sees no prospect of getting. That means that unless, the entirely unexpected happens, there is no chance of financing this scheme for any part of 1931-32."

The case was, therefore, taken up by His Excellency, the Governor –General, who approved the proposal of reviving the CABE and the Central Bureau of Education in principle. It was decided to address a letter to the provincial governments for ascertaining their views on the problem and to discuss the matter again in the light of replies that might be received. The letter addressed to provinces is important because it gives a glimpse into the history of the bodies in education sector that functioned at the headquarters.

Let me cite here a letter written by Mahatma Gandhi, which I am surprised, has been thoroughly misunderstood by many. The letter written on Feb. 21, 1947 relates to the Presidential Address delivered by Maulana Azad. The letter is critical of the message that Azad probably wished to communicate on issues like religious education, common script and the proposal for military training by the Indian youth. Read the following letter written to E.W.Aryanakum, Secretary, Hindustani Talimi Sangh and published in Harijan, 23-3-1947, i.e., only four months before India won its Independence. None of the three items he referred to was ever implemented for a variety of reasons. But the contents of the letter are nonetheless quite interesting to go through, largely because they continue to be relevant. But he somehow neither opposed the need for a body like the CABE nor did he say a word against the way it functioned.

The first item is about religious instruction / education and ethics on this Gandhi says" I do not believe that the State can concern itself or cope with religious education. I believe that religious education must be the sole concern of religious association. Do not mix up religion with ethics. I believe that fundamental ethics is common to all religions. Teaching of fundamental ethics is undoubtedly a function of State. By religion I have not in mind fundamental ethics but what goes by the name of denominationalism. We have suffered enough from State-aided religion and State Church. A society or a group, which depends partly or wholly on State aid for the existence of its religion, does not deserve or, better still, does not have any religion worth the name."

"The second point deserving attention in the report in question is," wrote Gandhi, "regarding the replacing of the Urdu and Nagari scripts by the Roman script. However attractive the proposition may appear to be and whatever is true of the Indian soldiers, in my opinion the replacing would be a fatal blunder and we would find ourselves in the fire having come out of the frying pan."

The third thing he went on to say was "reference to military education. I think we have to wait a long time before a nationwide decision on the point is made. Otherwise, we are likely to become a curse rather than a blessing to the world. Leaders are not made, they are born. Should the State be in a hurry over this matter even before full independence is established? Therefore I am surprised that the CABE should be a party to such a sweeping recommendation as they have made."

The Educational Advisor to the Government of India, Dr. Tara Chand, in his address to the CABE in January 1951 defined its functions a little differently than its alien forbears had done couple of decades back. He said, "This is as it should be. India is one and indivisible and so are its problems, especially of education. For the coherence, solidarity and strength of the nation largely depend upon common attitudes of mind and common ideals, which all strive to realize together and education is the means for the attainment of these ends.

"And if I may, shall I say that the Government of India look upon this all India Advisory Board as the extra-constitutional Parliament for the formulation of these ideas and ends? Although the Board has no legal or statutory authority, it has a moral authority, which the Government of India has treated as biding and which I hope the state governments are treating in the same manner. The authority of the Advisory Board is derived solely from the willing consent and cooperation of its members—among whom are responsible education ministers and accredited leaders of education in India. The cooperation of the Ministers gives that touch of realism and of what is capable of translation into practice without which our decisions would be like castles in the air, and the presence of eminent educationists guarantees that the Board will not allow itself to be overwhelmed by consideration of administrative convenience and will keep steadily before its gaze the goals towards which society should move.

"Education is an all-India affair, and education is an organic whole. It is difficult to determine priorities in its different aspects. We cannot say that for this year or during the next five years we will pay less attention to higher education or secondary education and concentrate only on basic and social education."

If read carefully the cited part of the Educational Advisor's speech suggests that despite the absence of any legislation regarding the powers of the CABE it in reality functioned as a very powerful instrument of implementing its own evolved policies. The various sub-committees of the CABE eventually found that their recommendations were uniformly and invariably accepted by all unhesitatingly. What greater power does a statutory body enjoy which this one without any such legal backup did not exercise in reality? The common perception is that power springs from the letters of the law but they apparently have no idea that this may not always happen. The springs of powers in Free India have their sources continuously changing course in accordance with the whims and fancies of the changed ruling party. Not unlike political ideologies education as an area of activity too these days evokes extraordinarily heightened emotional feelings.

We should also briefly mention that the CABE has seldom been criticized for its irrelevance and the desire of all governments down the history has been to control education in the interest of their own governments. It all depends on the efficiency or inefficiency of the government the way it achieves its objective. Some do it better than the others but act they must.

Performance Appraisal— (A study into its agenda items)

In the following few pages I present a brief note on the CABE and its various agenda items. The idea is to lay stress on the point that a huge, multi-lingual, multi-cultural and multi-party nation like India cannot survive without a forum like the CABE where the best available brains reflect on educational policies and offer their considered advice and make informed decisions. If past is any guide one can look forward to continue supporting an institution that has always stood in good stead.

We should remember that with the passage of time we have reached a stage when it has become necessary that someone should examine critically the performance of the CABE both as a forum for enlightened discussion and policy making. An attempt is therefore being made to present area-wise deliberations of the CABE and relate the same to the actions taken on each one of them. The success or failure of a suggestion / scheme reveals only a part of the tale whereas most of the indicators remain hidden from public view. Also, we cannot offer any opinion on the real constraints that made or marred the success of a given proposal. The important point to remember is that after 1951 the Center had the benefit of planning for the entire country through its Statutory Body—the Planning Commission. Still, the stand of the Government of India has been that "education needs a common platform where the center and the states can meet together and take joint decisions of policy. It is precisely this platform at the highest level, which the Central Advisory Board of Education has provided... It has been a practice of the Ministry of Education to refer every important problem in education to the Board for its opinion and advice." (Souvenir pp. IV and V).

Listed below are some of the major concerns of the Ministry of Education referred to the CABE for advice and opinion. Before India became free the CABE carried out the functions of policy making as well as of being a referral body. It also provided the alien rulers a forum where the elite among the subject people could help them appear both benign and open. Also, the idea was to appear to the natives that the rulers took them through their representatives into confidencc when taking policy decisions. Clearly, the CABE served several of the governments' explicit and implicit purposes. If the objectives and the uses of the CABE underwent a change with the change in Governments it does not imply that at any point in time it was set up or used merely as a front for soliciting public approval. The major difference after its revival in 1935 however lay mainly in the frequency of holding its meetings, which changed from being quarterly to annually probably purely for reasons of financial constraints both before and after Independence.

If one were to go through the list of MHRD's publications the one's ascribed to CABE make very interesting and informed reading. The list includes committee reports on subjects like Wardha Scheme, Teacher Training, consideration of topics like controversies in curriculum, Engineering Education, English Teaching, Equipments for Engineering Education, Examinations and Examination Reforms, Education in Foreign Countries especially Adult Education, Rural Education etc., Education of Factory Children, Textbooks Committee Report 1949; Religious Education, the question of medium of instruction in Higher Education, Agricultural Education etc.

Lest we forgot to analyze the content of the proceedings it may be remembered that the CABE conferences usually began with the address of the Ministers of Education, which in a way decided the agenda of the conference. These addresses are informative and carried contemporary concerns of the Ministry. As and when the Minister himself could not address, the substitute was rarely a person less than Education Secretary. This clearly shows that the Conference was taken seriously and the discussions remained well focused. It was here that all reports on education whether submitted by departmental committees, commissions or the committees appointed by the CABE were discussed. If no consensus could be evolved the matter was referred to a committee by it to report and then the same was taken up for discussion and resolution after the same had been submitted. The three topics that came for repeated discussion were religious education, basic education and the question of script for Hindi and Urdu. If teachers Training remained a matter of concern so did higher education, examination reforms and the like. The Hartog Committee, the report on Post-War Reconstruction—popularly known as Sargent Committee report, Wardha Scheme, Radhakrishnan Commission Report etc along with all policy resolutions of the Government were discussed at some stage in the CABE first. The 1968 and 1986 Policies on Education of the Government went through the CABE.

Today in the year 2005 the CABE stands revived and the work that it used to do in the past it has once again started undertaking. Whether or not it will ever have the same standing as originally it had; and, undertake research it did undertake once upon a time are doubtful assertions. But the fact remains that it has become functional.

It is fairly important that some serious research were undertaken on the proceedings of the CABE and reports brought out on all its committees —especially on those that were set up to come out with some meaningful recommendations that had future-oriented agenda in mind. It has been one area, which no one has so far found worth serious investigation. Personally I regret this neglect or shall I say over-sight? Who knows?

SECTION D
PROSPECTS AND THE ENDGAME

12

Revolutionalizing Rural Education – Reality Behind the Potential

(Designing New Strategies for Sarva Shiksha Abhiyan)

(We are on the threshold of a revolution that is bound to catapult the present rural infra-structural backwardness into modern day urban facilities and make available opportunities of the most advanced societies in our own backyard. We discuss here two unrelated exclusive Indian achievements and examine their potential for our use.)

According to an old and familiar saying "India lives in its villages." Their infra-structural backwardness continues to hog limelight. While lack of electricity is a national phenomenon lack of connectivity falls in the rural domain. Even so villages today are no longer idyllic. They are changing and changing very fast. Today's average villager expects to receive all that is freely available in the urban areas. He finds no reason to feel satisfied with his old ways of life and living. This means that education has become essential for the fructification for one's dreams. Any comprehensive analysis of India's illiterate population would reveal that most of this segment constitutes rural population, migrant labor, street children, tribal people and the physically or mentally challenged. The means to reach them out either do not exist or society per se has accepted that they are unreachable therefore they are unteachable as well. Even in the urban areas where education is seemingly being provided to all it has little to commend itself. In fact, the infrastructure that makes education an enjoyable experience (notwithstanding Prof. Yash Pal) simply does not exist.

Two unrelated exclusive Indian achievements have the potential to transform rural economy and connectivity. In fact, when fully operational the problems of rural migration to urban centers will become history. These are: an exclusive educational satellite in the space called Edusat and the use of hydrogen for running motors. In other words the best of education can now reach the remotest corners of the country and that too at a nominal cost and similarly electricity through hydrogen-driven motors without much bother. Within a couple of months (not years) we can see a transformation of Indian society never imagined ever before.

We have therefore to identify and target relevant groups where they exist and offer them an education, which is both 'relevant' and meaningful. The term 'relevant' here does not connote that education should merely enable one to remain rooted to way of life one has been used to living. Instead, it should succeed in breaking barriers that have forced one to start loving the monotony of routine in place of adventure. The reasons why the West could advance so much lay in its education becoming a source of adventure and innovation. The ability to take risks, think independently and create conditions that are conducive for growth besides being ambitious explain to a large extent the sprint the West took in the past couple of centuries. Things are changing in Asia and Oceania. I wish we too in India acknowledged this reality and encouraged the spirit.

In my view, we should prepare a blueprint for identifying different segments of population that need to be approached for getting educated. While collecting and interpreting Census data it is possible to prepare a comprehensive plan for an all-out approach to access target groups. The first step in the series of measures that we ought to take is to have access to educational institutions. With the help of current levels of technology it is no longer a pipedream to be able to do so. For once the technology would help the teacher to reach the target group. Distances can be covered in no time and meaningful education can be offered at the time convenient to the learner. It is now possible to create multiple plans of varying levels of specialization and offer them simultaneously. This is where the intelligent use of technology can yield the best of the results.

Now let us consider what needs to be provided first, i.e.,

what kind of infrastructure is imperative for our game plan to succeed. The entire modern technology is dependent on the process and availability of connectivity. If we are able to connect with our target groups / audience the first stage will have been covered. All kinds of problems exist in the first stage itself. We are woefully short of electricity. States like Uttar Pradesh, Bihar, Rajasthan and Madhya Pradesh have very little electricity. The alternative sources of providing the same too are in a miserable state of development. The wind power, sun power and even atomic power have failed to reach people. The technology to reach people is dependent on the availability of electricity or else how do we connect? This is one area that demands our attention on a priority basis. There is no alternative way to circumvent this stage of development. In fact, this question relates to a stark reality. We must continue to make efforts and keep thinking of tapping perennial energy sources. Indian scientists have already started working on these lines. One isn't sure though that they are anywhere near a breakthrough. The moment we are able to find or create alternatives for the availability of inexpensive energy sources half of the battle that we must wage to become an advanced nation will have been won. On December 2, 2004 the national dailies reported that hydrogen has been successfully tested to run motorcars and all kinds of engines. Tomorrow's electricity generators, if run on hydrogen, can give our rural schools both light and connectivity. We seem to be very close to a breakthrough in the field. In the meanwhile the rural areas where our eternal source of electricity generation exists its use is highly recommended. I am talking here about the sun-power. Also, there is a possibility to start using methane gas for generating power. At least in this regard villages are more suitably placed than the urban areas. In fact, the idea is to make each village independent in terms of power generation by using renewable sources of energy. Tomorrow's planning must concentrate on exploiting these perennially renewable sources of energy. The implications of this kind of approach, hardly needs any particular emphasis.

The second part of the plan constitutes identification and bringing together of the target groups to a common point where they could access 'virtual classroom' technology at any point of time without interruption. We may meantime recount that what is already available can be used with considerable acumen and economy for the benefit of our people. Let us not forget that we are the only country in the world, which has successfully placed an exclusive educational satellite (indigenously prepared and launched) in the orbit. The *Edusat* as it is being called is going to have 72 channels ready to be beamed from the height of 36,000 miles (i.e. from its geo-stationary orbit location). The entire program-preparation constituted three stages. When fully operational this satellite would offer connectivity to all levels and types of educational organizations. The second stage of the launch will cover deployment of hardware and the third or the final stage shall be reached when content-transmission starts. In fact, we are already in the game of providing education through our hub at IGNOU. The proposed satellite is going to give us far greater outreach and connectivity than hitherto possible. It is expected that this satellite would offer instructional facilities in the multi-media mode and video on demand service. We must not forget that numerous other agencies too are already providing similar services in India. They may not have educational channels like the DD at their command, but they are preparing course content in various formats and have a captive clientele too.

To cite ISRO Chairman, "Edusat is mainly intended to meet the demand for an interactive satellite–based distance education system through creating virtual classrooms at remote places in the country. It will provide connectivity to school, college and higher levels of education and also to support non-formal education including developmental communication. It is specially configured for audio-visual medium, employing digital interactive classroom and multi-media multi-centric system. Edusat will be ready for use in about two months (i.e. before Dec. 2004)."

He further explained, " Indian space program has been tuned to meet the national requirements in a self-reliant manner." This statement has significance for us. This means we can place other satellites in the space if this one fails to meet all our requirements. The scope of the Edusat program will be fully operational in three phases.

There are several agencies both at the center and the states levels that are already generating content for transmission. For instance, the CEC, IGNOU, NCERT, NCTE etc. have for long been generating content ready for transmission. In fact, 4 channels are already beaming educational programs for their respective audiences through the national network. The educational hub at the IGNOU campus was beaming NCERT programs for teachers and students, SITE programs for primary schools and NIOS programs for secondary levels. The 3 existing channels that are directed to address higher education clientele are called Gyan Darshan, Ek Lavya and Vyas. Thus far they have a captive audience. While the first channel telecasts 'enrichment' programs, the second channel addresses engineering requirements and the third channel caters to the needs of higher education sector respectively. But these channels currently offer their services only to those who had access through a specially designed medium or through cables. Despite best efforts these channels have failed to generate much interest outside a limited geographical area and a highly select number of viewers. The major difference between the existing and proposed scenario is that under the proposed scheme programs could be accessed anywhere and everywhere provided one had a DTH antenna, electricity and an ordinary Television set or even PC. For the first time ever the nation was going to be blessed with numerous educational channels that will meet all kinds of requirements—regional, linguistic and informational without any intermediary intervention.

It is quite obvious that for the first time content-generation has to be Gargantuan in proportion. Not only the existing content-generators both public and private have to redouble their efforts to meet national requirements, but also the variety in terms of languages, levels, and types was expected to be enormous. The challenges posed by the Edusat launch need to be addressed on top priority basis.

A given type of technology best suited for India has been selected. The principal objective is to reach out people both nationally and regionally almost simultaneously. Therefore, 2000kg class satellite was selected, which could beam nationally as well as regionally. Since the idea was to impart instruction through this satellite, linking facilities had also to be kept in mind. The infrastructure for teaching–end had to be created and put in place. The reason why DTH was chosen is because it was thought that alternative to it was going to be both difficult and expensive. Considering future requirements, expansion of facilities and the cost of maintenance etc. besides simple features for application and speed, KU-band was found to be most suitable. Firstly, it was an international band and secondly, its vendors were easily available. This band could provide national coverage. It was a kind of extension of the existing facilities.

The basic elements of the satellite constitute a centralized Hub, various sub-Hubs and cost-wise having a receiving terminal (ROT), i.e., a passive classroom, would cost a mere Rs. 20, 000/- only. The setting up of an interactive terminal (SIT) would cost somewhere around Rs. 1.1 lakh only.

In the present case while the number of Hubs were limited, the ROTs could be as numerous as one desired. This means that signals with the help of DTH facility could be received anywhere across the country, irrespective of the terrain or the type of receiver one had – an ordinary PC or a television. The technology will suit any classroom with any number of students or the size of the classroom. In fact, for a country like India the cost of a technology mattered the most. The selected technology is most suited from this point of view as well.

One has to be introduced to two-way communication of interactive traffic, which is to be offered and explained how live programmes would be transmitted and interactivity is likely to take place. This is one stage when any place could be converted into a virtual classroom. This technology offered the facility of both on-line and off-line accessing.

Initially the network capacity will be to have a thousand terminals but later on when the Edusat is fully operational the number could be expanded to 5000 terminals.

The Times of India (21.X.2004) editorially commented, "A focused campaign to appraise educational benefits of using EDUSAT must be initiated. The potential to network the leading hubs of technical education in the country must also be actively utilized. Further, with the satellite, literacy levels could well take a quantum leap forward. The arithmetic is easy. In the fully operational phase, the EDUSAT network is expected to support up to 1.5 lakh reception terminals. With 50 students per terminal, that works out to a figure of 7.5 million. If five such satellites can be set up, then a staggering 37 million children in remote areas could benefit at a fraction of the cost it takes the government to set up primary schools. Obviously, there will be several hurdles in the implementation process. But here at last is an opportunity provided by technology for a complete paradigm shift in our approach to education for all is no longer a pie in the sky. The answer is actually up there."

The planning has to be done at the grass-root levels. We have not only to provide connectivity but also to see that the process remains operative all the while. I think this is where we have to avoid taking risk. We cannot afford to overlook the NGOs, village elders, tribal chiefs etc. In case this is feasible one should involve social workers too but care should be taken to keep politicians away. Once the plan starts succeeding the politicians will certainly like to join the bandwagon. Care may also be taken that money required for the purpose is either minimal or it is routed through responsible hands who can be held accountable.

We have thus far never used high-tech for rural primary schools. But the stage has been reached when this process must be adopted. This technology can be used for offering the most interesting and advanced course content for the rural children. Also, it is not a very expensive process. It costs a bit in the initial stages but there after the maintenance cost alone has to be taken care of.

The third stage is to select target groups for specialized community-based learning. For instance, universities and colleges have necessarily to be selected for offering content learning. Here one visualizes the possibility of organizing virtual classroom conditions for two-way connectivity. At a given hour an entire state or the country as a whole can be covered. Of course, most of the places will have single-mode connectivity only, i.e., they merely receive a programme and for necessary guidance and question-answer sessions to be offered they wait for a while. Apart from the institutional arrangement of the type with which we are very familiar, we have to go out and interact and offer services that are beyond the ordinary. For instance, we can have programs for the working children that vary in levels and content in different rural centers. For arranging a program of this nature careful planning is imperative both for selecting content and organize target audience as and when the same can be assembled in groups. It is not only the content but also the ambience for learning is necessary. This is the most difficult part of the program. Lot of initial research into the psychology of these groups is imperative. The planning at this stage has to be delayed if it is not possible to organize classes for them or before any meaningful program is feasible to chalk out. But we must also remember that this is the largest single group that needs essential educational service. This is one group, which has not been properly addressed thus far and therefore it has remained outside both the formal and the non-formal education orbit.

The reason why I am laying more emphasis on this aspect of planning is the common desire to overlook the inconvenient parts of any process. We must resist the temptation to neglect important sectors of a plan. This planning has to be bottom up and not the vice versa, which is the usual mode. I believe that for a plan to succeed the involvement of people on a large scale is always helpful. People refuse to involve themselves in any scheme if they find that it has no meaning to them. A meaningful scheme will automatically elicit a level of public involvement that will ensure a long and enduring relationship. By implication it is bound to be an insurance against possible difficulties and glitches. Thus far our planning has been top-down. For once let us reverse the process. This would also be a measure of our testing whether or not we can become good salesmen of ideas and schemes. Only a few decades back Agriculture universities brought about a change in the age-old agricultural practices by involving farmers who were not even literates. If they sold better future the present technology is selling both – the present as well as future. Education empowers. It enriches. On top of it all it enables one to be creative. All one needs is a slight nudging and a push. And the path shall have been traversed.

13

Information Technology and The Digital Divide

Contemporary education is witness to far greater changes in both the curricula and methods of instruction in the past couple of decades than in the past couple of centuries put together. Not only we have larger numbers of peripatetic teachers, but also we have tremendous variety of institutional mobility. The tools of instruction also appear to have changed in very many ways. In a way all this constitutes globalization. Globalization per se as a concept and practice both are not new to an Indian. Indian literature both ancient and modern is replete with references declaring the world as being a single large unit and most of the time we also practice the idea literally, which holds that "the entire human race is but one family". What greater proof for this practice could one offer than to point out the presence of millions of Indians living abroad. Indian religions too have unhesitatingly been unanimous about endorsing this view. Since this concept is embedded naturally in the Indian psyche we seldom face problems on that score. We could easily cite numerous hymns and verses from Indian literature both ancient and modern to endorse the statements made here.

The theme implies that if material conditions remained unchanged the process of globalization, the world would continue to remain homogeneous and basically equal. The fact is that thus far we have neither knowledge nor experience of any society that could ever qualify to be called either equal or homogenous. To me it looks as though the Divine intention itself was not to create a world that would ever *be* so boring as to be either equal or homogenous. What perhaps is possible is *to offer an infrastructure that makes equity an achievable object.* There are several philosophical systems that decry equality but support equality of opportunity. In brief, they are all for equity. The tragedy with this almost universal desire is that it is a mere formulation of a concept and not a roadmap for an action plan.

It would be advisable not to overlook the fact that equality is an unachievable goal. In reality it is a virtual impossibility to succeed in this direction. It is both sensible and relevant to say that it is also an undesirable value because no society could ever function with that kind of an impossible reality. All of us are aware that there are two types of constructs—the real and the ideal. An Ideal is what inspires one to work hard and compete and the Real is wherein one shall always fall short of the Ideal. Life acquires meaning by our efforts to bridge the distance between the Real and the Ideal. What the ancient Indians were talking of (vasudhaiva kutumbkam) will forever remain an ideal construct even as our dream to have equity practiced in today's world becomes a virtual reality. This diversion was intentional lest we overlooked the main issues involved here. The main issue for debate in my opinion is whether or not globalization is bound to lead to digital divide. My contention in this regard is that globalization will have its impact in several other ways rather than create inequality. No society was ever equal and neither it is likely to ever become so. Inequality is embedded in the nature of society itself.

The other points relate to poverty and co-existence of numerous hierarchical layers of social and economic existence and progress. At no point of time in Indian history have we been free from the misery of poverty. Indeed, the very progress of our society has been totally unrelated to the reality of prosperity. Certain classes or castes in India have traditionally been rich at the expense of others. One needs to consult the history of our society to get an idea why prosperity has been praised by so many. Praise is invariably reserved for the rare and the exclusive. We take for granted what is readily available. Riches or fortunes are destined to be in the hands of few. We must also acknowledge the reality that Indian society is inherently and basically unequal. It is not merely the caste that divides us all but the political system that has grown overtime too has acquired a vested interest in poverty. For instance, what would happen to the Left parties if for some reason India came out of its vice-like grip of poverty? Not only will they become irrelevant because they will then lose the constituency they have thus far cultivated, they will also be forced to look for some other ideology to survive. Without going into a diversionary mode let me state here that it is not true that we have waited for countless centuries to see that as a society we should get divided digitally, we have been and are a remorselessly divided society with or without any innovation or scientific advancement. Therefore, what happens now will in no way be worse than what the existing reality is. In other words, what I am saying is that the so-called digital divide is likely to do us some good instead of something unimaginably worse.

I refuse to mourn the absence of equality in our society. The gadgetry involved in modern-day information technology and its mastery and command by a few will have on those means of transmission compares well with the inventions of gunpowder or paper or the wheel etc. Every time something new comes it takes time to percolate down to deliver its benefits universally. The ones who are fortunate or intelligent enough constitute the vanguard of prosperity. In the process they are likely to accumulate unprecedented power either of expertise or the riches. This is some kind of universal law. Nothing new is likely to happen even now. The very concept of digital divide is contextually misplaced and ill conceived.

What we must note at this juncture are a few important facts about India's new class structures. We already know that India is caste-ridden and is afflicted with regional biases with plenty of tribal dominated areas. Still, in order to describe this social reality we might as well use the well-known terms Lord C.P. Snow used some five decades back to describe the British society. *India lives on in numerous concentric circles of parallel societies with minimum number of communication channels open for any kind of dialogue.* The English speaking/knowing urban elite knows nothing or very little about the majority of non-English speaking/ knowing Indians. Thanks to oil boom the non-English knowing India's unskilled workers suddenly hit the jackpot. They built big mansions from their earnings abroad in remote villages and are even willing to invest in education for children. The classical example of this trend can be witnessed both in Kerala and Bihar. The results of their monetary investment have not been universally beneficial.

India's traditional urban elites continue to have a vested interest in the preservation of the once discredited 'British heritage.' Therefore, they read, speak and think in English and attend the same clubs as their erstwhile rulers did. They have their exclusive schools, which charge heavy fees just 'to maintain standards.' Their children go to Mission Colleges and join All-India services or the multinationals. They marry within their class and should the caste also match they then have the best of both the worlds.

India has accepted the West as a model for modernization. In the process, Indians have ceased to be prejudiced against the use of English language, which during India's struggle for freedom symbolized foreign domination. Indeed, after independence, the mastery of this language has been instrumental in creating a class of rulers who are imposing Western ideas and institutions on the non-English knowing people. If this has led to a social division of Indian people, it is helping a few to attain a good deal of prosperity at the cost of others. More so now that India has joined the WTO regime, the information technology has come to rule the roost. The implications are there for all to witness. There was a time when the Tatas and the Birlas were the richest Indian business families. Today they stand outclassed by Premji & Co.

The majority of the non-elites join government run/ grants-in-aid/charity/ municipal schools. These schools may teach the same curriculum as the elites do but here the teaching is carried on in Hindi or some regional language. And from then onwards starts the discriminatory process eventually leading these children to a future of becoming second-grade citizens. Couple of decades back there was always a possibility that few of the non-elites will crossover the dividing lines and join the mainstream elites. This is going to become unlikely now.

Educationally the great urban-rural divide has become glaring in most parts of the country. The villages do have their schools—a vast majority of them being single-teacher. The re-affirmation of faith in the Sarva Shiksha Abhiyan by the UPA notwithstanding the village school retains, by and large, its 'community center character' where all varieties of social functions including political meetings and gram panchayat sessions are held. During summer and winter breaks its buildings serves as a barat ghar (wedding-hall) or when the teacher is away which is fairly frequent the students indulge in free-for-all games. The seriousness with which the government issues fiats for running these schools is truly a mockery of commitment where even the barest minimum facilities and climate for teaching happen to be non-existent. Expecting such schools to bring up rural / tribal children ready for a highly competitive world is surely a cruel joke on an unsuspecting crowd.

All Indian cities are facing an explosion in population, a large chunk of which consists of migrant, unskilled labor, adding a shanty township each month. Since they serve as vote-banks for the ruling party before every municipal or parliamentary election, they are regularized. The inhuman conditions in which these people live are seasonally improved and gradually municipal schools start appearing as pleasant surprises in an otherwise bleak surrounding. However, what is shocking is that villages are gradually becoming slums—where the landless laborer and the old cobbler or blacksmith finds it difficult to survive. With the arrival of technology in Indian farming and the formation of co-operatives in states like Maharashtra, Gujarat, etc. rural life has become quite comfortable for the landowners even when their landholdings are not very large. With television covering most of the country's population and pocket radios available almost universally the complexion of social life is gradually getting urbanized even in remote corners of the country. While the banking services have now become available in majority of rural pockets, hoards of urban entrepreneurs have landed up in rural areas in search of cheap labor and land for their industries. The mushroom growth of plantation societies has more or less established that Indians can smell economic benefits from miles away. What I am trying to say is that even without much effort Indians seem to be happy with their socially divided existence and highly discriminating school system. If one added the presence of antiquated religious schools to this list, the divisions already in existence are arguably not dependent on any digital phenomenon.

Human progress since primitive times could be defined in terms of its march towards providing basic necessities of life to all. This progress should be seen as an effort to be creating conditions under which one could claim to have some dignity attached to human life. These efforts are definable in terms of one's ability to earn one's livelihood and to live in reasonable safety. One should also see that even this modest goal has remained elusive in majority of the cases. The enlightened people are interested to see that human past does not extend beyond the pages of history read in school days. Probably this seems to explain the choice of the present sub-theme.

Let me now take up seriatim the problems of globalization vis-à-vis India as they cover areas beyond the territorial boundaries defined in terms of nation states. However, most of the problems arise when one talks in terms of Nation-States. Several thinkers believe that since all humans belong to the same race the world must be treated as a common habitat. The political process that led to the formation of Nation States has now to be put into the reverse gear. To that end we have several world organizations trying to iron out political and other varieties of rivalries. Besides, it makes economic sense to fight jointly when faced with a common yet strong enemy. Modern technology and innovations and research are an expensive business. The EU experiment therefore should be seen against that background. This holds out a hope that something like this may have to be evolved in the Asian region too. The SAARC strikes immediately as our response to the EU model.

We can see that Europe has gradually overcome the concept of nation states and is becoming socially and economically a cohesive, competitive society. Others who had thus far not refused to be part of it are queuing up to join in. A typically Christian Europe is being wooed by a dominant Islamic country like Turkey to become a part of it. The very concept of Europe trying to unite is the result of an American threat to dominate and weaken it. Besides being a question of survival and acquiring the ability to stand up to American challenge, the economic reasons have far out-weighed other considerations. Educational system is getting defined to become an instrument of the latest warfare. Research is getting due weightage and the mobility of scholars is being deliberately promoted and encouraged. Without going into details let us accept that EU is emerging as a model of future trans-border arrangement to meet challenges of WTO and the IPR etc. The march of globalization is largely livelihood-driven. An eminent economist of Indian origin Jagdish Bhagwati is responsible for the establishment of *World Migration Organisation* and editorially The Times of India (Dec.18, 2002) has called for India to opt for Akhand pluralism. This is one reason why India has started looking invitingly toward the East. Recent moves to get gas via Bangladesh or the trading co-operation with China are all examples of our acknowledgement of the changing reality. The world has somehow been unsuccessful in retaining sacrosanct the existing political arrangement called the nation-states and its boundaries and even the national languages are gradually losing out to the dominant world language. We have today numerous world organizations promoting socio-economic unity and almost all governments are a party to their running. Even in India the dominant languages that help one to migrate from one state to another are either English or Hindi. Therefore, one must acknowledge the reality of local and regional languages losing out to politically dominant and economically helpful languages. DTH might prove to be a great help in retaining and even enriching regional and local languages. But one is unsure about their bright future.

India is unfortunately facing tremendous internal ethnic and religious problems. These biases and disagreements are preventing it to become a Nation. The tribes, castes and regions besides multiplicity of languages are preventing it to put up a combined fight on any front.

Consequently, it is the 'minority groups' among Indians that are reaping all the benefits, but as a nation we are losing out on almost all fronts. We not only lack imaginative leadership but the irresponsible behavior of the majority of our legislators gives us no hope for a better future.

Microsoft entry defines "globalization as a concept that encapsulates the growth of connections between people on a planetary scale." Globalization involves the reduction of barriers to trans-world contacts. Many believe that through it people become more able—physically, legally, culturally, and psychologically—to engage with each other in "one world".

The same write-up continues to say:

"Global connections take many forms. For instance, jet aeroplanes transport passengers and cargo across any distance on the planet within a day. Telephone and computer networks effect near-instantaneous interpersonal communication between points all over the Earth. Electronic mass media broadcast messages to world audiences. Countless goods and services (such as Nissan cars and Club Med holidays) are supplied to consumers in global markets. Moreover, some articles (including much clothing and electronics) are manufactured through trans-world processes, where different stages of production are located at widely dispersed locations on the Earth. The US dollar and the Euro are examples of currencies that have global circulation. In global finance, various types of savings and credits (for example, offshore bank deposits and Eurobonds) flow in the world as a single space. Many firms (for example, Exxon), voluntary associations (for instance, Amnesty International), and regulatory agencies (such as the World Trade Organization) operate across the globe. Climate change (so-called "global warming") and stratospheric ozone depletion are instances of anthropogenic (that is, human-induced) ecological developments that unfold on a planetary scale. Finally, people experience global consciousness, in as much as we define the realm of our lives in trans-world, planetary terms."

With globalization the world as a whole also becomes a social space in its own right. Thus global connections entail a different kind of geography. Whereas other social contexts are territorially delimited, global relations transcend territorial distances and territorial borders to unfold on planet Earth as a single social space. In this sense globalization might be characterized as the rise of "supra-territoriality". Whatever it may mean to others for an Indian it is not easy to eliminate the significance of localities, countries, and regions. Nor does the spread of trans-world connections abolish territorial governments or dissolve territorial identities. The global coexists and interrelates with the local, the national, the regional, and other dimensions of geography.

Globalization has also not encompassed all of humanity to the same extent. In terms of territorial location, for example, global networks have involved the populations of North America, Western Europe, and East Asia much more than other parts of the world. In terms of class, global finance has been a domain of the wealthy far more than the poor. In terms of gender, men have linked up to global computer networks much more than women. This kind of gender bias was somehow only to be expected.

Needless to say, this unevenness of globalization has important implications for social power relations. One could easily witness the impact of power relations. People with connections to supraterritorial spaces have access to important resources and influence that are denied to those who are left outside. In this regard, some commentators have 'deplored "global apartheid", as manifested in the so-called "digital divide" and other inequalities. Others have objected to a "cultural imperialism" of Hollywood and McDonald's in contemporary globalization. Since the mid-1990s such discontents have provoked a so-called "anti-globalization movement" marked by regular mass protests against global companies, the International Monetary Fund, and other prominent agents of trans-world relations.

Conceptually globalization may be easy to define but its practices remain both unclear and indistinct. Semantically or even contextually too it fails to be distinct. Perhaps it has its origins mainly in business and operationally it borrows its attributes and the definition of its characteristics from the models offered by the MNCs. Politically it has its bases in the power equations. Each country is today defined in terms of political power it has or does not have. It would appear that the USA has the monopoly of defining who will do what and how. Deviations from that definition are not permitted. Those that defy her authority to do so face armed intervention. When applied to education it would mean IPR and world rating of institutions. By implications it means that standards of educational degrees will have to be defined in the international context. The analogy is available in the world of patents of drugs or industrial products. The copyrights and patents give certain privileges to their original creators/ innovators and others. From now on, the formerly shared intellectual privileges would stand withdrawn from common use without meeting the conditions imposed by the bodies where they are either patented or given copyrights. As of today richer countries are educationally advanced as well. Globalization both as a concept and practice is intended to retain that monopoly. The G-eight countries can today decide about other non-G-eight countries. They have every power to dictate in other areas as well. The present day concept of globalization is but an extension of the same power configuration. Education is just one of the several areas that will get stifled by the few that have the power which unfortunately others do not have. And in this area India has much to worry about. With 3.5 crore remaining outside the schooling system we may have think of some other plan than Sarva Shiksha Abhiyan.

'Imagine There's no Country' by Dr. Surjit Bhalla is the title of a recently published book taken from John Lennon's song. The context is globalization. In the midst of all kinds of depressing debates about the impact of globalization on poorer countries his findings suggest that in the two decades from 1980 to 2000, the proportion of poor people in the world has fallen from 40% to 13%. In these two decades poorer countries have grown twice as fast as rich ones. The respective ratios are 3.1 per cent to 1.6 per cent. According to Dr. Bhalla one third of the global population resides in China and India. In the same two decades these two countries have witnessed record income growth. In a way, these figures persuade us to believe that globalization is not too bad after all. There are numerous other forms of globalization, just as there is a variety in the reactions to the hegemony of American power. If European Union has been formed to meet that kind of challenge, SAARC is the other alternative model. WTO and IPR are the byproducts of the same process. The eventual goal may remain full integration of all nations or may be total dissolution of the concept of division of people on any bases whatever but today we are nowhere near realizing this kind of goal.

I am not competent to discuss either the political or the economic impact of globalization. I could however go into its impact on Indian culture, languages and education. I share the commonly held view that an already fractured and divided society will get further subdivided and the technological revolution may sound the death knell to many languages, multiple cultures and create unbridgeable gaps between the 'digital have's' and the 'non-have's'.

The premise on which I am discussing the question of 'digital divide' is that we are well past that stage when we were being consulted whether or not we have any wish to join the bandwagon. *Today there are no choices.* Either join the mainstream or become extinct like dinosaurs or dodo. Having joined willy-nilly the rat race, as it were, there is no point in looking back. We are in the center-stage. We must take stock of what lies ahead of us and whether or not there is any possibility that we might still retrieve part of the lost ground. Each of these points has to be considered separately and contextually. We could react euphorically and say that a fraction of our population has done well both here and abroad. Hence, we are not likely to suffer too much as compared to X or Y. We may also stand up to say that the present scenario is too grim to describe therefore all that lies ahead of us is a grim reality and the chances are that we may do very poorly. I hold the view that neither of the two is a certainty provided we know what we want and are willing to act rationally and with good deal of determination and foresight. But first we should wake up to the impending reality.

The fact of the matter is that even in the USA the

Government has come to realize that their society has been impacted very badly by the digital divide. In a paper written by *Beverly P. Lynch* titled "The Digital Divide or the Digital Connection: A U.S. Perspective" the multi-dimensionality of the concept has been framed by Pippa Norris into three distinct aspects:

1. Global divide – divergence of Internet access between industrialized and developing countries.

2. Social divide – gap between information rich and information poor in each nation.

3. Democratic divide- difference between those who do and those who do not use the new technologies to further political participation.

The above-cited paper emphasized the digital divide in its social aspects in the U.S. and paid particular attention to the role of the library in furthering equity of access to information. How much of this discussion will be valid for us in India could be imagined by the simple fact that majority of even urban population in India has only limited access to the Internet and few schools have libraries and the books and journals are equally dated or tattered, if they have any. For the sake of discussion only I am citing some figures from the most powerful and perhaps the richest country in the world.

In 1994, as the U.S. policy makers measured telephone penetration in the country since they realized that telecommunications policy would be influenced by the growing importance of computer and modem availability in households they created database. In 1995 the first Report, on " Falling Through the Net: A Survey of the "Have-Nots" in Rural and Urban America" was issued. Following its earlier formats of gathering data by household, the survey gathered household data on availability of computers and modems and analyzed data by income, race, age, educational attainment, and geographic region (rural, urban, central city). The report gave interesting data and provided benchmark data, against which subsequent studies have been compared showing the phenomenal growth in computing availability and Internet access between 1994-2001. In 1997 the telephone penetration was 94%. Computer penetration was 36.6% and PC growth by household was up 42.1% from 24.1% in 1994. The assumption was that the rural PC penetration would be less than in urban areas. In 2000 the PC penetration had climbed to 51.1. During 2002 the results show that currently two million new Internet users are added each month. Children and teen-agers use computers more than others. In the lowest income groups too the growth was around 25% annually. The use of the Internet among the richest and the poorest was 77% and 35% respectively. Efforts are on to bridge the gap between those who have access to Internet and others who do not have such facility.

Compared with what obtains in the USA, now let us have figures given by Mumbai-based *Strategic Foresight Group* for India. The Times of India Dec.1, 2002, reported these figures. The report said," with different segments of the population and different regions of the country moving in various directions. India may formally remain united (note the word 'may'), but in every other respect, it will go to pieces within the lifetime of an Indian who has just stepped into adulthood. The report asserts that the disparities engendered by India's current development model have given rise to three broad kinds of economies. The Business class economy, which gives access to luxuries, constitutes a bare 2% of the population. The Business class is the one about which we talk the most. Then we have the Bike economy comprising 15% of the population—its consumption includes television, the telephone, the radio the motorbike and gas and water connections. The remaining 85% belong to the Bullock cart economy. While 50% of this class has access to the barest minimum consumer comfort, the rest however are just about surviving.

The figures in this regard appear to have slightly improved. With the coming in of the broadband and wireless telephony the above-cited figures are bound to undergo a sea-change.

Now to think of being able to compete with nations like China or any other country in Asia, the report has its serious doubts. The report would like us to have proper policies if the nation has to survive let alone compete and compete successfully, failing which we are likely to break up. The minimum we could expect from the Government is to reduce corruption and increase governing efficiency. An *ORG-Marg* survey reports that Indians pay Rs. 26,728 crores in bribe in a single year (Times of India Dec.18, 2002). In the year 2005 the data as reported in the Times of India (14th March) endorses the statement made by an Indian Prime Minister almost a decade back that the subsidized food-grain intended for the poor does not reach the target groups because of the immense corruption in the system. Surprising as it might appear, the teaching profession (something least expected) figures in one of the three top-most corrupt categories. This question needs to be addressed by the apex body of the teachers called the NCTE.

In a country like India governance is simply unknown and the rule of law is restricted to those that are poor and politically unconnected. If there is one country in the world where legislatures function overtime to make laws but no one is worried about their observance. The rich and mighty are as a rule above law and if one is also politically well connected then he / she commands more power than even the best paid executive from any walk in life. Now, this reality is not dependent on Information Technology or computers. The Indian lawmakers ceased to be role models long back. In the year 2006 the situation is much worse than it ever was. The Indian lawmakers have outsmarted the underworld in more ways than one.

With more than a billion people India remains both a zoo – with tremendous variety of human existence and a museum where all historical periods continue to co-exist in chronological frames almost simultaneously. Few nations could boast of this singular achievement. When we can take pride in our cultural, religious and economic diversities and suffer social, regional (cow-belt and the non cow-belt areas), and geographical differences without demur what then is going to bother us? Under the circumstances, I think the idea of 'digital divide' is in reality no more than a mosquito bite or a minor irritant that will be taken care of in the process itself. However, if we are of the worrying type then we shall have to think of millions that are likely to die of hunger, unemployment and a whole lot of diseases without any medical aid. Depending on the type of category one belongs to 'the digital divide' will have its meaning and perception. By itself this term defines an idea and ideas have the unfortunate tendency of being interpreted according to the interest groups.

Index

B

C

D

J

K

L

M

S

T